# Making Ends Meet

# Making Ends Meet

*How Single Mothers Survive Welfare
and Low-Wage Work*

Kathryn Edin and Laura Lein

Russell Sage Foundation • New York

## The Russell Sage Foundation

The Russell Sage Foundation, one of the oldest of America's general-purpose foundations, was established in 1907 by Mrs. Margaret Olivia Sage for "the improvement of social and living conditions in the United States." The Foundation seeks to fulfill this mandate by fostering the development and dissemination of knowledge about the country's political, social, and economic problems. While the Foundation endeavors to assure the accuracy and objectivity of each book it publishes, the conclusions and interpretations in Russell Sage Foundation publications are those of the authors and not of the Foundation, its Trustees, or its staff. Publication by Russell Sage, therefore, does not imply Foundation endorsement.

**Library of Congress Cataloging-in-Publication Data**

Edin, Kathryn, 1962-
    Making ends meet: how single mothers survive welfare and low-wage work /
    Kathryn Edin and Laura Lein.
        P.   cm.
    Includes bibliographical references and index.
    ISBN 0-8175-4229-3 (hardbound)   ISBN 0-8175-4234-X (paperback)
    1. Single mothers—United States—Social conditions. 2. Single mothers—
    Employment—United States. 3. Maternal and infant welfare—United States.
    4. Welfare recipients—Employment—United States. Wages—Minimum wage—
    United States.   I. Lein, Laura.   II. Title.
    HQ759.915.E34   1997
    306.85'6—dc21                                                           96-40379
                                                                                CIP

RUSSELL SAGE FOUNDATION
112 East 64th Street, New York, New York 10021
10 9 8 7 6 5 4

*To our children*

*Anna, Rebecca, David, Kaitlin, and Marisa*

# Contents

# —— Foreword ——

Ever since Lyndon Johnson first asked his Council of Economic Advisors to estimate how many Americans were poor, public officials, policy analysts, and journalists have relied on the Census Bureau for information about poverty. When the bureau reports that poverty has become less common among the elderly, as it has over the past generation, we congratulate ourselves. When the bureau reports that poverty has become more common among children, we wring our hands.

In *Making Ends Meet*, Kathryn Edin and Laura Lein present powerful evidence that the Census Bureau's measures of poverty are often quite misleading. The good news is that poor families have more resources than a naive reader of census statistics might think. The bad news is that the official poverty thresholds also underestimate poor people's needs. Because of these problems, the official poverty count may be either too high or too low. Fortunately, almost everyone recognizes that the line between the poor and the nonpoor is somewhat arbitrary, so it does not much matter whether we say that 10 or 20 percent of the population is "poor." What does matter is that poverty rates for different groups reflect the frequency of destitution in each group. When the poverty rate is higher among children than among the elderly, for example, we need to be confident that children are in fact more likely to lack basic necessities. It is also important that changes in the official poverty rate mirror changes in people's ability to buy basic necessities. If the official poverty rate frequently rises while material hardship falls, or vice versa, poverty statistics are worse than useless.

*Making Ends Meet* focuses on the group that has traditionally had the highest poverty rate in America: unskilled single mothers and their children. Edin and Lein's findings suggest that, at least for the next few years, official poverty statistics will probably provide a quite misleading picture of how these families' economic status is changing. As the new time limits on welfare receipt begin to take effect, more and more single mothers will have to take jobs. Most of these newly employed mothers will have more income than they had on welfare, so their official poverty rate will fall. But they will also have more expenses than they had on welfare, and they will get fewer noncash benefits. Edin and Lein's findings dramatize the likely result. Between 1988 and 1992, mothers who held low-wage jobs reported substantially more income than those who collected welfare, but they also reported more hardship. If this pattern persists in the years ahead, time limits will probably bring both a decline in the official poverty rate and an increase in material hardship.

## OFFICIAL STATISTICS VERSUS REAL BUDGETS

Measuring income is extraordinarily difficult. Until 1940 the Census Bureau did not even try to ask Americans about their income because the subject was considered too sensitive. Now the bureau asks people about their income all the time, but only two-thirds of the nation's households answer all the bureau's questions. Those who do answer often make mistakes. Some even provide deliberately misleading information. In general, families that get most of their income from a regular paycheck or pension check seem to report their income quite accurately. But the poor get more of their income from irregular sources, and such income is not well reported.

Sometimes the resulting data seem implausible at best. According to the Census Bureau, for example, 1.5 million single mothers had cash incomes below $5,000 in 1992. These mothers typically had two children. Most got food stamps and Medicaid, but only a minority lived in subsidized housing.[1] Taking these women's reported income at face value implies that they paid for their rent, utilities, transportation, clothing, laundry, and other expenses from a monthly budget of less than $420. Almost half appeared to be living on less than $200 a month.

One way to see whether families really live on such tiny sums is to look at the Labor Department's Consumer Expenditure Survey (CES). According to the CES, families with incomes below $5,000 in 1992 took in an average of only $180 a month.[2] Yet these families told the CES that they had spent an average of $1,100 a month. This confirms the common-sense belief that families cannot live on air. But we still need to explain how these families manage to spend six times as much as they take in.

Ask an economist this question and you will get a standard answer. Low-income families appear to live beyond their means because they are only temporarily poor. When their incomes dip, they use savings, credit cards, or loans from relatives to smooth their consumption. When their incomes rise, they repay their debts. This explanation makes sense for families in which the breadwinner has just lost a steady job or the family business is losing money. But single mothers who report incomes below $5,000 seldom have savings or credit cards, and most stay poor for a long time. How do they manage?

*Making Ends Meet* shows that almost all poor single mothers supplement their regular income with some combination of off-the-books employment and money from relatives, lovers, and the fathers of their children. Few keep a record of such income. Even if they knew the annual total, they would not necessarily report it to the Census Bureau, since they do not report it to the Internal Revenue Service. Secretiveness is especially common among welfare recipients, almost all of whom have non-welfare income that they conceal from the welfare department.

Taking account of irregular income has a dramatic effect on our picture of welfare mothers' economic status. Consider Illinois, a fairly typical state that Edin studied intensively from 1988 to 1990. During 1990 an Illinois mother with two children and no other income got $367 a month from Aid to Families with Dependent Children (AFDC).[3] She got another $50 a month if the father of her children made child support payments to the state. (If the father paid more than $50, the state kept the rest.) If she worked, she could keep a small part of her earnings to cover work-related expenses, but anything beyond that amount was subtracted from her AFDC check. Most Illinois welfare recipients were therefore expected to live on less than $5,000 a year in cash, plus food stamps and Medicaid.

Most Illinois welfare recipients live in the Chicago area, and most live in unsubsidized housing. Even in Chicago's worst neighborhoods, unsubsidized apartments almost always cost at least $350 a month in 1990. An optimist might think that welfare mothers somehow found unusually cheap apartments, but when Edin asked forty Chicago mothers in unsubsidized housing how much they paid, only one spent less than $300 and only five spent less than $350. Edin also interviewed frontline welfare workers who routinely checked recipients' rent stubs. These informants confirmed that when welfare recipients lived in unsubsidized apartments they usually spent about as much for rent as they got from AFDC.

Nonetheless, there was no public discussion of how welfare recipients paid their other bills. The most obvious explanation for this was political. Conservatives did not raise the question because they did not want to draw attention to the fact that AFDC benefits were too low to support a family. Liberals were equally reluctant to discuss the issue, because they did not want to admit that recipients were balancing their budgets with unreported income. This conspiracy of silence encouraged the public to imagine that welfare recipients could get by on whatever the legislature chose to give them. Once the public accepts this comforting assumption, it becomes natural to cut benefits whenever the state budget tightens.

I myself never thought seriously about how welfare recipients could live on $300 or $400 a month until Kathryn Edin forced me to do so. This happened quite fortuitously. In 1983 and 1985 Fay Cook and Susan Mayer, my colleagues at Northwestern University, and I had conducted two telephone surveys in which we asked Chicago residents whether they had recently experienced various material hardships, such as going hungry, not seeing a doctor when they thought they needed treatment, or having their utilities shut off. We found a lot of hardship. But a lot of families with very low incomes also said that they had not experienced any of the hardships we listed. Following standard economic logic, we assumed that most of these families either spent an unusually large fraction of their income on the things we had asked about or that they spent this money unusually efficiently.[4]

To see if these speculations were correct, we hired Kathryn Edin (who was then a graduate student at Northwestern) to reinterview some of our respondents. After a few weeks she reported that she was getting nowhere. When she called back low-income respondents who had not reported any hardships and asked how they managed, they were reluctant to talk with her. Many seemed to suspect that she was working for the welfare department or some other government agency. She therefore proposed a different approach. Instead of interviewing respondents who had no reason to trust her, she would ask people who worked with welfare recipients to introduce her and vouch for her trustworthiness. She would then build a "snowball" sample by asking each initial respondent to introduce her to additional welfare mothers.

Edin asked each mother in this new sample how much money she spent in an average month on different goods and services. Having established the family's average monthly expenditures, she asked mothers how they paid their bills. Piecing this story together often took many interviews spread over several months, but eventually all her respondents provided budgets that more or less balanced. None of them lived on AFDC alone, and none of them reported all their income to the welfare department. The average mother got only half her cash from AFDC. The remainder came primarily from off-the-books employment, family members, boyfriends, and absent fathers.

After interviewing fifty welfare recipients, Edin received a grant from the Russell Sage Foundation to support a comparative study of unmarried Chicago mothers who worked at regular jobs paying less than $7.50 an hour. Then she and Laura Lein proposed a collaborative study of Boston, Charleston, and San Antonio. Once again they approached respondents through trusted intermediaries. This inevitably meant that they oversampled people with a lot of friends, especially friends on welfare or with low-wage jobs. Fortunately, there is no obvious reason why that fact should distort conclusions about single mothers' budgets.

## DRAWING THE LINE

*Making Ends Meet* describes what Edin and Lein found in Boston, Charleston, Chicago, and San Antonio. It shows that all but a handful of single mothers consumed goods and services whose value exceeded the official poverty line. This does not mean they were living well. Edin and Lein found widespread material hardship. Based on what they found, I would argue that the official poverty threshold is too low. But the evidence is not clear-cut, and not all readers will agree.

Everyone who studies these mothers' budgets will find a few items they regard as "luxuries" rather than "necessities." This is consistent with everyday experience. All of us have seen poor people buy things that we ourselves would not buy, and most of us have occasionally felt that such behavior was extravagant. One reason food stamps have become so unpopular is that millions of Americans have watched the woman ahead of them in the checkout line use stamps to pay for something they judged too expensive for their own family. Such judgments flow partly from the fact that no two people seem to agree on what constitutes a necessity. But there is also another more fundamental problem: most people find that spending all their money on necessities is unbearably depressing. The poor are as subject to this dilemma as the rest of us.

In American usage, a necessity is something essential for physical survival or a moderate level of physical comfort. Food, shelter, heat, light, warm clothing, and medical care are the standard examples. Purchases that merely generate pleasure, like a television set or a birthday present, or that generate self-respect, like attractive clothes or cosmetics, are not defined as necessities. Nonetheless, poor people in every culture occasionally forgo physical necessities in order to obtain luxuries that they value for non-material reasons. This always seems extravagant to outsiders for whom the luxuries in question have less symbolic significance. But neither morality nor common sense requires human beings to value their health and physical comfort more than their honor, pleasure, or self-respect. Once we concede that people cannot live by bread alone, we should not expect poor people to spend all their money on either bread or its equivalent.

This logic suggests that the mother who takes her children to McDonald's once a month is not necessarily being extravagant or foolish, even if her treat means that there is not enough for breakfast or dinner later in the week. Such a mother may have a better sense of what her children need than the nutritionist who tells her to buy more beans and rice. The fact that she buys occasional treats does not mean that she has more money than she needs for necessities. It just means that for most people an occasional luxury is a necessity, and that the line between the two is less clear-cut than some of my New England ancestors might have wished.

Edin and Lein's budgets also provide useful evidence about how much money a mother needs to keep her family together. The crucial clue here is that Edin and Lein found no single mothers who lived on welfare alone. In theory, this could just mean that every mother is capable of supplementing her welfare check in some way, and that every mother prefers more income to less. But this explanation stretches credulity. In order to supplement her welfare check, a mother must have either job skills that some employer values, interpersonal skills that allow her to make continuing claims on her relatives, or a capacity to trade her charms for some man's money. Many mothers lack at least one of these resources. It follows that some mothers almost surely lack them all. If such mothers cannot supplement their welfare checks, what becomes of them?

The fact that Edin and Lein did not find such mothers suggests to me that they cannot maintain their own households. Edin and Lein also interviewed welfare mothers who shared housing. They too had some supplementary income. (A mother who cannot earn any money on the side, has no boyfriend, and cannot get help from her relatives is unlikely to have the makings of a good roommate.) Some mothers who cannot supplement their check presumably live with their parents. This is especially common among teenage mothers, whom Edin and Lein did not interview. But as teenage mothers grow up, they usually move out of their parents' (or mother's) household. Some teenage mothers may leave their children with the grandmother. Others move out with their children but later find that they cannot pay their bills and move back in with their parents or other relatives, or show up in shelters. If a mother has exhausted these sources of help, she may send her children to live with her mother or some other relative. In a few cases her children end up in foster care.

How common are such family breakups? The 1992 Current Population Survey (CPS) found that 2.6 percent of children under the age of eighteen lived with neither their mother nor their father.[5] About 2 percent lived with a grandparent, aunt, sibling, or other relative. The remaining 0.6 percent lived with non-relatives (usually foster parents). Anecdotal evidence suggests that most of these children had a living mother, but statistical data is not currently available on this topic or on the reasons why children live with people other than their natural parents.

An interpretation of Edin and Lein's budgets suggests, the official poverty thresholds underestimate poor families' needs by roughly 25 percent—though there is clearly much individual variation around this (or any other) estimate. Moreover, this threshold is not the level at which families begin to experience material hardship and therefore seem "poor." Rather, the threshold represents the lowest level of resources that allows a family to live independently. When families appear to be living on significantly less than this, we are underestimating their resources, either because they do not report all their income or because they are not paying cash for a lot of what they consume.

## PREDICTING THE FUTURE

In August 1996, President Clinton signed legislation abolishing AFDC and replacing it with Temporary Assistance for Needy Families (TANF). TANF's most widely publicized feature is its requirement that able-bodied welfare recipients work after two years. But the new law also gives states a lot of freedom to design their own TANF rules. A generous state that wants to get around the federal time limits can probably do so. Few states will try, however, because the new law also gives them strong financial incentives to cut their overall level of welfare spending.

Under the pre-1996 system, every dollar that a state appropriated for AFDC was matched by one to four dollars of federal money. (The matching formula was more generous for poorer states.) Under TANF, states get a block grant whose size does not depend on how much of their own money they spend.[6] If a state decides to spend more because the number of TANF applicants has risen, because the cost of living has risen, or because recipients who hit their time limit cannot find work, it will have to pay the additional cost from its own treasury. Conversely, if states cut limit eligibility or cut benefit levels, they will be able to keep every dollar they save. Instead of paying twenty to fifty cents for a dollar's worth of charity, states will now have to pay a full dollar.

Raising the cost of altruism almost always reduces its frequency. Once legislators digest the fact that spending a dollar on welfare means that they have a full dollar less for hospitals, schools, highways, or tax cuts, welfare will almost inevitably get a smaller share of every state's budget. Most states are already setting even tighter time limits than federal law requires. Some are also cutting benefits. As time goes on, the real value of the federal block grants will fall. As a result, most states will probably let real benefit levels fall and tighten their time limits.

The combination of lower real benefits and tighter eligibility standards will push more mothers into the labor force. No one knows for sure how single mothers will fare, but the evidence assembled in *Making Ends Meet* is probably our best currently available guide to the economic impact of this change. Edin and Lein's data bear both on what is likely to happen and how we will interpret these changes. I take these issues up in reverse order.

## Measuring Change

If past experience is any guide, policy analysts, journalists, and social scientists will all turn to the Census Bureau's poverty statistics for evidence about TANF's economic impact. If the poverty rate among single mothers rises, liberals will say "I told you so." If it falls, conservatives will say the same thing. Yet for reasons to which I have already alluded, official poverty statistics will almost inevitably overstate TANF's benefits or understate its costs.

When TANF pushes mothers into the labor force, they will usually earn more than they got from welfare. But newly employed mothers will also need more cash to pay their bills.

- Newly employed mothers will usually have to pay for child care. (Most mothers who can get free child care are already working, either formally or informally.)

- Most newly employed mothers will have to pay for transportation to work. In cities without efficient public transit systems, they will usually need an automobile.

- Because newly employed mothers will usually have more income, their food stamp allotment will be cut. Every $100 of extra cash income will mean $30 less in food stamps.

- If newly employed mothers have a federal housing subsidy, every extra $100 in cash income will also raise their rent by $30.

- In most cases taking a job will mean that the mother eventually loses her Medicaid benefits. In some cases her children will also lose their benefits. Some newly employed mothers will get health insurance at work, but many will not. Working mothers will therefore have more out-of-pocket medical expenses.

The official poverty measure does not take account of such changes. The Census Bureau does publish an unofficial poverty series that incorporates the estimated value of food stamps, housing subsidies, and Medicaid, but even this series ignores work-related expenses. All the bureau's current poverty estimates will therefore exaggerate the economic benefits of TANF. In order to eliminate this bias, the bureau would have to create a new series that not only added the value of noncash benefits to income but subtracted work-related expenses.[7]

Political support for such a change may be hard to find. Both the president and Congress are now irrevocably committed to the idea that single mothers should work. Both therefore want to show that working can improve a single mother's economic status. Neither the president nor Congress wants to deal with evidence suggesting that Washington will have to spend more money if it wants to make this hope a reality. The Census Bureau is not oblivious to its political environment, and it may decide to treat the biases built into its current poverty statistics as a low priority problem.

## Forecasting Change

Edin and Lein found that single mothers who earned $5 to $7 an hour between 1988 and 1992 experienced slightly more material hardship than those who relied primarily on welfare. This makes it tempting to predict that hardship will increase as TANF pushes more mothers into such jobs. But before accepting this gloomy prophecy we need to ask how closely "post-TANF" working mothers will resemble the mothers whom Edin and Lein studied. Post-TANF mothers will probably earn less than the mothers Edin and Lein studied, and they will probably have to spend more for child care and medical care. Recent increases in the earned income tax credit (EITC) should offset some of these disadvantages, but probably not all of them.

Edin and Lein looked hard for single mothers in minimum-wage jobs. They found hardly any. This was because they did their fieldwork at a time when single mothers still had a choice between work and welfare. Minimum-wage jobs left single mothers worse off than they were on welfare, so they seldom took such jobs. Once mothers hit their TANF time limits, however, those who cannot find jobs paying $6 or $7 an hour will have to settle for whatever they can get. Post-TANF mothers are therefore likely to earn less than the working mothers whom Edin and Lein interviewed.[8] Indeed, the main goal of time limits was to push single mothers into jobs they would not otherwise take. In most cases that will mean jobs paying close to the minimum wage.

Edin and Lein did not interview working mothers who were currently unemployed, and they did not factor unemployment into working mothers' monthly budgets. This was not because single mothers never lost their jobs or always found other positions immediately. But when single mothers lost their jobs, they could go back on AFDC while they looked for work. Under TANF, a steadily rising fraction of single mothers will lose this safety net and will have to plan on periods without income.

History suggests that the American economy can create some kind of work for almost every pair of willing hands. But history also suggests that American employers usually reserve steady work for those who are unusually reliable or have valuable firm-specific skills. If a firm can train someone to do a job in a few days, it has no incentive to keep her on the payroll when business is slow, when she misses work because her children are sick, or when she irritates her supervisor. Most employers see a former welfare recipient as a risky hire. They will hire her only if they know they can easily replace her should things not work out. As a result, the jobs open to former recipients tend to be those with high turnover and frequent layoffs.

Unskilled adults almost always have unemployment rates at least twice the national average. Since the national unemployment rate seldom falls below 5 percent, we have to assume that "post-TANF" welfare mothers will be unemployed at least 10 percent of the time when the economy is doing well and even more during recessions. In poor inner-city neighborhoods and depressed rural areas, the rate is likely to be even higher. The least skilled and least reliable mothers will often have trouble finding any kind of work.

For all these reasons, it seems unlikely that welfare mothers who hit their TANF time limit will earn as much (at least in real terms) as the mothers whom Edin and Lein interviewed. Nonetheless, their annual income may be higher because Congress has made the EITC considerably more generous since 1992. If a single mother with two children works regularly at $5.15 an hour, which will become the legal minimum wage in September 1997, the EITC will now give her an extra $2 an hour. If she works thirty-five hours a week and is unemployed 10 percent of the time, she will end up with about $12,000 for the year. If she can work forty hours a week at $6 an hour and is never laid off, she can end up with about $16,000. In real terms, that is not far from what Edin and Lein's working mothers earned.

The mothers whom TANF pushes into the labor force will, however, need to spend more on child care and medical care than Edin and Lein's mothers spent. Single mothers with low-wage jobs seldom paid market rates for child care between 1988 and 1992. Some got a government subsidy. Some had a relative who watched their children. Some had older children who did not need (or at least did not get) regular supervision. Mothers who had to pay market rates for child care rarely worked. When time limits push such mothers into the labor force, their child care bills will be much higher than those of the mothers who chose to work under the old system.

Edin and Lein's working families also needed less medical care than their welfare families. Chronic illness, whether of a child or a mother, makes it hard for the mother to work. In addition, AFDC recipients got automatic Medicaid coverage, whereas low-wage workers got more limited coverage or none at all. TANF will push more mothers with high medical bills into the labor force. How they will pay these bills once they lose their Medicaid coverage remains a mystery.

Judging by Edin and Lein's data, working mothers who can earn $16,000 (including EITC) in 1997 should be close to self-sufficiency. If they get either child support or a child care subsidy and are either healthy or insured, they should be able to make ends meet. If a mother earns only $12,000, however, she will usually need a lot of outside help to balance her budget.

If these predictions are correct, implementing TANF is likely to cause a lot of hardship. The country could then respond in either of two ways. One option would be for states to make TANF's time limits more flexible. Most liberals will support this solution, but this may be a mistake. Supporting single mothers who did not work was politically defensible in an era when married mothers seldom worked, but that era is long gone. Today, few Americans believe that poor children will suffer if their mother takes a job, and most therefore think that single mothers should work.[9] A system predicated on single mothers staying home will never again win political support or provide decent benefits. And it will always treat recipients as scum.

The better option is to accept the public's judgment that no able-bodied adult should get something for nothing, assume that single mothers ought to work whenever jobs are available, and build a support system that also allows such mothers to care for their children and pay their bills. How might we do this?

## Raising the Minimum Wage

The minimum wage will rise to $5.15 an hour in September 1997. This will be about 40 percent of what the average blue-collar worker earns in manufacturing. During the 1950s and 1960s, unions were stronger and the minimum wage was about 50 percent of the blue-collar average in manufacturing. One obvious way to mitigate TANF's adverse impact on single mothers would be to raise the minimum to at least $6 or perhaps even $6.50 an hour. While a $6 minimum would probably eliminate some marginal jobs, past experience suggests that the reduction would be small. The wage gain for single mothers would, in contrast, be quite large.

## Child Care Subsidies

For mothers with young children, the cost of child care is the most obvious obstacle to working. While some former welfare recipients get child care subsidies, there is not enough money available to cover everyone who will need help once TANF's time limits begin to take effect. Expanding the number of subsidized child care slots would be expensive, partly because a lot of mothers who currently rely on informal care would apply for slots. But all schemes for moving single mothers into the labor force are expensive. Putting these women to work is simply not cost-effective. The rationale for TANF has to be political, social, and cultural, not economic. And while child care subsidies do not make economic sense, they are probably the most politically plausible way of ensuring that single mothers who work can also pay their bills.

## Federal Housing Subsidies

The single mothers who experience the greatest economic hardship when they take minimum-wage jobs will be those in high-rent areas like Boston, California, and New York. One simple way to help these mothers would be for Congress to alter the rules governing the distribution of federal housing subsidies. If families with a full-time worker went to the head of the waiting list, and if Congress set these families' rent at 25 percent rather than 30 percent of their income, single mothers would have more incentive to find work. Increasing the proportion of working adults in public housing would also improve the social environment in the projects. Even if working mothers paid only 25 percent of their income in rent, they would usually pay more in dollars than welfare recipients do, so the cost to the taxpayer would fall.

## Health Insurance

Allowing all low-income families to buy into Medicaid for 10 percent of their earnings would go a long way towards making work pay for many unskilled single mothers.

## Child Support Enforcement

Some TANF enthusiasts believe that absent fathers can be forced to hand over significant amounts of money to the mothers of their children. This is probably true for fathers who hold steady, well-paid jobs. But women who end up in minimum-wage jobs have seldom had children by men who now work steadily at a good job. Such women are more likely to have had a child with a man whom they cannot identify or who is now dead, in jail, homeless, or addicted to drugs. Pursuing absent fathers is a positive step, but it is not likely to raise much money for the single mothers who will need the most help.

A higher minimum wage plus a mix of health care subsidies, housing subsidies, and child care subsidies would allow even single mothers with unstable low-wage jobs to make ends meet. At the moment, however, Congress and the president are preoccupied with budget cutting. If they add any new federal outlays, these will probably go either to the Pentagon or to middle-income voters, not to the poor. Middle-of-the road legislators may eventually become convinced that the country should do more to supplement the earnings of poor single mothers, but not until they have read a lot of horror stories about working mothers who end up in shelters or have to send their children away to live with their relatives. Meanwhile, a lot of women and children are likely to suffer.

## WOULD HELPING SINGLE MOTHERS MAKE THEM MORE NUMEROUS?

Some conservatives oppose all efforts to help single mothers balance their budgets, even when the mother works. They argue that making life easier for single mothers will just make them more numerous. For those who see single mothers as a major cause of the nation's social problems, cutting their numbers is even more important than reducing material hardship.

Although liberals scoff publicly at these arguments, few really doubt that changing the economic consequences of single motherhood can affect its frequency. Imagine a society in which unmarried women knew that if they had a baby out of wedlock their family would turn them out, the father would never contribute to the baby's support, the government would give them no help, and no employer would hire them. Hardly anyone, liberal or conservative, doubts that unwed motherhood would be rarer in such a society than it is in the United States today. In the United States, however, traditionalists who want to discourage unwed motherhood have a limited array of policy levers to pull. They cannot prevent parents from helping out daughters who become single mothers, employers from hiring such women, or men from marrying them. Those who want to discourage single motherhood are left with only one lever: they can reduce single mothers' government benefits.

Economists have tried to estimate the effect of this strategy by studying state-to-state differences in AFDC benefits. At first glance, these look huge. In 1994, monthly cash benefits for a family of three ranged from $680 in Connecticut to $120 in Mississippi. Unfortunately for social science, these differences are more apparent than real. First, federal food stamp benefits are lower in high-benefit states. Second, rents also tend to be lower in low-benefit states. Susan Mayer found that when two states' nominal 1990 benefits differed by $100, welfare recipients' disposable income (after paying for food and rent) typically differed by only $30.[10] The true difference between high- and low-benefit states thus turns out to be closer to $175 than $560. Judging by current evidence, differences of this size exert little influence on fertility decisions and only a modest influence on living arrangements.[11]

The economic consequences of becoming a single mother vary more from country to country than they do within the United States. Cross-national comparisons therefore provide a useful check on how the risk of ending up poor affects a woman's decision about whether to become (or remain) a single mother.[12] Using data from the Luxembourg Income Study (LIS), Lee Rainwater and Tim Smeeding have estimated poverty rates and living arrangements for children in fourteen rich countries during the early 1990s.[13] They define a child as poor if the child's family income (adjusted for family size) is less than half that of the median family income in the same country. They treat a mother as "single" if she did not live with either a husband or a male partner. To get a rough estimate of how costly it was to become a single mother in each of the fourteen countries, I subtracted the (logged) odds that children who lived with a married couple would be poor from the odds that children who lived with a single mother would be poor.

Among children who lived with a single mother in the early 1990s, Rainwater and Smeeding found poverty rates ranging from a high of 56 percent in the United States and Australia to lows of 5 percent in Sweden and 7 percent in Finland. The gap between the rates for single and married mothers also varied dramatically, exceeding 40 percentage points in Australia, Canada, and the United States but falling below 10 percentage points in Denmark, Finland, Sweden, Belgium, and Italy.

If fear of poverty discouraged single motherhood, we would expect to find relatively few single mothers in English-speaking countries and far more in Scandinavia. Figure F-1 shows no such pattern. Instead, single motherhood appears to be more common in the countries where its cost is highest.[14] Single motherhood increases the odds of being poor in Australia, Canada, and the United States more than in most other countries. (The Norwegian observation reflects the near-zero probability that Norwegian couples will be poor.) But the number of single mothers is far higher in the United States than elsewhere and is as high in Australia and Canada as in Sweden and Denmark. European rates of single motherhood seem to be more influenced by proximity to the North Sea than by the risk that becoming a single mother will make you poor. These comparisons suggest that the frequency of single motherhood in rich countries depends mainly on its cultural rather than its economic cost.[15]

Both domestic and international evidence thus suggests that the United States could do substantially more than it now does to help single mothers without appreciably increasing the percentage of women who raise their children alone. But evidence

**FIGURE F–1.    Relationship Between the Incidence of Single Motherhood and the Relative Odds that Single Mothers and Couples Will Be Poor: Fourteen Rich Countries Circa 1990**

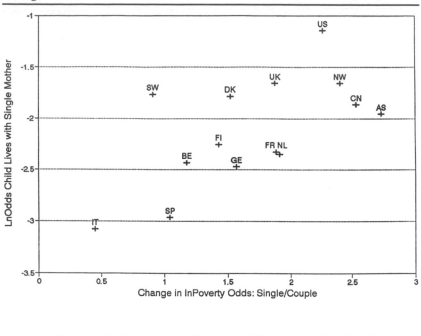

AS = Australia, BE = Belgium, CN = Canada, DK = Denmark, FI = Finland, FR = France, GE = West Germany (1989), IT = Italy, NL = Netherlands, NW = Norway, SP = Spain, SW = Switzerland, UK = United Kingdom, US = United States.

Source: Tabulations by Lee Rainwater using national surveys conducted between 1989 and 1994 and available through the Luxembourg Income Study. Note: All estimates are weighted by the number of children in the household.

of this kind is unlikely to affect many American legislators' willingness to support such policies. For conservative legislators and voters, single motherhood is a moral rather than a practical problem. They want the government to punish what they see as bad behavior, regardless of whether such punishment has any deterrent value.

Some American liberals and progressives are equally passionate in their defense of single motherhood. American feminists often see divorce and unwed motherhood as sensible responses to the defects of American men. From their vantage point, having to depend on a potentially abusive or unreliable man is even worse than having to depend on the government. Because relations between the sexes are particularly strained among African Americans, black women are especially likely to raise children on their own. Some black nationalists like to portray the two-parent family as a European invention that whites should not impose on people of color, and white multiculturalists often echo this view.

The "culture wars" between liberals and conservatives have left American children worse off than they would be if either liberalism or conservatism were hegemonic. Because so many Americans see single motherhood as a legitimate and perhaps even prudent choice, our children are unusually likely to live in households without a male breadwinner. Because so many conservatives regard single motherhood as a menace, the government does little to help, and these households are unusually likely to be poor. What really harms children, it seems to me, is America's much-vaunted diversity. What children need is consensus—any kind of consensus will do—about how they should be supported. But consensus is precisely what America seems least likely to produce.

If this argument is correct, the United States is unlikely to do much to improve single mothers' economic status in the near future. But if TANF makes single mothers significantly worse off, as seems to me likely, legislators will probably initiate some new programs for helping single mothers who work. Anyone who wants to approach that challenge realistically should read *Making Ends Meet*.

CHRISTOPHER JENCKS
Kennedy School of Government, Harvard University

# Acknowledgments

This research involved the collaborative efforts of dozens of community organizations, grassroots community leaders, academic colleagues, and graduate students in each of the cities we studied. We cannot thank all of them here, but some deserve special mention.

In Chicago, Shirlee Garcia, Sonja Grant, and North Park College's Urban Outreach staff were extraordinarily helpful in teaching Kathryn Edin the ropes and introducing her to some of her initial respondents. William Julius Wilson and Jolene Kirschenman also provided Edin with assistance in gaining entrée into several Chicago communities. Kim Allen, Deborah Buffo, Sharon Fredricksen Bjorkman, Shirlee Garcia, Sonja Grant, Arwen Murray, and Nancy Nelson assisted Edin with interviewing, transcribing, and data coding. Sharon Fredricksen Bjorkman was indispensable in her role as project manager. At various stages, Edin's Chicago research was supported by grants from Northwestern University's Law and Social Sciences program, The Ford Foundation, a Faculty Department Grant from the Eli Lilly Foundation, and the generous support of the Russell Sage Foundation.

In Charleston, Penny Todd of the East Cooper Community Outreach program, Bill Davis of the Eastside Neighborhood Council, Janice May of Big Brother/Big Sister, Reverend Roger L. Washington of Greater Beard Chapel AME church, Dorothy Givens of the *Charleston News and Courier*, Sylvia Folk, and T. C. Drayton provided crucial assistance. Sharon Fredricksen Bjorkman traveled from Chicago to Charleston for a semester to offer her excellent managerial skills, and she and Sylvia Folk assisted in interviewing Charleston respondents.

In rural Minnesota, Mary Jo Hofer, Sheri Peterson, and Carol Weber helped Kathryn Edin to gain entree into the community, and Sheri Peterson managed the project and conducted several of the interviews.

In San Antonio, Robert Brischetto, Patti Radle, Rod Radle, many participants in Inner City Development, and Henry Rodriguez all helped enormously in introducing Laura Lein to the city and its neighborhoods. At various stages, Lein's work in San Antonio was supported by the Rockefeller Foundation, the Hogg Foundation for Mental Health, and the Center for Research on Dispute Resolution. Roy Feldman introduced Lein to several service institutions in San Antonio. Erica David, Michael Duke, Robin Gingerich, Eva Lee, Sharon Mann, Jane Parker, DeAnn Pendry, Rose Mary Penzerro, Diane Ancilio, Pamela Smith, and E. Michael Symonds assisted in interviewing respondents and data coding there.

In Boston these tasks were handled by Amy Abraham, Rosemarie Wells Day, Karen Hullenbaught, Susan Lusi, LaDonna Pavetti, Teresa Eckrich Sommer, and Jane Wiseman. Pamela Hormuth contributed considerably to the organization of the two-city effort.

Irene Brown, Irwin Garfinkel, Christopher Jencks, Robin Jared, Deborah Stone, Roberta Splater-Roth, and Anne Sparks all read various drafts of the book and gave us excellent suggestions. Christopher Jencks helped us raise the money to fund the project and offered us wonderful advice throughout each stage of research and writing. Mary Jo Bane alerted us to each other's work and recruited a group of wonderful graduate students to conduct interviews in the Boston area. Dr. Eric Wanner and the Russell Sage Foundation Board were extraordinarily supportive of the project from the beginning and not only provided most of the funding for the research but arranged for one of us (Kathryn Edin) to spend a year at the foundation's headquarters in New York City writing up the results. Timothy J. Nelson masterminded the database that allowed us to code, store, and efficiently retrieve the massive amount of data we collected. Pauline Jones transcribed copious amounts of data. When the time came to publish the book, we were grateful for the proofreading skills of Joan Bosi and the editorial assistance of Rosyln Coleman and Suzanne Nichols.

Finally, both of our families were extremely supportive of our work. Kathryn Edin's husband joined her for a year in Charleston,

South Carolina, and two summers in Minnesota. He and their infant daughter also traveled with Edin to New York City so she could spend the year working on this book. Laura Lein's husband and three children spent one summer living across the street from a San Antonio housing project, and another summer in Boston so she could train interviewers there. One way or another, each of these family members participated in the research, and the authors are grateful to them.

KATHRYN EDIN
LAURA LEIN

—— Chapter 1 ——

# Single Mothers, Welfare, and Low-Wage Work

O N DECEMBER 18, 1994, the cover of the *New York Times Magazine* featured an African American single mother of four. In the photograph, Mary Ann Moore stands in an apron and sanitary cap in front of an industrial-sized stove, ready to start her ten-hour work day as a cook in a Chicago soup kitchen. When *New York Times* journalist Jason DeParle interviewed Moore in the fall of that year, she had been working at this job for almost twelve months.

As the article revealed, thirty-three-year-old Moore had held at least two dozen service-sector jobs since leaving high school. Between these jobs she had relied on Aid to Families with Dependent Children (AFDC). At the time DeParle interviewed her, Moore was paid $8 an hour and could work up to sixty hours a week. It was the highest-paying position she had ever held. To land the job, she had to complete training at a Chicago city college and obtain a food and sanitation license. To keep the job, she had to wake her family at 3:30 each morning; dress, feed, and transport them eleven miles from her subsidized South Chicago apartment to her mother's apartment in the Cabrini Green housing project (her mother got the older children to school and the younger children to their day care center); and then travel six more miles to the North Side to begin her work day at 6:00 A.M.

Although this job netted Moore about $1,600 in a typical month (she worked an average of fifty-six hours a week), leaving welfare for work had substantially increased her expenses. The Chicago Housing Authority raised her rent from roughly $100

1

to $300 a month; she had to purchase a used car that cost her $300 a month; she had to pay for liability insurance and gasoline ($100 a month); and she had to spend $100 a month on day care for her two-year-old twins. This left Moore with roughly $800 a month with which to feed and clothe her family of five, buy diapers for the twins and school supplies for her two school-aged boys, pay her phone bill and household expenses, and meet out-of-pocket medical expenses. In addition, she paid $67 a month toward a student loan for the training she had needed to land her job.

Of the thousands of welfare-related stories appearing in major newspapers in recent years, DeParle's rendering of Mary Ann Moore's situation was one of only a handful that took a serious look at the working lives of former welfare recipients. DeParle used Moore's story to test the assumptions of those who wanted to replace welfare with work. After spending several weeks living with Moore's family, observing her daily routine, asking countless questions, and tallying up her monthly budget, DeParle concluded that, even for mothers who can get a relatively good job like Moore's, trading welfare for work is far more problematic than most reformers presume. Moore was—and would almost certainly remain—one sick child away from destitution.

## ECONOMIC WELL-BEING OF
## MOTHER-ONLY FAMILIES

National data suggest that despite her tight budget, Moore was more fortunate than most former welfare recipients. Not only did she earn more money per hour than most women with similar skills and education, she was able to work more hours than most, and she had not been laid off. She was fortunate enough to live in a subsidized apartment and had a day care subsidy for her preschool children. Finally, Moore's mother was willing and able to take on many of the parenting tasks while Moore was at work.

Moore's income placed her just above the official poverty line, but about half of all single mothers and their children fall below this threshold. Fifty-five percent of all African American children living in a mother-only family were officially poor in 1990, as were 41 percent of white children. Twenty-two percent of all children lived in mother-only families in that year, up from 11 percent in 1970. Among whites, the proportion of children living with two parents fell from nine in ten to roughly seven in ten. For African Americans, the proportion dropped from about six in ten to just under four of every ten children (Levy 1995, 40).[1] Some of this decline was due to growing nonmarital births (three of Moore's children were born while she was unmarried) and some to divorce or separation.

Like Moore, most unskilled and semiskilled mothers who try to support their children by working are hard-pressed to find a job that pays a living wage (see chapter 5).[2] In the 1970s, few unskilled and semiskilled women who worked full time earned enough to support a family (for a discussion of what constitutes a living wage, see chapter 8). During the 1980s and 1990s, these mothers' prospects for a living wage job did not improve (Bianchi 1995, 127–33).

Neither did their chances of getting financial help from their children's fathers, though federal and state lawmakers have made repeated efforts to improve these chances. In 1988, the Family Support Act required states to increase the percentage of welfare-reliant children who had legally identifiable fathers, mandated improvements in collection rates, forced fathers' employers to begin withholding child support from their wages, required states to adopt uniform standards for setting child support awards, and obligated child support officials to update these awards at least every three years. In addition, some states implemented computerized systems for locating delinquent parents and have required the putative fathers of nonmarital children to take genetic paternity tests. Other states intercept tax returns and lottery winnings, garnish bank accounts, suspend driver's licenses, and put nonpaying fathers in jail. Unfortunately, these measures have not improved the financial situations of most low-income single mothers (Edin 1994; Edin 1995; Sorensen and Turner 1996).

Given their limited ability to glean income from either work or their children's fathers, it is not surprising that, at any given point over the last few decades, half of all mothers raising children alone have relied on welfare to help pay their bills. However, the value of a welfare check declined dramatically (more than 40 percent) between the mid-1970s and the mid-1990s as inflation eroded the purchasing power of benefits. As welfare devolves to the states, this erosion will almost certainly continue because federal block grants to states are not likely to increase as living costs rise. As states begin to implement the new federal work requirements and time limits, fewer mothers will be eligible for the program at all.

Nearly three decades of stagnant wages, ineffective child support enforcement, and dwindling welfare benefits have made single mothers and their children America's poorest demographic group. Because 60 percent of all children born during the 1980s will spend part of their childhood in a mother-only family, and because current trends suggest that an even higher proportion of children born during the current decade will be raised by single mothers, we believe the economic well-being of mother-only families should be of concern to every American (Martin and Bumpass 1989; Sweet and Bumpass 1987).

## Welfare, Work, and Motherhood
## in Four U.S. Cities

Even before welfare was time-limited, a substantial majority of those who collected welfare got off the rolls within two years, and hardly any stayed on the rolls continuously for more than eight years (Harris 1993; Pavetti 1992). Just about all of those who received any welfare spent three times as many of their adult years off the rolls as on it (Harris 1997), and only about one-fifth of the daughters of highly dependent mothers became highly dependent themselves (two-thirds of these daughters never even used welfare) (Duncan, Hill, and Hoffman 1988).

Despite these realities, taxpayers have generally viewed welfare recipients as wastrels who were willing to spend their adult years living off the hard work of others while raising children who were likely to do the same (Bobo and Smith 1994). In the 1990s, even the relatively sympathetic renderings of many liberals portrayed welfare mothers as trapped in a vicious cycle of dependency from which many of them could not escape. Lawmakers of both parties and a Democratic president used these claims to justify their support of the Republican welfare reform bill of 1996. They reasoned that the only way to rid society of current and future generations of dependent women and children was to toughen up the rules regarding welfare. As the government got tough, they believed poor women would behave more responsibly. They defined "responsible" behavior on the part of parents rather narrowly as the willingness to engage in wage-earning labor (and on the part of nonparents as the willingness to forgo child-bearing until they could support their children on their earnings).

This book is about 379 low-income single mothers who, in future years, will likely be affected in some way by changes in federal and state welfare policies. When we interviewed them, their lives were somewhat similar to Mary Ann Moore's. Most were similarly skilled and had a good deal of experience with the world of low-wage work. Most also had personal experience with welfare. None of the single mothers we spoke to, however, earned as much as Moore. Nor did most have housing and day care subsidies plus a supportive relative with enough free time to take a major role in parenting their children.

Our conversations with these mothers show that low-income single mothers have a much broader view of what constitutes responsible behavior than policymakers do. Not only must mothers ensure that their children are sheltered, fed, and clothed, they must also see that they are supervised, educated, disciplined, and loved. As any parent knows, these goals often conflict. Few affluent Americans realize the depth of this conflict for poor or near-poor single mothers. The mothers we interviewed had to choose between a welfare system that paid far too little to provide for their basic needs and a labor market that offered them little more than they could have gotten by staying home. Since neither affordable health insurance nor child care was available to most low-wage workers, mothers who chose work over welfare often had to trust their family's medical care to county hospital emergency rooms and their children's upbringing to the streets. The lack of affordable housing for low-income families meant that many low-wage working mothers (particularly African Americans and Latinas) had to raise their children in some of the country's most dangerous neighborhoods—neighborhoods many Americans are afraid even to drive through.

The women we interviewed were fairly evenly divided between those who received cash benefits from welfare and those who did not. We refer to those who were receiving cash welfare benefits as welfare-reliant, and to those who were not receiving cash welfare but had low-wage jobs as wage-reliant. Yet like their counterparts nationwide, most of the welfare-reliant mothers had substantial work experience, and most of the wage-reliant mothers had received cash welfare in the past. This reflects the fact that over the last few decades, many unskilled and semiskilled single mothers have cycled between welfare and work (Edin and Harris forthcoming; Harris 1993; Harris and Edin 1996; Pavetti 1992).

We have chosen the term "reliant" over the more commonly used "dependent" because neither welfare nor work provided enough income for families to live on.[3] Because of this, all but one of the 379 mothers we spoke with engaged in other income-generating strategies to supplement their income and ensure their economic survival. The one mother who did not, a publicly housed Boston-area resident, provided the quintessential exception that proves the rule. Her child went without food and adequate clothing on a regular basis, and she was in danger of losing custody of the child due to "neglect."

The mothers we interviewed were drawn from four U.S. cities: Chicago, Boston, San Antonio, and Charleston, South Carolina. None of the cities we studied provided mothers nearly enough in welfare benefits to cover their expenditures. Yet because of state differences in welfare payments, mothers' benefits varied broadly across our four sites, and these variations had real consequences for the women and children we studied. Welfare-reliant mothers living in cities in low-benefit states (the Charleston and San Antonio mothers) experienced significantly more material hardship than those either in Chicago, a city in an average-benefit state, or in the Boston area, which offered higher-than-average benefits (see chapter 2). Overall, the welfare-reliant mothers covered only three-fifths of their expenditures with their welfare benefits.

The working mothers covered about two-thirds of their monthly expenses with wages from their main jobs. Yet in dollar terms, the wage-reliant mothers faced the largest gap between their income and expenses. Their material hardship rates reflected this large gap: wage reliant mothers reported experiencing more material hardship than those who relied primarily on welfare (see chapter 4).

Because of their constant budget shortfall, mothers in both groups had to generate additional revenue to make ends meet. Welfare-reliant mothers had to keep these activities hidden from their welfare caseworkers and other government bureaucrats. The federal rules that applied to these mothers required them to report any cash income to their welfare caseworker, who then would have reduced their welfare checks by nearly the same amount. In most states, these rules still apply. Therefore, in order to supplement their welfare income, recipients concealed the extra money. Although the federal tax rate on income is far less punitive than the penalties of most welfare departments, many of the wage-reliant mothers we interviewed also hid their side-income. This was because many received means-tested food stamps, housing subsidies, or other benefits that would have been reduced or eliminated if program officials knew about their supplementary income.

## The Dual Demands on Single Mothers

It is virtually impossible to understand the economic behavior of the mothers we interviewed without considering the overall context within which this behavior occurred—that of single motherhood. Our mothers' accounts show that all over America, unskilled and semiskilled single mothers face desperate economic and personal situations that they can seldom resolve satisfactorily. Most want to be good providers *and* good mothers. For these parents, good mothering means, at minimum, keeping their children out of danger—off the streets, off drugs, out of gangs, not pregnant, and in school. Most of us would endorse these goals, but few realize just how difficult they are to achieve for mothers who must support their children on low-wage employment.

These widely shared social definitions of good mothering affected how our respondents spent their money. Good mothers, they believed, should treat their children on occasion. Consequently, some mothers would occasionally forgo necessities to pay for a basic cable television subscription, a movie rental, a trip to a fast food restaurant, new clothes for the first day of school, or name-brand sneakers. Although these items are not essential for a child's material well-being, a cable television subscription is a relatively inexpensive way for mothers to keep their children off the streets and away from undesirable peers. Likewise, buying a pair of expensive sneakers is insurance against the possibility that children will be tempted to steal them or sell drugs to get them.

The importance of being a good mother also limited women's access to the more financially lucrative survival strategies available to them. Although a few mothers sold sex, drugs, or stolen goods when other strategies failed, almost all believed that good mothering and routine criminal activity were incompatible. Thus, few mothers engaged in well-paid side-work like prostitution. Instead, they opted for cleaning houses, maintaining apartment buildings, mowing lawns, babysitting, collecting bottles and aluminum cans, or other poorly paid work.[4]

Finally, concerns about good mothering profoundly affected the way that mothers thought about the advantages of welfare and low-wage work. The regular jobs open to unskilled and semi-skilled women were precisely those jobs that are least compatible with mothering. The jobs our mothers held seldom provided health benefits, so mothers who chose them often had to forgo medical care for themselves or their children. Many of these jobs offered unpredictable or limited hours, required workers to take shifts at odd or irregular times, provided few if any paid vacation or sick days, and did not allow mothers to take or make personal calls to check on children left home alone. In sum, the nature of their jobs often made it difficult for mothers to fulfill their parenting roles satisfactorily.

Because virtually all the women we interviewed were at least as concerned with parenting as with providing, many chose not to work for a time. As low-income single mothers' option to withdraw from the labor market and rely on welfare is increasingly restricted, it is hard to gauge what impact this may have on their ability to parent their children effectively. We believe that this will largely depend on the type of jobs and the kinds of long-term support services states will be able to provide unskilled and semi-skilled single mothers who work.

## PROJECT HISTORY AND RESEARCH DESIGN

This research grew out of two previous studies on how low-income single mothers made ends meet. Kathryn Edin began her research in Chicago after working with Susan Mayer and Christopher Jencks on the 1983–1985 Chicago Survey of Poverty and Material Hardship.[5] The survey showed that nearly half of the families with incomes below the official poverty threshold reported that their expenditures on food, housing, and medical care exceeded their entire incomes (Mayer and Jencks 1989).

This finding led Edin to ask how poor families—particularly poor mother-only families—make ends meet. Her first attempt to find the answer to this question involved reinterviewing poor single mothers who had participated in the 1985 survey, first by telephone and then in person. While a few of those she contacted were forthcoming, most were unwilling to offer information about how they made ends meet. Their hesitancy arose because they had no personal introduction to her and therefore suspected she was "checking up" on them in some official capacity.

Edin concluded that she could not get accurate responses from low-income single mothers using survey research methods. She therefore took a different tack, contacting a wide variety of individuals who knew welfare mothers in various capacities and asking them for personal introductions to potential respondents. She then arranged a series of informal semistructured interviews with each respondent.

Edin's initial interviews took place in Chicago, a city with average welfare benefits and living costs. For the most part, Chicago welfare recipients lived bleak lives, often in dangerous neighborhoods, and spent little or nothing for extras. Their welfare checks and food stamps often did not cover rent and food, much less the rest of the items their families needed each month. If the mothers had tried to live on their welfare benefits alone, most would have exposed their children to serious material hardship. To avoid this, the mothers devised a set of survival strategies to supplement their welfare benefits and pay their bills. Virtually none of the mothers reported any of this supplementary income to their caseworkers. Though no mother Edin contacted in Chicago went without such supplemental income, many people doubted that the patterns one had observed in Chicago—a city with a reputation for vice and corruption—occurred with equal frequency elsewhere.

At about this time, Laura Lein was conducting similar research among Mexican American welfare recipients in a San Antonio public housing project. These families could not make ends meet on their welfare checks either. In order to get the goods and services their families needed each month, the San Antonio families garnered assistance from as many as twenty-five different public and private service agencies each year. Each agency had different regulatory requirements, eligibility criteria, and routines for service delivery. Thus, using agencies as a survival strategy took a lot of time, energy, and know-how. Yet even when parents undertook such efforts, they barely raised their families above destitution.

Edin and Lein pooled their data from Chicago and San Antonio welfare recipients and extended their work to two additional cities: Boston and Charleston, South Carolina. Two of the cities (Charleston and San Antonio) offered very little in cash welfare benefits, whereas the other cities offered average (Chicago) or above-average (Boston) welfare payments. Edin and Lein also extended the study to include a sample of low-wage working single mothers in each site, since Edin's Chicago research had suggested that low-wage workers were in a financial bind similar to that of welfare-reliant mothers. One of the low-benefit cities offered these single mothers a tight labor market (Charleston), while the other was slack (San Antonio). Similar labor-market differences were evident in the higher-benefit cities (Chicago's was average whereas Boston's was slack). In addition, there were substantial variations in living costs between the sites. Thus, extending our work in these ways allowed us to observe the effects of welfare benefit levels, labor-market conditions, and living costs on low-income single mothers' economic situations and survival strategies.

When Edin conducted her Chicago interviews, Illinois mothers received cash welfare benefits approximating the national average, and they faced a moderate cost of living and a relatively tight labor market (unemployment ranged from 5.3 to 6.2 percent in 1989). When Lein collected her data in San Antonio, cash benefits were among the lowest in the nation (though the cost of living was also low) and unemployment rates were quite high (ranging from 6.2 to 7.3 percent in 1991). Charleston, South Carolina, also offered very low welfare benefits, but the cost of living in Charleston was much higher than in San Antonio and the labor market there was quite tight (unemployment ranged between 4.1 and 5.3 percent in 1991). Finally, the Boston area provided relatively high welfare benefits, matched by a high cost of living. Unemployment was also well above the national average (ranging from 7.2 to 8.6 percent in 1991 and 1992).[6]

## SAMPLING AND INTERVIEWING TECHNIQUES

In each of these metropolitan areas, we sampled two basic populations of single mothers: welfare recipients and nonrecipients who held low-wage jobs. We also stratified our sample by two additional criteria: race and whether the respondent got a housing subsidy. We looked primarily at African Americans and whites, not because we expected to find substantial racial differences, but because we wanted to ensure adequate representation of both groups. We also stratified by whether a mother paid market rent or had some level of rent subsidy, on the grounds that mothers in subsidized housing have a better chance than others of making ends meet on their welfare benefits or wages alone.

We allowed one deviation from this design. San Antonio, like most Southwestern cities, has a large Mexican American community with large numbers of mother-only families, so we added Mexican Americans who were U.S. residents to our San Antonio sample. We included this group because Lein's previous research indicated that San Antonio's Mexican American mother-only families had little access to the kind of income-generating strategies that Edin's Chicago mothers had used, and we wanted to see how these constraints affected these mothers' budgeting strategies and material well-being.

Gathering accurate budget information from a large group of single mothers living in a variety of places proved to be a huge task. Mothers who are used to keeping their survival strategies a secret from caseworkers, housing authorities, the Internal Revenue Service (IRS), and unfriendly neighbors who might turn them in hesitate before trusting anyone outside of their personal networks. In our initial fieldwork, we both learned that a stranger had almost no chance of getting an accurate accounting of these mothers' income-generating strategies (see Edin 1993; Lein 1994).

Data from large nationally representative surveys were consistent with our experiences. Poor or near-poor persons who participate in such surveys typically report incomes that are far below their expenditures. In analyzing the results of the Consumer Expenditure Survey (CES), Edin and Jencks (1992) found that mothers who received something from public assistance (which includes welfare) typically reported enough income to cover only three-fifths of their expenditures. Since these mothers were unlikely to have any savings to fall back on, Edin and Jencks concluded that welfare-reliant CES respondents were as likely to hide their side-income from survey researchers as from welfare officials.

Because reliable data on survival strategies proved so hard to obtain, we recruited mothers with the assistance of a wide variety of trusted community residents, including members of neighborhood block groups, housing authority residents' councils, churches, local community organizations, and local charities that the community held in high regard. These personal introductions were crucial to our ability to gain the mothers' trust.

To guard against interviewing only those mothers who were well connected to community leaders, organizations, and charities, we asked the mothers we interviewed to refer us to one or two friends whom they thought we would not be able to contact through other channels. In this way, we were able to get to less-connected mothers. All in all, we were able to tap into over fifty independent networks in each of the four cities. This technique ensured an extremely cooperative and yet relatively heterogeneous group of prospective respondents, almost 90 percent of whom agreed to be interviewed.

After contacting each mother, we arranged multiple semi-structured in-depth interviews with her. Interviewing more than once proved just as important to our data-gathering efforts as personal introductions. First, we found that the more conversations we had with a mother, the more likely she was to give us the whole story. The whole story was hard to get not only because mothers were sometimes hesitant to tell it but also because we did not always know how to interpret their words when they did.[7] For example, when we initially asked mothers if they engaged in prostitution to make ends meet, virtually every woman denied doing so. However, a small number of women told us they had several "boyfriends" who would "help them out" with a bill in exchange for "going out." Others admitted to "selling sex" or "selling ass." When we pressed them, we found that the women used these terms to distinguish their activities from those of "professionals"—women who worked for a pimp and solicited on a daily basis.

Questions regarding support from absent fathers provide another example of how difficult it could be to interpret mothers' initial responses. In this case, some mothers who insisted they received nothing in child support later told us that the child's father "helped out" each week. At first, we assumed this meant that the father provided only in-kind support. Later, we discovered that many of these fathers also contributed cash outside of official channels. Finally, we learned that most mothers only termed absent fathers' cash contributions as "child support" if it was collected by the state.

Questions about household composition provide yet another example of interpretive difficulties. When we asked mothers if boyfriends or absent fathers lived with them, they would often tell us "no, but he stays sometimes." Over time, we discovered that mothers in certain communities do not generally refer to a boyfriend as "living in" unless his name is on the lease. In subsidized housing, boyfriends never signed the lease—if they did so, their income would raise the rent. In private housing, boyfriends seldom signed leases either since they frequently moved between the households of relatives and girlfriends.

Some of these problems (such as distinguishing between prostitution and help from boyfriends) arose in all groups, but others applied only to specific sites, racial or ethnic groups, or neighborhoods. In San Antonio, for instance, some mothers told us that they purchased their clothing from "boosters." We soon learned that "boosters" were professional shoplifters who contracted with the family to steal preselected clothing in the sizes needed. Families then paid boosters an agreed-upon fraction of the sticker price. Thinking we had stumbled across a folk term that might apply across all poor communities, we began to ask respondents in other sites if they purchased clothing from boosters. They were mystified. This type of professional shoplifting was not common in other sites, and the term was seldom used.[8]

Among Charleston's central-city African Americans, to offer another example, mothers who turned their child's father over to the Child Support Enforcement authority told us they "put him on the green." Some respondents believed this phrase referred to the color of money. Others told us they thought it referred to the large park in front of the central-city welfare office—which resembled a village green—since this was where mothers signed the necessary forms to begin child support proceedings. However, neither whites nor African Americans living in the semirural areas on the outskirts of the city had any familiarity with that term.

In short, gathering accurate data regarding income-generating strategies required not only trust but learning to ask the questions properly and interpret the answers correctly. However, there were also other reasons for multiple interviews. First, mothers who were unclear about their expenditures the first time we interviewed them could keep careful track of what they spent between interviews and give a more precise accounting of their budget the second or third time around. Second, multiple contacts gave interviewers a chance to double- and triple-check budget information, probing for more information when budgets were not in balance or did not make sense. We deemed a case finished when the respondent came within $50 of reconciling her monthly expenses to her income and when the interviewers felt confident that the overall budget made sense given what else we knew about that family's situation.

In a typical initial interview, we gathered a topical life history. In subsequent interviews, we collected detailed income and expenditure data. We first asked respondents to estimate expenditures during the previous month. We then asked how much these monthly amounts had varied over the previous twelve months. Finally, we asked if they had made large one-time purchases during the previous year (VCRs, furniture, appliances, bicycles, and so forth) that were not included in their monthly account.

For mothers who had moved from welfare to work or back to welfare within the prior twelve months, we gathered expenditure data for only those months since their change in status but asked them to describe how their economic situation had changed as well. If they had changed status within the last month or two, we spaced the first and second interviews several months apart, so the women could accurately calculate the impact of the status change on their budgets. We used the same practice for mothers who moved from a subsidized to a private apartment or vice versa, or for mothers who had recently doubled up or moved out of a shared-housing situation.

After gathering a detailed account of each respondent's monthly expenditures, we asked her to tally her total income, both from AFDC and other welfare programs and from outside sources. Asking the expenditure question first was crucial for getting an accurate budget. In one or two of our very early interviews, we felt that respondents who had talked about their income first had adjusted their expenditures downward to fit those descriptions, and almost never talked about outside income. Then, once mothers made the claim that they spent nothing for clothing, school supplies, transportation, Christmas presents, entertainment, and so on, it was very hard to get them to change their stories, even when we ran into them at a bus stop or saw the newly purchased items in their homes. Though we finally generated budgets from these respondents that made sense, it took repeated interactions (twelve in one case) and a lot of persistence.

We asked respondents to detail their monthly expenditures and income at least twice and asked them to account for any discrepancies. Once we persuaded a mother to trust us, getting an accurate accounting of her expenditures was relatively easy. Unlike more affluent consumers, most single mothers who live on very little keep careful track of every dollar they spend. Since the food stamp program required that mothers keep records of rent and utility bills and pay stubs, mothers generally had these on hand. Any purchase the mothers made beyond these necessities usually involved careful planning. Expenditures for nonnecessary items often required that mothers skimp on necessities. For these reasons, mothers were generally able to construct sensible budgets over time. The principal exception was a very small group of drug-addicted mothers whose spending patterns were erratic and hard to tally. In these cases, we worked with the respondent to make the best estimate possible.

## RESEARCH QUESTIONS

Five central questions drove our research design:

1. How much money do unskilled and semiskilled single mothers spend in different locations?
2. Where do unskilled and semiskilled single mothers get their money?
3. What kinds of material hardships do single mothers experience in different locations, and how much do these conditions vary between welfare- and wage-reliant mothers?
4. How do single mothers assess the economic and noneconomic consequences of choosing work or welfare?
5. Are single mothers' spending patterns influenced by their welfare or marital status, their family background, the neighborhoods in which they live, or their racial or ethnic group?

In each city, our first goal was to construct expenditure and income figures that made sense and were roughly in balance. One might think that such figures already exist.[9] After all, the Census Bureau is constantly asking people about their incomes, and it also has an ongoing Consumer Expenditure Survey. As we mentioned earlier, this survey and others taken at the national level have failed to produce budgets that balance for poor and near-poor single mothers. We thought there were three possible reasons for the discrepancy these surveys show in mothers' budgets: they could underreport their income, they could exaggerate their expenditures, or they could borrow to meet temporary deficits. Our goal in collecting budget data was purely descriptive—to discover how much money unskilled and semiskilled single mothers really spent, both when they received welfare and when they did not.

Once we collected all of the expenditure data, we asked mothers about how they generated the income—both official and unofficial—to meet these expenses. We expected that mothers' unofficial income sources would vary from city to city, because some cities would offer more unofficial moneymaking opportunities than others. We expected these opportunities would depend, in turn, on labor-market conditions, on the character of each city's informal economy, and on how effectively welfare officials could enforce rules about reporting side-income (which, it turned out, depended mostly upon city size).

Over time, we found that mothers in both groups relied on three basic strategies to bring their income in line with their expenses: work in the formal, informal, or underground economy; cash assistance from absent fathers, boyfriends, relatives, and friends; and cash assistance or help from agencies, community groups, or charities in paying overdue bills. Mothers employed all these strategies in all four cities, but to varying degrees.

Our third question was one of objective well-being. Until recently, no government agency regularly kept track of how often a family goes without food, needed medical care, adequate housing, or warm clothing during a given year. Given the widely varying sites we chose to study, we thought that variations in mothers' economic situations might have an effect on whether they suffered hardships. We also believed that by measuring hardship, we might gain some insight into the trade-offs involved in moving from welfare to work. Specifically, we wanted to know whether mothers who lived in cities with lower welfare benefit levels or wage rates experienced more hardship, whether welfare-reliant mothers experienced more or less hardship than wage-reliant mothers, and what level of spending was necessary for mothers of both groups to avoid hardships.

Fourth, we were interested in how mothers who received welfare viewed their own prospects for work, and how these perceptions compared with the situations of the workers we interviewed. Several surveys have asked welfare-reliant women whether they want to work (see chapter 3), yet no study we know of has captured detailed open-ended accounts of the work attitudes and plans of such a large and heterogeneous group of welfare recipients. We asked mothers to talk at length about what kind of job (in terms of salary, benefits, job security, and other less tangible job attributes) they believed they would need to provide a viable long-term alternative to welfare. Since we could not follow mothers as they moved on and off welfare, we paid special attention to the accounts of people who had recently moved from work to welfare and compared them with those of people who had recently moved from welfare to work. These comparisons involved people who were "at the margin" with respect to the welfare/work choice.

Finally, we wanted to know whether the economic lives of unskilled and semiskilled single mothers were similar for all groups of mothers, or whether mothers from different backgrounds had different economic situations. Although there has been renewed interest among social scientists in the role that culture plays in the lives of the poor, no other study has gathered data that allow comparisons of the income-generating survival strategies of mothers from different backgrounds. In particular, we hoped to address the question of whether mothers' economic situations and survival strategies are largely driven by shared structural opportunities and constraints or whether subgroups exhibit distinctive patterns that cannot be explained merely by reference to their position within the social structure.

## LISTENING TO
## LOW-INCOME SINGLE MOTHERS

We believe that the in-depth accounts of these 379 single mothers' real-life economic situations and the survival strategies they employed to resolve these situations can shed new light on welfare reform efforts across states. In the scholarly debate about welfare reform, the voices and lived experiences of single mothers are often drowned out by reams of statistics, usually aggregate numbers that, while useful, can distance us from the daily struggles poor single women face as they try to both parent and provide for their children. As states take on the hard task of creating welfare systems that are more effective than the federal system which preceded them, legislators who hope to succeed will need

to recognize that implementing the mandate of the federal government to get mothers to work in two years will make daily life
harder for many of these women and their children. Mothers who
made ends meet by combining informal work with welfare under
the old welfare rules will have to quit their informal jobs to meet
workfare requirements and will have less net income with which
to pay their bills. Mothers who managed before by waiting for
hours in the lines of local charities in hopes of getting help in
paying an overdue bill will face similar constraints under the new
rules. Less income for the mothers will almost certainly mean that
their children will be worse off, both materially and develop-
mentally (Brooks-Gunn and Duncan forthcoming). The harm to
children will be particularly severe if states cannot find a way to
pay for long-term child care and health care for unskilled and
semiskilled working mothers. Because the kinds of jobs most of
these mothers will likely get offer virtually no premium on experience, transitional child care subsidies and health benefits will
not be enough.

States who want to meet the twin goals of getting welfare
mothers to work while safeguarding the well-being of their children must understand that the real problem with the federal welfare system is primarily a labor-market problem. For the large
majority of the mothers we interviewed, it was lack of access to
a living wage and not a pervasive and disabling poverty culture
that made working so difficult. Unless states can manage to equip
welfare-reliant single mothers with the skills that will lead to living wage jobs, single mothers who work will continue to need
government help.

# — Chapter 2 —

# Making Ends Meet on a Welfare Check

A LONG MINNESOTA'S HIGHWAY 72—which runs between the Canadian border town of Rainy River and Bemidji, Minnesota—a large, crudely lettered billboard greets the southbound traveler:

> WELCOME TO MINNESOTA
> LAND OF 10,000 TAXES
> BUT WELFARE PAYS GOOD

Antiwelfare sentiment is common among Minnesotans, who live in a state with high personal income taxes and cash welfare benefits substantially above the national median (see chapter 8). But even in southern states, where cash welfare benefits are very low and taxes modest, citizens are likely to denigrate welfare. In 1990, about 40 percent of respondents in each region told interviewers from the National Opinion Research Center that the United States spends too much on welfare.[1] In 1994, another nationally representative survey found that 65 percent of Americans believed welfare spending was too high (Blendon et al. 1995).

Legislators recognize welfare's unpopularity. In the first half of the 1990s, several states cut benefits, and all let their value lag behind inflation. In addition, most states applied for federal waivers to experiment with benefit limitations or sanctions not allowed by the old federal rules. Some states established a "family cap," which denied additional cash to mothers who had another child while receiving welfare. In other states, mothers whose children were truant from school lost a portion of their cash grant. Furthermore, under the new federal rules, all states

20

must limit the amount of time a mother spends on welfare to five years.

Public dissatisfaction with welfare persists despite the fact that cash benefits to welfare recipients have declined by more than 40 percent in real terms since the mid-1970s (Blank 1994, 179). The reasons for the continuing public discontent throughout this period are complex, but probably rest on the widespread belief that the federal welfare entitlement perpetuated laziness and promiscuity (Bobo and Smith 1994; Page and Shapiro 1992).[2] Lazy women had babies to get money from the welfare system, the story went, and then let lazy boyfriends share their beds and live off their benefits. These lazy and immoral adults then raised lazy and immoral children, creating a vicious cycle of dependency.

Those who have promoted this view include the news media and talk show hosts, but social scientists also have contributed. The most widely known "scientific" argument was developed by Charles Murray, who in 1984 claimed that welfare actually makes the poor worse off. Federal welfare became too generous during the 1960s and 1970s, Murray argued, and began to reward unwed motherhood and indolence over marriage and jobs (Murray 1984). Social scientists spent much of the late 1980s attempting to discover whether Murray was right. Typically, economists judged the merits of the claim by estimating the disincentive effects of more or less generous state welfare benefits on work (for a review of this literature, see Moffitt 1992). Other researchers attempted to measure the effect of varying state benefits on marriage, divorce, and remarriage (Bane and Ellwood 1994).

The task we set for ourselves in this chapter is a more fundamental one. In order to assess whether any welfare program is too generous, one must compare its benefits to the cost of living faced by that program's recipients. An obvious starting point is to ask how much families headed by single mothers spend each month to make ends meet, and how that income compares with what they receive from welfare.

## HOW MUCH DO WELFARE-RELIANT MOTHERS SPEND?

In 1992, Donna Carson, a forty-year-old African American mother of two living in San Antonio, characterized herself as "ambitious and determined." She had spent most of her adult life playing by the rules. After high school graduation, she got a job and got married. She conceived her first child at age twenty-five, but her husband left before the child was born. Soon after her son's birth, she arranged for her mother to take care of him and went back to work. Because she did not have to pay for child care, her wages from her nurse's aide job combined with the child support she received from her ex-husband were enough to pay the bills. Ten years later, when she turned thirty-six, she had a second child. This time she was not married to the father. Carson's mother was willing to watch this child as well, so again she returned to work. Shortly thereafter, Carson's father's diabetes worsened and both of his legs were amputated. Her mother was overwhelmed by the tragedy and checked herself into a psychiatric hospital, leaving Carson to care for her two children and her disabled father alone. Seeing no other way out, she quit her job and turned to welfare. That was 1989.

Three years later, when we were talking with her, Carson was still on welfare, and her budget was tight. Her typical monthly expenditures were about $920 a month. One-third of that amount went to rent and utilities, another third went to food, and the rest went to cover her children's clothing, their school supplies, her transportation, and all the other things the family needed. Her combined monthly benefits from AFDC and food stamps, however, came to only $477.

Some months, she received a "pass through" child support payment of $50 from the father of her first child, who was legally obligated to pay. Although this payment did not reduce her AFDC benefits, her food stamps did go down by about $15 every time she received it. The father of her second child bypassed the formal child support system and paid her $60 directly each month. To get the rest of the money she needed, Carson took care of a working neighbor's child during the day. This neighbor could pay only $100 a month, but gave her the money in cash so that Carson's welfare caseworker could not detect the earnings and reduce her check. She got the rest of the money she needed from her father, who paid her $250 in cash each month to care for him.

Though Carson had more personal tragedy than most, her budget was similar to that of most other welfare recipients we talked with. Table 2-1 gives the monthly expenses of the 214 welfare-reliant mothers we interviewed (and their 464 children). It shows that our respondents averaged $213 a month on housing, $262 on food, $336 on other necessary expenses, and $64 on items that were arguably not essential—a total of $876 for an average family of 3.17 people.[3]

## Housing Expenses

The housing expenses of welfare-reliant families varied substantially. This variation depended on whether recipients paid market rent, had a housing subsidy in a public housing project or a

**TABLE 2-1. Monthly Expenses of 214 AFDC Recipients: Means and Standard Deviations**

|  | Mean | SD |
|---|---|---|
| Housing costs | $213 | $187 |
| Food costs | 262 | 112 |
| Other necessities | 336 | 176 |
| Medical | 18 | 43 |
| Clothing | 69 | 62 |
| Transportation | 62 | 83 |
| Child care | 7 | 32 |
| Phone | 31 | 35 |
| Laundry/toiletries/cleaning supplies | 52 | 31 |
| Baby care | 18 | 32 |
| School supplies and fees | 14 | 48 |
| Appliance and furniture | 17 | 39 |
| Miscellaneous | 47 | 59 |
| Nonessentials | 64 | 63 |
| Entertainment | 20 | 31 |
| Cable TV | 6 | 14 |
| Cigarettes and alcohol | 22 | 30 |
| Eat out | 13 | 27 |
| Lottery costs | 3 | 16 |
| TOTAL EXPENSES | 876 | 283 |

*Source:* Authors' calculations using Edin and Lein survival strategies data.
*Note:* The mean family size is 3.17 people. Numbers do not total due to rounding.

private building (Section 8), or shared housing with a relative or friend. Donna Carson paid market rent, which in San Antonio was quite low but still higher than what most mothers pay in subsidized units. However, apartments that meet the physical criteria required for Section 8 tended to be in neighborhoods with less access to public transportation than the neighborhoods where housing projects were generally located, so these families usually had to maintain an automobile. Consequently, while public housing and Section 8 residents paid roughly the same amount for housing, Section 8 families spent far more for transportation.

In most cases, the welfare-reliant families who shared housing with a friend or relative were able to split the rent, utilities, telephone bill, and other household expenses. Thus, their expenses for rent and these other items were relatively low. About half of those who shared housing lived with one or both parents. The other half lived with siblings or friends. Mothers who lived with a parent usually made only token contributions toward the rent and took some portion of the responsibility for utilities and household maintenance. Most lived with their parents precisely because they could not afford to maintain their own households. Those who lived with a sibling or friend usually paid half of the household expenses. Sometimes, however, mothers "rented" only a portion of the living space (a single room, for example) and paid only a quarter or a third of the household costs.[4]

## Food Expenses

Food expenditures averaged $262 a month for the welfare-reliant families we interviewed. This means that these mothers spent $19 per person on food in a typical week. This amount is nearly identical to the federal government's cheap food plan (the "thrifty food budget"), which uses as its base what poor mothers bought for their families in the 1950s and adjusts the prices in that "basket" for inflation each year (Ruggles 1990; Schwarz and Volgy 1992). The average weekly food stamp allotment for the families we interviewed, however, was slightly lower than this amount—$16 per person. This is because we oversampled mothers with housing subsidies to try to find mothers who could live on their benefits alone, and they do not qualify for the maximum amount of food stamps (food stamps are adjusted for living costs). This meant that the average mother had to cover $40 of food expenses each month with income from some source other than food stamps.[5]

Food stamp benefits also varied with family income, including cash welfare. In the lowest AFDC benefit states, therefore, families could receive up to $292 a month in food stamps for a family of three, or $21 per person per week in 1991, and families in these sites who reported no outside income received this maximum. Most found it sufficient to cover the bulk of their food expenditures. Families in states that paid more generous welfare benefits received roughly 30 cents less in food stamps for each additional dollar in cash welfare benefits. Because of this, hardly anyone who lived outside the South could pay their food bills with food stamps alone.[6] In San Antonio, food stamps covered 99 percent of respondents' average food expenditures; in Charleston, 88 percent; in Chicago, 80 percent; and in high-benefit Boston, only 65 percent.

## Other Expenses

Besides housing and food, clothing took the next biggest bite out of the average family's monthly budget, followed by transportation, laundry and toiletries, telephone charges, medical expenses, baby care, and appliance and furniture costs. On average, welfare-reliant mothers spent $69 a month on clothing. This means that the mothers with whom we spoke typically purchased $261 worth of shoes, coats, and other apparel for each family member in a year.[7] Most of this was for their children, since children continually grow out of their clothing.

Welfare-reliant mothers employed a number of strategies to contain their clothing expenditures. Virtually all purchased some of their clothing at thrift or second-hand stores, and most scoured neighborhood yard sales. During our interviews, many mothers proudly showed us their second-hand buys: a barely worn pair of name-brand jeans or a winter coat that was practically new and only a bit too small. A mother's largest expense in the clothing category was for children's shoes. Children not only went through two or more pairs of shoes a year, but shoes in children's sizes and in good condition were seldom available at neighborhood thrift stores. Winter coats, hats, mittens, and boots were also expensive, and most children grew out of them every other winter. Thus in the winter months, clothing needs could become an added hardship. One mother told us,

> In the winter months, I have had to keep my children at home on the really cold days because I didn't have warm enough clothes to dress them. I have learned to swallow my pride, though, and go to the second-hand shops and try to get the right kind of winter clothes for the boys.

The welfare-reliant mothers we interviewed felt that second-hand clothing was acceptable for younger children, whose peers were still largely unconcerned with appearance. One mother told us,

> For shopping I go to yard sales and the Salvation Army for Jay's clothes. Fortunately, he isn't the type of kid who always has to have Nike sneakers or he won't go to school. I get him K-Mart ones, or I go to the used clothes store [on] Belmont [Avenue]. I probably spend $200 a season on new clothes for him, but some of those he can wear from season to season.

Other mothers reported that their older children—especially high school boys—felt they could not maintain their self-respect or the respect of their peers while wearing K-Mart shoes to school. Some mothers felt that if they did not purchase name-brand sneakers, an athletic jacket, or other popular items for their teenagers, their children might be lured into criminal activity so they could buy these items themselves:

> My boy, he sees these kids that sell drugs. They can afford to buy these [tennis shoes] and he can't. So I have my little side-job and [I buy them for him]. You got to do it to keep them away from drugs, from the streets.

One mother told us that in order to buy her child a $50 pair of tennis shoes, she ate only one meal a day for a month. The savings in her food bill were enough to cover the purchase of the shoes. Most mothers in her neighborhood did not feel it was necessary to go hungry to meet their children's clothing needs, because they could generate the extra cash in other ways, which we discuss later.

Mothers who bought new clothing generally had to put the clothing on layaway. They paid a small portion of the purchase price each month. Some others found professional shoplifters who would note the children's sizes, shoplift the clothing, and sell it for a fraction of the ticket price to the mother.

Transportation cost the average welfare-reliant family $62 a month. Families living in Charleston (where there was little access to public transportation) and families living outside central cities spent more because they had to maintain automobiles or pay for taxis. At the time of our interviews, welfare rules limited the value of a family's automobile to $2,500. This meant that mothers had older cars, which generally required more frequent repair and got poorer gas mileage. All of the states we studied had mandatory insurance laws, and respondents told us that minimum insurance coverage cost at least $40 a month. In addition, Chicago and metropolitan Boston required that families purchase city stickers to park on the street, and South Carolina taxed the value of a family's car each year.

Although mothers who had access to public transportation spent less than those mothers who maintained cars, bus and subway transportation cost the average mother who used it more than $60 a month. Few mothers lived in areas where they could walk to the laundromat or the grocery store. In neighborhoods that provided these amenities, rents were higher. Since few mothers could afford child care, a shopping trip required that mothers bring their children with them and pay the bus or subway fares for the older children as well (younger children often ride free).

Laundry, toiletries, and cleaning supplies also constituted a significant proportion of monthly expenses. Some mothers washed their clothing in the bathtub and let it air-dry in their apartment or outside. This was a time-consuming task, however, and mothers complained that their clothes did not get as clean as machine-washed clothing. A few mothers owned or rented their own washers and dryers, but most used local laundromats. Because most families' clothing stock was slim (for example, two or three pairs of pants for each person was typical), mothers usually washed their clothing once each week or more. Laundromat prices varied, but mothers seldom spent less than $6 for coin machines each time they visited the laundromat, for roughly three loads.

All told, the welfare-reliant mothers had to spend $23 in a typical month to wash and dry their clothing and an additional $29 on toiletries and cleaning supplies. Food stamps could not be used to purchase toiletries or cleaning supplies, so mothers had to pay for sponges, cleaning fluids, dishwashing liquid, hand and laundry soap, bleach, toilet paper, hair care products, deodorant, disposable razors, and feminine products with cash.

Ninety-two percent of our sample had telephone service for at least part of the year. On average, families spent $31 monthly on telephone charges. Twenty-six percent of the welfare recipients had their phone disconnected at least once during the past year because of nonpayment. When mothers ran short of money, they were usually more willing to do without a phone than to neglect rent, utilities, food, clothing, transportation, or other essentials. Basic service charges also varied widely by site. In San Antonio, where basic local service cost about $12 a month, families spent only $18 a month for phone-related costs. In all other sites, comparable service ranged from $20 to $25 a month, and families spent much more. These costs included not only charges for local and long-distance calls but connection and reconnection charges as well. Although not strictly necessary for a family's material well-being, mothers without telephones had a difficult time maintaining contact with welfare caseworkers and their children's schools. It was also more difficult to apply for jobs because prospective employers could not reach them to set up an interview. Some solved this dilemma by sharing a phone with a neighbor; messages left with neighbors, however, were not always promptly forwarded.

Medicaid, the government's health insurance program for low-income families, offered free emergency care and routine physician care. All the households in our welfare-reliant sample were covered by Medicaid. Over-the-counter medicines and other medical services, however, were not covered and constituted another $18 of the average welfare-reliant mother's monthly budget. These expenses included routine drugstore costs, such as those for pain relievers, cough syrup, adhesive bandages, vitamin tablets, or other medicines families frequently used. In addition, few state Medicaid programs pay for prescription birth control pills, abortions, antidepressants, or other mental health drugs. Nor do most Medicaid plans pay for dental care, except for emergency oral surgery.

Diapers and other baby care products cost an average welfare-reliant family $18 a month (37 percent of the welfare recipients in our sample had babies in diapers). Welfare-reliant mothers with infants and young toddlers typically received formula, milk, eggs, and cheese from WIC (Women's, Infants', and Children's nutritional program). Most mothers told us, however, that they were usually one or two cans short of formula each month and had to purchase them at the grocery store. In addition, WIC does not provide disposable diapers, which constituted roughly 80 percent of the cash welfare-reliant mothers had to spend on baby care. Only a tiny minority of the mothers we interviewed used cloth diapers; although cheaper than disposables, cloth diapering was not practicable for mothers who relied on laundromats. In addition, mothers who used cloth diapers reported substantial up-front costs (they had to buy the diapers), and these mothers spent substantially more for laundry supplies than other mothers. Mothers also averaged $14 a month on school-related expenses and $7 a month on child care.

Appliances and furniture cost the typical family another $17 a month. Generally mothers purchased both new and used furniture and appliances with installment payments. Because they could not get bank credit, these mothers would often arrange credit at local thrift shops and "rent to own" furniture stores. Although local thrift stores did not generally apply finance charges to mothers' purchases (they usually held the item until it was fully paid for), rent-to-own furniture stores did. Because the latter stores charged very high interest rates and allowed long repayment periods, mothers sometimes ended up paying two to three times the actual value of the item. Meanwhile, mothers who missed a payment could have the furniture repossessed, losing whatever equity they had built up.

Miscellaneous items in the families' budgets included check-cashing fees and fees for money orders, debt service, burial insurance (discussed later in this chapter), and haircuts. These items totaled $47 in the average month.

## Nonessentials

Entertainment cost the typical family $20 each month and was usually limited to video rentals; occasionally it included movies, trips to amusement parks, and travel (mothers sometimes sent their children to relatives during the summer). Mothers spent an average of $22 for cigarettes and alcohol each month, mostly on cigarettes. Mothers seldom bought their own alcohol, and those who drank depended on boyfriends, friends, and family members to pay for their drinks. This was also true for most mothers who used marijuana or other drugs. In addition, mothers spent an average of $3 a month for the lottery, $6 a month for cable television, and $13 a month to eat out. All told, the typical welfare-reliant family spent $64 a month on these nonnecessary items, or about 7 percent of their total budget.[8] Although not physical necessities, the items met crucial psychological needs.

Although the mothers in our sample worried about day-to-day material survival, most saw survival as having broader "psychological" and "social" dimensions. One mother commented:

> You know, we live in such a materialistic world. Our welfare babies have needs and wants too. They see other kids going to the circus, having toys and stuff like that. You gotta do what you gotta do to make your kid feel normal. There is no way you can deprive your child.

This woman's statement captures a common sentiment among the welfare recipients we interviewed: children need to have an occasional treat, and mothers who refuse them may deprive their offspring of normalcy. Even among Mexican American mothers in San Antonio, who spent less than any of the other welfare-reliant mothers, one family in six paid a small monthly fee for a basic cable subscription. These mothers told us they saw the cable subscription as a cheap way of keeping their kids off the streets and out of trouble.

The mothers themselves needed an occasional boost too. Many reported that by spending small amounts on soda pop, cosmetics, cigarettes, alcohol, or the lottery, they avoided feeling like they were "completely on the bottom," or that their lives were "completely hopeless." When we asked respondents if they could do without them, they replied that these items gave them some measure of self-respect, and without them they would lose hope of bettering their situations:

> I never buy for myself, only for my son. Well, I take that back. I allow myself two of what I guess you would call luxuries. Well, I guess three. First, I buy soda pop. I do not eat meals hardly ever, but I always have to have a can of Pepsi in my hand. I drink Pepsi nonstop. My boyfriend, he buys it for me by the case 'cause he knows how much I like it, and I guess it's the pop that gives me my energy for dealing with my son—you know, the sugar and caffeine and stuff.
>
> And then I treat myself to the cigarettes. Without the smoking, I would just worry all the time about how we was going to eat and would never relax. I feel like I deserve some little pleasure, you know, and so those cigarettes keep me up, keep me feeling that things aren't so bad.
>
> And the other thing is, I buy my cosmetics. I mean, I go around feeling so low all the time, and the makeup makes me feel, you know, better about myself. I feel like I'm not so poor when I can buy myself some cosmetics at the discount house.

The few respondents who spent money on alcohol reported similar sentiments:

> Oh, sometimes, you know, just to relax or somethin', I just go out and have a few. And when I'm really low, I sometimes go out and tie one on, if you know what I mean. Sometimes I think I'll go crazy all day in the house if I can't get out once in a while. I just couldn't take it.

Although few mothers played the lottery with any regularity, those who did also viewed it as a sort of escape:

> I just can't afford not to buy some tickets when the pot gets real big. I sometimes buy five tickets if I can afford it. I like to plan what I'm going to do with it, you know, fantasize and stuff—dream of what it would be like to own nice things and such.

## Variations in Expenditures by Site

As we show in table 2-2, housing costs account for the bulk of variation in monthly expenditures between cities. Half of the welfare-reliant mothers interviewed in each city lived in federal, city, or county subsidized housing. These mothers' rent was set at 30

TABLE 2-2. **Average Monthly Expenses of 214 AFDC Recipients by Site**

| | Charles-ton | San Antonio | Chicago | Boston | Sig. |
|---|---|---|---|---|---|
| Family size | 2.95 | 3.40 | 3.32 | 2.87 | * |
| Housing costs | $224 | $112 | $289 | $239 | *** |
| % paying all of their own rent | 34% | 14% | 34% | 11% | *** |
| Food costs | $249 | $278 | $288 | $217 | *** |
| Food per person | 87 | 84 | 91 | 80 | |
| | | | | | |
| Other necessities | 372 | 258 | 365 | 372 | *** |
| Medical | 28 | 17 | 15 | 15 | |
| Clothing | 70 | 58 | 75 | 74 | |
| Transportation | 97 | 34 | 67 | 62 | *** |
| Child care | 12 | 4 | 5 | 10 | |
| Phone | 25 | 18 | 36 | 47 | *** |
| Laundry/toiletries/ cleaning supplies | 46 | 40 | 67 | 53 | |
| Baby care | 27 | 19 | 8 | 20 | ** |
| School supplies | 11 | 13 | 24 | 8 | |
| Appliances/furniture | 21 | 10 | 18 | 23 | |
| Miscellaneous | 36 | 45 | 50 | 59 | |
| | | | | | |
| Nonessentials | 46 | 55 | 60 | 99 | *** |
| Entertainment | 14 | 14 | 24 | 26 | * |
| Cable TV | 6 | 6 | 2 | 13 | *** |
| Cigarettes and alcohol | 16 | 15 | 29 | 26 | ** |
| Eat out | 10 | 19 | 2 | 24 | *** |
| Lottery costs | 0 | 1 | 3 | 10 | ** |
| | | | | | |
| TOTAL EXPENSES | 891 | 704 | 1,003 | 927 | *** |

*Sources:* Authors' calculations using Edin and Lein survival strategies data.
*Note:* Columns do not total due to rounding. Two-tailed tests for significance of differences between cities given by * > .10; ** > .05; *** > .01.

percent of their reported incomes. In most cases, this also covered electricity and heat. The other half of our welfare-reliant sample lived in private housing, either on their own or with another family. Private housing costs varied dramatically by site. In 1990, the census found that Boston landlords were able to charge a median $656 a month for rent; such rents were also typical of New England and California cities, as well as suburban New York. In Chicago the median was $507. Chicago rents were similar to those in Atlanta, Baltimore, Miami, Minneapolis/St. Paul, Philadelphia, Sacramento, and Seattle. In Charleston, the median rent was $411, similar to those rents paid by residents of other fast-growing sunbelt cities like Austin, Charlotte, Dallas/Fort Worth, Houston, Jacksonville, Nashville, Raleigh/Durham, Richmond, and Tampa/St. Petersburg. In San Antonio, median rent was only $363, resembling those in other southern cities like Little Rock, Louisville, Memphis, and New Orleans (U.S. Bureau of the Census 1994b).

Mothers' average transportation costs also varied significantly across cities. Boston and its inner suburbs were densely populated and close together. Here, public transportation was readily accessible and relatively inexpensive. Chicago was larger, but its central city was also well served by buses and elevated trains. The Chicago and Boston-area mothers we interviewed spent between $60 and $70 each month on transportation.

Charleston mothers spent the most on transportation—an average of $97 a month—because more had cars (45 percent in Charleston versus 21 percent in Chicago, 24 percent in Boston, and 8 percent in San Antonio). In Charleston, respondents complained that regular bus service was largely confined to tourist districts and did not serve poor or near-poor areas. The Charleston Transit Authority eliminated service to the city's most notorious public housing project after gunfire shattered several bus windows. Because the complex was so isolated from the rest of the city, residents had to walk a mile to the nearest bus stop, and the path was dangerous; it wound through a series of vacant lots and abandoned warehouses where muggings, rapes, and shootings are commonplace. The project's physical isolation from the remainder of the city also meant no laundromat or grocery stores were within walking distance. Because other poor Charleston neighborhoods were also isolated, the major forms of transportation were private automobiles and unlicensed neighborhood taxis.

Residents of San Antonio's largest housing project were not quite as isolated. Though they had access to some public transportation, only one city bus line ran within walking distance of the project. Laundry facilities and small corner grocery stores were close by, but these businesses charged somewhat inflated prices.

Thus in both Charleston and San Antonio, mothers who could not maintain or borrow cars seldom traveled out of their immediate neighborhoods. Those who did were largely at the mercy of unlicensed neighborhood taxi drivers—local men (and sometimes women) who took mothers to the grocery store, laundromat, welfare office, or other destinations for about $10 per round trip. They had little competition from licensed cabs, since taxicab companies did not like to send drivers into poor neighborhoods or projects because they feared their drivers would be mugged or cheated out of their fares.

On average, the mothers we interviewed spent just over $600 a month on nonhousing and nontransportation items; mothers in San Antonio spent less ($558) and mothers in Boston more ($626). If we adjust for family size—San Antonio households were the largest, while Boston-area households were the smallest—the site differences in nonhousing and nontransportation spending were greater. This does not necessarily mean that the Boston-area mothers wasted more money than those in San Antonio. As we will show, mothers who spent more exposed their families to less material hardship.

## HOW MUCH COULD A SINGLE MOTHER
## RECEIVE FROM WELFARE IN THE EARLY 1990s?

Ordinary Americans usually use the term "welfare" to refer to the whole package of federal and state programs serving working-age adults and their children. Virtually no cash benefits are available to childless working-age adults unless they are disabled (only a few states offer General Assistance benefits to the childless).[9] Nor are there many welfare benefits available to married parents.[10] Unmarried fathers receive little welfare because mothers nearly always keep the children when marriages or other partnerships break up. Therefore, when people speak of "welfare" they are nearly always referring to the programs that target single mothers and their children.

## The Federal Welfare System

Under the old federal welfare rules, a single mother with no outside income was entitled to a number of cash and in-kind welfare benefits from the government, with Aid to Families with Dependent Children providing the main cash benefit. (Under the new rules, the federal entitlement has ended, but states will likely continue to provide cash welfare to poor single mothers and their children for up to five years.) Some mothers were also eligible for a small amount of energy assistance and, in a handful of states, could qualify for additional cash to help them purchase school clothes for their children or pay for a small part of their utilities (see chapter 6).

Under both the old and the new rules, welfare programs are jointly funded by the state and federal governments and wholly administered by the state, which sets benefit levels and eligibility criteria within federally defined limits. In 1993, cash welfare benefits for a family of three varied between $120 a month in Mississippi and $680 a month in Connecticut. Illinois, which fell at the U.S. median, offered a family of three a maximum of $367 a month (U.S. House of Representatives 1994).[11] Roughly 5 million families received welfare in 1993, and 9.5 million American children lived in a household that depended in some part on welfare benefits (U.S. House of Representatives 1995, table 10-24).

## Medicaid

Low-income mothers could have been eligible for four noncash programs: Medicaid, food stamps, WIC, and housing subsidies. Only Medicaid and food stamps were entitlements—that is, anyone who qualified could receive the benefit. Medicaid programs varied somewhat by state, but most entitled welfare-reliant mothers and their children to free doctor visits, hospitalization, and routine prescription drugs. If these families were to have purchased this kind of health insurance on the open market, the cost would probably have exceeded $300 a month (see Jencks and Edin 1995). Thus, the average value of Medicaid exceeded the value of cash welfare in many states.

It is important to recognize, however, that this average con-
ceals immense variation among families. For families with few
medical problems, Medicaid was worth relatively little; for those
with serious problems, it was very valuable. Since single-parent
families receiving federal welfare benefits in the late 1980s and
early 1990s were significantly more likely to have serious health
care problems than other single-parent families, Medicaid provided a crucial safety net for many of these families (Wolfe
1994).

## Food Stamps

Nationwide, nine out of ten mothers who received cash welfare
in 1993 also participated in the Food Stamp Program.[12] Because
federal food stamps were means-tested—adjusted for a recipient's
total income—they were somewhat higher in states where AFDC
benefits were lower. In states where welfare paid a single mother
with two children $324 a month or less, a family of three with no
outside income could get food stamps worth $292 in 1993 (see
table 2-3). Although the higher benefits in some states reduced
assistance from the food stamp program, no state paid so much
in cash welfare that families become ineligible for food stamps.[13]

## Housing Subsidies

Nationwide, about one welfare-reliant mother in ten lived in public housing and one in ten received a Section 8–type subsidy to
live in private housing in 1995 (U.S. House of Representatives
1995, table 10-27). All mothers with subsidies paid roughly 30 percent of their cash income for rent—roughly $120 for a mother
with two children who received median cash benefits. Many
mothers with whom we spoke had reservations about living in
public housing projects because they were generally located in
high crime ghettos of central cities. Section 8 subsidies, which set
rents at the same level as public housing but allowed recipients
to live in privately owned buildings in mixed-income neighborhoods, were therefore much more attractive. But the supply of
these subsidies was limited. Because of this, the program was
overwhelmed by demand, and mothers usually waited for many
months, sometimes years, to obtain Section 8 housing.

TABLE 2-3. **Maximum AFDC Benefits for a Family of Three in the Four Cities**

|  | Charleston | San Antonio | Chicago | Boston |
|---|---|---|---|---|
| 1993 maximum AFDC benefits | $200 | $184 | $367 | $539 |
| Maximum food stamps | $292 | $292 | $285 | $228 |
| TOTAL | $492 | $476 | $652 | $767 |
| Median rents for MSA in 1990 | $411 | $363 | $507 | $656 |
| 25th-percentile rents in 1990 | $346 | $292 | $375 | $446 |
| Cost of subsidized housing (3 persons, 1990) | $60 | $55 | $110 | $162 |
| Food stamp "tax" if in subsidized housing | $22 | $18 | $60 | $60 |
| AFDC and food stamps minus food costs, and private rent at 25th percentile | $−146 | $−108 | $−15 | $29 |
| AFDC and food stamps minus food costs, and subsidized rent | $140 | $129 | $250 | $313 |

*Sources:* AFDC levels from U.S. House of Representatives (1993). Rents from U.S. Bureau of the Census (1994a), table 245, pp. 440–44. Median rents from U.S. House of Representatives (1993).

*Note:* The table shows benefit levels available in 1993. Benefits are calculated using 1990 rents and 1993 cash welfare and food stamp benefits in each city.

## Variations in Benefits by Site

We chose research sites with a broad range of both cash and in-kind welfare benefits (see table 2-3). Chicago offered cash benefits at the national median. Boston's benefits were much more generous. In Charleston and San Antonio, benefits were among the lowest in the nation. In the early 1990s, cash benefit levels were set so that no family in any of the cities we studied could afford to pay average market rent.[14]

Table 2-3 shows how median rents and rents at the 25th percentile compared with cash and in-kind welfare benefits in each site. In Chicago and Boston, mothers paying modest rents needed to spend virtually all of their cash welfare benefits on rent.[15] The gap between welfare benefits and rents at the 25th percentile was even greater in San Antonio and Charleston.

In San Antonio, cash welfare did not cover the rent at the 25th percentile, and most poor families could afford only the very worst private housing. Some welfare-reliant families we interviewed there lived in dilapidated shacks that sometimes had no heat or electricity, or had backed-up sewage systems or dirt floors. Others doubled up in slightly better quarters or moved to housing projects.

In Charleston, Hurricane Hugo eliminated many of the cheapest private rental units in September 1989. In response, families either doubled up with their relatives or remained in their half-ruined homes. As was true in San Antonio, the only private housing mothers could afford on their own was usually in deplorable condition. Some mothers lived in trailers or run-down dwellings on the outskirts of the city where rents were more affordable.[16]

By 1990, rents for even relatively cheap housing units in Charleston ranged from $200 to $300 a month (U.S. Bureau of the Census 1994b, 347).[17] Though the city was under pressure to provide more subsidized housing, it did not respond. Instead, it closed one of its largest housing projects—Ansonborough Homes—to make room for a multimillion-dollar aquarium. At about the same time, the Section 8 housing program stopped taking new applications, informing marginally-housed families that they could not apply until they became literally homeless. Three of the families we interviewed tried this strategy and waited for several months in overcrowded family shelters until a Section 8 subsidy became available.

## "IT'S JUST NOT ENOUGH"

Table 2-4 shows that the 214 welfare-reliant mothers we interviewed received an average $307 in cash a month from AFDC and another $222 in food stamps. Mothers also received $36, on average, from federal welfare program for the financially-needy disabled, the Supplemental Security Income (SSI) program.[18] Thus, the combined welfare incomes of the families with whom

TABLE 2-4. **Summary of Benefits for 214 Welfare-Reliant Mothers by Site (1991 dollars)**

|  | Total Sample | Charleston | San Antonio | Chicago | Boston |
|---|---|---|---|---|---|
| TOTAL WELFARE | $565 | $493 | $488 | $599 | $696 |
| AFDC | 307 | 193 | 192 | 368 | 495 |
| Food stamps | 222 | 220 | 276 | 230 | 140 |
| SSI[a] | 36 | 81 | 21 | 1 | 61 |

*Source:* Authors' calculations using Edin and Lein survival strategies data.
[a]In 1990, federal rule changes allowed children with serious disabilities to receive SSI benefits. Since the Chicago respondents were all interviewed before 1990, they could not take advantage of this benefit for their children.
*Note:* Differences between the cities all significant at the .01 level. Numbers do not total due to rounding.

we spoke averaged $565 a month. Because of our stratified sampling strategy, roughly half of the welfare-reliant mothers interviewed in each site received housing subsidies, which lowered their food stamp benefits.

How far did these benefits go toward meeting the needs of welfare-reliant families? All 214 of our welfare-reliant respondents reported that their combined benefits ran out long before the month was over. One mother told us: "I don't ever pay off all my bills so there isn't ever anything left over. As soon as I get my check, it's gone and I don't have anything left." Another respondent said:

> What you have to live off isn't enough. Me myself, I just got back on and I had been off for about six years because I was working. But [I had some health problems and needed some medical insurance so] I had to get back on the program. It's just not enough. You just can't live off it especially with three kids or two kids. It is impossible, the things you have to do to last you until the next month. Me myself, I get $380 [in cash] for three kids [plus food stamps]. The rent I pay is just impossible plus my other little bills.

Only a handful of the welfare-reliant mothers with whom we spoke came close to meeting their expenses with combined welfare benefits, and only one got by on these benefits alone.

When mothers received their check, they prioritized their expenses, usually paying for housing (rent, electricity, gas) and purchasing food before attending to their other bills. After housing and food, the typical family had $90 left to pay for their other expenses: clothing, transportation, laundry, school supplies, furniture and appliances, over-the-counter medicines and toiletries, haircuts, telephone calls, and items such as diapers and routine dental care.

As table 2-5 shows, mothers who lived in public housing projects came the closest to meeting their expenses with their benefits. Because their families were somewhat larger than average, they received $639 a month from cash welfare, food stamps, and SSI. To meet the needs of a mother and three children (the most common family size in this group), project-based families, who constituted 31 percent of our welfare-reliant sample, typically spent $828 each month. This meant that their expenses exceeded their total welfare income by roughly $189. The budgets of Section 8 families (24 percent of the sample) were somewhat tighter

## TABLE 2-5. Welfare Income and Expenses of 214 AFDC Recipients by Housing Category

| | Project-Based Subsidy | Section 8 Subsidy | Shared Housing | Private Housing | Sig. |
|---|---|---|---|---|---|
| Number of families | 66 | 51 | 47 | 50 | N/A |
| Family size | 3.80 | 3.00 | 2.55 | 3.12 | *** |
| Total welfare benefits | 639 | 552 | 483 | 558 | *** |
| Total expenses | 828 | 886 | 717 | 1,077 | *** |
|   Housing | 122 | 157 | 147 | 453 | *** |
|   Food | 289 | 269 | 222 | 258 | ** |
|   Transportation | 32 | 99 | 58 | 69 | *** |
|   Other | 385 | 361 | 290 | 297 | |
| Welfare minus housing and food expenses | 228 | 126 | 114 | −153 | *** |
| Welfare minus total expenses | −189 | −334 | −234 | −519 | *** |

*Source:* Authors' calculations using Edin and Lein survival strategies data.
*Note:* Two-tailed tests for significance of differences in means between housing types given by * > .10; ** > .05; *** > .01.

because, as we discussed earlier, they had to pay more for transportation than publicly-housed mothers. Furthermore, their families were smaller (generally three persons), so they received nearly $100 less in welfare benefits than their publicly-housed counterparts. Overall, Section 8 mothers' welfare benefits left them $334 short each month.

The 22 percent of welfare-reliant families who shared housing with a friend or relative had smaller-than-average families (2.5 persons versus 3.17 persons) and received only $483 a month from AFDC, food stamps, and SSI. Because they often split the rent, utilities, telephone, and sometimes the food bill with another family, they spent only $717 a month on average, but their $234 shortfall each month was still substantial (see table 2-5).

The final group of mothers we interviewed, those in private unshared housing, faced the largest gap between income and expenditures. They received $558 from AFDC, food stamps, and SSI and spent $1,077 in an average month, leaving them $519 short. Their situation was truly desperate: they were $153 in the red after paying only for housing and food. Overall, 36 percent of the welfare-reliant families in our sample got less from AFDC, food stamps, and SSI than they paid for housing and food. Among privately-housed mothers, 84 percent fell into this category. Perhaps more worrisome, the budgets of privately-housed mothers are probably the most representative of welfare recipients nationwide, since program statistics show that only about one-fifth of welfare recipients receive housing subsidies (U.S. House of Representatives 1995, table 10-27).

One mother in eight came within $50 of covering her expenditures with her welfare benefits. As a group, these twenty-six mothers were unusual in several ways. First, all of them received subsidized housing or shared housing costs with a friend or relative. Second, half of them received substantial in-kind assistance from a variety of community organizations (in some cases, between twenty and thirty organizations per family over the course of a year) and from their families and friends. Third, half sold most of their food stamps for cash. They then got their food from community organizations and purchased almost all their other necessities from neighborhood fences who sold stolen groceries, clothing, and toiletries at cut-rate prices. Our best guess is that in the absence of these strategies, these mothers would have had to spend between $200 and $300 more a month to keep their families together.

Only one of our 214 mothers—an extremely frugal, publicly-housed Boston-area resident—was able to meet her expenses with her welfare benefits. She made ends meet because she lived in an unusually generous state and spent nothing whatsoever on entertainment, alcohol, cigarettes, or the lottery; nothing on child care; nothing on school supplies (what the school did not provide, her son did not get); and nothing on furniture or appliances (she scavenged broken-down furniture from alleys). She spent nothing on transportation, since all her friends lived in the projects and she walked nearly everywhere she needed to go. She also spent very little on laundry because she washed clothes in the bathtub and let them air-dry. She spent little on clothing because she purchased the majority of the family's clothes (the few there were) at thrift stores. Finally, she spent nothing for Christmas, birthdays, or any other special occasion. No other respondent in *any* site made ends meet on so little. Since her child frequently went hungry, had only one change of clothes, and often missed school because he lacked adequate winter clothing, several of this woman's neighbors (whom we interviewed) had reported her to child protective services for neglect.

## HOW DO WELFARE-RELIANT MOTHERS
## MAKE ENDS MEET?

No one without substantial assets can spend more than they take in for long. The welfare-reliant women we interviewed had few savings, no IRA accounts, no stocks or bonds, and no valuable assets. If they had and if their caseworkers had known, they would have been ineligible for welfare. When they ran out of cash and food stamps, those who did not have a generous parent or boyfriend worked at regular or informal jobs. They also had to "work" the system, making sure that neither their earnings nor the contributions they received came to the attention of the welfare department. If they reported such income, their welfare checks would soon be reduced by almost the full amount of this income, leaving them as poor as before.

Table 2-6 shows that, on average, cash welfare, food stamps, and SSI covered only about three-fifths of welfare-reliant mothers' expenses.[19] A small amount also came from the earned income tax credit (EITC) for wages earned in the prior year. From our conversations with mothers, we learned that they made up the remaining gap by generating extra cash, garnering in-kind contributions, and purchasing stolen goods at below market value. We found it difficult to estimate, however, how much each mother saved by using the latter two techniques (see chapter 6). Therefore, we only present figures for those strategies that generated extra cash.

Earnings from reported work, unreported work (off the books or under a false identity), or work in the underground economy (selling sex, drugs, or stolen goods) made up 15 percent of welfare-reliant mothers' total monthly income.[20] Another chunk (17 percent) came from members of their personal networks and went unreported. Agency-based contributions—usually cash contributions, direct payment of mothers' bills, or the portion of student grants and loans that could be squeezed for extra household cash after paying for tuition and books—covered the last 4 percent of the average welfare-reliant mother's budget.

To get a clearer sense of how welfare-reliant mothers generated extra income, table 2-6 also shows the degree to which mothers relied on various sources of income each month. By definition, all the mothers we coded as welfare-reliant received something from the AFDC program. Table 2-6 shows that almost all of them also received food stamps (95 percent), compared with 87 percent of welfare recipients nationwide (U.S. House of Representatives 1993, 711).[21] Nine percent of the sample received SSI or payments for the care of foster children. Seven percent received money from the EITC because they reported income from work during the previous calendar year.

Table 2-6 gives further detail on how mothers' earnings from work contributed to their family budgets. Five percent worked in the formal economy at reported jobs, compared with 6 percent nationally (U.S. House of Representatives 1993, 696). Others were also working and not reporting it. Approximately two-fifths (39

**TABLE 2-6. Survival Strategies of 214 Welfare-Reliant Mothers**

| Variable | Amount of Income Generated Through Each Survival Strategy | Percentage of Total Budget | Percent of Mothers Engaging in Each Survival Strategy[a] |
|---|---|---|---|
| TOTAL EXPENSES | $876 | 100% | N/A |
| Housing costs | 213 | 24 | N/A |
| Food costs | 262 | 30 | N/A |
| Other necessities | 336 | 39 | N/A |
| Nonessentials | 64 | 7 | N/A |
| | | | |
| Welfare benefits | 565 | 64 | N/A |
| AFDC | 307 | 35 | 100% |
| Food stamps | 222 | 25 | 95 |
| SSI | 36 | 4 | 9 |
| | | | |
| EITC | 3 | 2 | 7 |
| | | | |
| Work-based strategies | 128 | 15 | 46 |
| Reported work | 19 | 2 | 5 |
| Unreported work | 90 | 10 | 39 |
| Underground work | 19 | 2 | 8 |
| | | | |
| Network-based strategies | 151 | 17 | 77 |
| Family and friends | 62 | 7 | 46 |
| Men | 95 | 11 | 52 |
| Boyfriends | 56 | 6 | 29 |
| Absent fathers | 39 | 4 | 33 |
| Covert system | 33 | 4 | 23 |
| Formal system | 7 | 1 | 14 |
| | | | |
| Agency-based strategies | 37 | 4 | 31 |
| | | | |
| TOTAL INCOME | 883 | 100% | N/A |

Source: Authors' calculations using Edin and Lein survival strategies data.
Note: These income-generating strategies do not include in-kind contributions or purchasing goods illegally because these figures were difficult to estimate. Columns do not total due to rounding.
[a]The sum of the percentages exceeds the total because some mothers engaged in more than one strategy.

percent) worked off the books or under a false identity to generate additional income, and 8 percent worked in the underground economy selling sex, drugs, or stolen goods. (The percentages do not sum to 46 percent because some mothers engaged in more than one strategy.) Table 2-6 also shows that 77 percent of mothers were currently receiving covert contributions from family, boyfriends, or absent fathers in order to make ends meet.[22] Nearly half (46 percent) of welfare-reliant mothers relied on family and friends for financial help each month. Even more, 52 percent, received help from a man: 29 percent from boyfriends on a regular basis, 14 percent through the formal child support collection system, and 23 percent from the fathers of their children on a covert basis. In addition, 31 percent received cash, voucher, or direct assistance in paying a bill from a community group, charity, or student aid program.

## COULD THEY HAVE SPENT LESS?

Critics of welfare programs often suspect that low-income families cause their material poverty through poor money management (Heclo 1994). By comparing the expenses that our mothers reported, however, with those of the poorest income group in the Consumer Expenditure Survey (CES), we show that our welfare-reliant mothers spent substantially less than most American households in the early 1990s.[23]

Table 2-7 compares our mothers' expenditures with those households surveyed by the CES. Column 2 shows the monthly expenditures of CES one-parent households with at least one child under age eighteen—a rough proxy for single-mother households. Column 3 shows expenditures by all CES households that reported incomes below $5,000 (not including food stamps or other in-kind benefits), which is just above the average annual cash benefit for welfare recipients in the early 1990s. The main story here is that the CES families reported spending far more for necessary and nonnecessary items than our mothers did, suggesting that our mothers' expenses reflect the very low end of national consumption patterns.

TABLE 2-7. **Average Expenses of 214 Welfare-Reliant Mothers Compared with Those of Poor Households in the Consumer Expenditure Survey**

| | Mean | CES 90-91 One-Parent Households with at Least One Child Under 18 | CES 90-91 Two or More Person Households with Very Low Incomes (less than $5,000 a year)[f] |
|---|---|---|---|
| TOTAL EXPENSES[a] | 876 | 1,804 | 1,563 |
| Size | 3.17 | 2.9 | 3.0 |
| Housing[b] | 213 | 469 | 394 |
| Food | 275 | 303 | 289 |
| Food (at home) | 262 | 217 | 193 |
| Food (eat out) | 13 | 88 | 97 |
| Medical | 18 | 65 | 97 |
| Clothing | 69 | 147 | 103 |
| Transportation | 62 | 260 | 247 |
| Phone | 31 | 51 | 44 |
| Laundry/toiletries/ cleaning[c] | 52 | 45 | 42 |
| School supplies | 14 | 22 | 23 |
| Appliances/furniture | 17 | 61 | 64 |
| Entertainment[d] | 26 | 81 | 86 |
| Cigarettes/alcohol | 22 | 32 | 42 |
| Miscellaneous[e] | 47 | 259 | 130 |
| Child care/baby care/ lottery | 75 | N/A | N/A |

*Sources:* Column 1, Edin and Lein survival strategies data. Column 2, extracted from U.S. Bureau of Labor Statistics (1993), pp. 146–49, table 34. Column 3, extracted from U.S. Bureau of Labor Statistics (1993), pp. 30–33, table 5.

[a]Although we include child care ($7 a month) and lottery expenses ($3 a month) in the total, we do not itemize them, because they were not included in CES categories. We calculated these levels simply by adding the standard work-expenses deduction available to AFDC mothers after twelve months on the job ($90). We then subtracted $10 to take into account the fact that mothers must be eligible for at least $10 in benefits to receive anything. Columns do not add due to rounding.

[b]In the CES estimates, housing costs include the following: All shelter costs, costs of fuel and electricity, and costs of water and public services. We have excluded "household operations" and telephone services. The family size is rounded to match CES figures.

[c]In the CES estimates, this figure includes laundry and cleaning supplies and other household products, as well as personal care products and services. In our calculations, haircuts were included under miscellaneous, but all other personal care products and services were included under toiletries.

[d]Includes all entertainment and cable TV costs.

[e]The CES figures used here include "household operations," "postage and stationery," "reading," "miscellaneous," "cash contributions," and "personal insurance and pensions." Our figures also included these items, but we added haircuts to this category as well.

[f]According to these data, families in this category spend several times what they earn.

Another way to evaluate mothers' expenditures is to ask how much these expenditures secured in the way of material well-being. Of the 214 welfare-reliant mothers we interviewed, the vast majority were living significantly below what most Americans would think an adequate standard. Recall that the average welfare-reliant mother in our sample had a total monthly cash income of $883, or $10,596 a year, on which to support herself and her children. The poverty line for a three-person family was $11,521 in 1992. During our interviews, we learned that about half of the mothers reported total expenditures of less than 75 percent of the poverty threshold for their family size, and more than four-fifths spent less than the official threshold. Although 18 percent did spend more than the official poverty line, only 4 percent spent more than 133 percent, and none exceeded 160 percent of the federal threshold. Not surprisingly then, most welfare-reliant mothers reported that their families regularly went without items that virtually every American would consider necessities.

Until very recently, no federal government agency regularly surveyed Americans about food or medical hardships, about whether they have recently been evicted, whether they have had their utilities shut off, or whether they have enough warm clothing for the winter.[24] In 1983 and 1985, Fay Cook and Christopher Jencks took a first step toward filling this gap by surveying over two thousand Chicago-area households across the full range of incomes; 1,617 respondents answered all the questions that concern us here.[25] Cook and Jencks asked about hardship in four main areas: food, housing, utilities, and health care. In their analysis of these data, Mayer and Jencks (1989) documented a fairly strong relationship between these hardships and a family's income-to-needs ratio.

Cook and Jencks's questions are nearly identical to those we asked of our respondents in the late 1980s and early 1990s; our questions are presented in appendix A. We asked about hardships relating to food, housing, utilities, and health care and added some hardship questions of our own based on mothers' open-ended accounts of their lives. We asked each welfare-reliant mother if there had been a time during the past year when she did not have enough money to buy the food her family needed, if she or her children had gone hungry, if the family had gone without a doctor or dentist when she thought treatment was needed, if the family had had their utilities shut off for nonpayment, and if they had substantial problems with housing. We also ventured beyond Cook and Jencks's framework by asking mothers if they had been evicted or become homeless in the last two years (see table 2-8).[26] Finally, based on our open-ended discussions with welfare-reliant mothers, we added questions about whether a mother or her children had gone without winter clothing she thought the family needed or whether the household had gone without a telephone. In sum, we asked questions in five hardship domains: food, clothing, utilities, health care, and housing.

Despite our addition of a few more questions, enough similarities remain between our work and that of Cook and Jencks that their results can serve as a reference point by suggesting the degree to which the average urban American household experiences deprivation relative to a household headed by a poor single mother. In the following sections, we therefore compare the responses of our sample with those of Cook and Jencks.

## Food and Hunger

We asked welfare-reliant mothers in each site, "Has there been a time in the last year when you needed food but couldn't afford to buy it?" and "Was there a time in the last year when you or your children actually went hungry?" Except in Boston, about a third of the families we interviewed had run out of food during the previous twelve months despite the fact that nearly all of the welfare families received food stamps (compared with one-fourth of Cook and Jencks's nonelderly respondents).[27] The relatively high cash benefits and numerous services (including food pantries) available to Boston-area mothers meant that only one-fourth of them had run out of food.

Although some welfare-reliant mothers turned to relatives or food pantries in this situation, other mothers could not depend on this type of help. Fifteen percent of our welfare-reliant families had actually gone hungry during the previous year (compared with 7 percent of the Cook and Jencks group). Mothers who regularly ran out of food found that food pantries put strict limits on the number of times a given mother could receive assistance. Nor

**TABLE 2-8. Measures of Material Hardship for 214 Welfare-Reliant Mothers by Site**

| Hardship | All Welfare | San Antonio | Charles-ton | Chicago | Boston | Sig. |
|---|---|---|---|---|---|---|
| *N* | *214* | *63* | *44* | *62* | *45* | *N/A* |
| 1. No food | 31% | 33% | 34% | 32% | 24% | |
| 2. Hungry | 15 | 16 | 23 | 13 | 11 | |
| 3. Doctor[a] | 7 | 6 | 9 | 5 | 9 | |
| 4. No health benefits | 0 | 0 | 0 | 0 | 0 | N/A |
| 5. Utilities off | 17 | 16 | 25 | 13 | 16 | |
| 6. At least two housing-quality problems | 25 | 46 | 18 | 13 | 18 | *** |
| 7. Public housing | 31 | 40 | 11 | 26 | 44 | *** |
| 8. Shared housing | 22 | 27 | 25 | 18 | 18 | |
| Evicted | 9 | 10 | 16 | 8 | 4 | |
| Homeless | 16 | 11 | 27 | 18 | 9 | * |
| Winter clothes | 12 | 11 | 16 | 11 | 9 | |
| Phone off or no phone | 34 | 43 | 40 | 32 | 20 | |
| Core hardships[b] (1 to 6) | 1.06 | 1.46 | 1.25 | .71 | .78 | *** |
| Weighted core hardships | .66 | .99 | .78 | .40 | .47 | *** |
| Hardship I (1 to 8) | 1.58 | 2.13 | 1.61 | 1.15 | 1.40 | *** |
| Weighted hardship I | .88 | 1.24 | .91 | .58 | .76 | *** |

*Source:* Authors' calculations using Edin and Lein survival strategies data.
[a]This includes mothers who said they went without a medical or eye doctors' care, but does not include lack of access to a dentist, chiropractor, or any other health practitioner.
[b]Unweighted scores are the sum of the individual hardships.
*Note:* Two-tailed tests for significance of differences in means between cities given by * > .10; ** > .05; *** > .01.

was persuading neighbors and friends to share their food as easy as one might expect, especially for those mothers living in poor communities. Many mothers managed to keep themselves and their families safe by affiliating only with a small group of trusted family and friends with whom they shared resources. Even among these trusted few, the norms of reciprocity were strong, and mothers who could not give something in return found that loyalty quickly wore thin. Any researcher who has spent substantial time in blighted inner-city neighborhoods knows that residents do not readily trust others outside of their limited networks, often with good reason.

Hunger did not always affect both the mother and her children, but this was often the case since children who ate school breakfast and lunch missed the evening meal if the family had no food. We estimate that roughly 75 percent of children shared their mother's hunger hardship. So whereas 31 percent of the children in our welfare-reliant sample had experienced shortages of food, we estimate that about 15 percent had actually gone hungry. If these figures were representative of welfare recipients nationwide, which they may not be, roughly two million children receiving cash welfare went hungry for lack of money each year in the early 1990s.

## Winter Clothing

Rather than ask mothers if they had been unable to afford *all* the clothing their families needed during the past twelve months (virtually everyone would have answered affirmatively), we restricted our inquiry to whether families had gone without the winter clothing the mother felt the family needed. Cook and Jencks did not ask this question. We included it because early on in our research many mothers told us that a lack of adequate winter clothing was a common hardship and that they had kept their children home from school in cold weather because of it. Overall, 12 percent of mothers answered this question affirmatively. The rate in Charleston was higher than in other sites, because relatively high rents and low cash benefits left the largest gap between welfare income and expenses.[28]

## Telephone and Utilities

Overall, about one-third of the welfare-reliant mothers had their telephone disconnected or went without any phone service throughout the previous year.[29] That average masks a revealing variation across the four sites, however. Between 40 and 43 percent of the welfare-reliant mothers living in the low-benefit South had gone without a telephone at some time in the prior year. In Chicago, where benefits were higher, 32 percent had been without a telephone. In Boston, where benefits substantially exceeded the national median, only 20 percent had gone without telephone service during the prior twelve months. (Cook and Jencks did not ask about telephone service because they conducted their survey by telephone.) More than any other hardship, lack of telephone service mirrors welfare benefit levels.

Seventeen percent reported having had their electricity or gas shut off during the past year because they could not pay the bill (compared with 8 percent of the Cook and Jencks group). This hardship affected 21 percent of the children of the welfare-reliant mothers we interviewed (larger families experienced more utility shutoff than smaller ones). Utility-related hardships were most common in Charleston, where people relied on electric heat, the price of which was particularly high. Furthermore, in some of Charleston's subsidized housing, utility bills were not included in the rent. In these units, the housing authority provided large electric space-heaters that were old and inefficient. Despite Charleston's relatively mild climate, winter electric bills often exceeded $200 a month.

## Medical Hardship

We also asked each mother, "Is everyone in your household covered by health insurance, such as Medicare, Medicaid, or another plan?" "Has there been a time in the last year when you or anyone else in your family needed to see a doctor or go to the hospital but didn't go because they couldn't afford it?" and "Has there been any time in the last year when you or anyone else in your family needed to see a dentist but didn't go because they couldn't afford it?" Though all of the mothers in the welfare-reliant group had Medicaid for themselves and their children, between 5 and 9 percent of respondents in each site said that either they or one of their children had needed to see a doctor during the previous year but could not afford it (compared with 9 percent of those whom Cook and Jencks surveyed).[30] Our figure included mothers who said they could not afford medical treatment that Medicaid did not cover. We did not include the dental hardship because virtually no one in the welfare-reliant group was able to afford routine dental care, though most recognized the need for such care (15 percent of the Cook and Jencks group had recently gone without needed dental care because they could not afford it).

## Housing-Quality Hardships

Like Cook and Jencks, we coded respondents as having experienced a housing-quality hardship if during the preceding twelve months they had experienced at least two of the following: inadequate garbage pickup, a stove or refrigerator that did not work, a leaky toilet or other plumbing problem, faulty electricity, broken heating system, a broken window, rat or roach infestation, or a leaky roof. Overall, one-quarter of mothers said they had two or more of these problems with their housing (as opposed to 14 percent of Cook and Jencks's respondents). Because these hardships were positively related to family size, fully one-third of all children lived in poor-quality housing.

In San Antonio, 46 percent of welfare-reliant respondents reported two or more housing-quality hardships; elsewhere the figure was between 13 and 18 percent. The high rates in San Antonio reflected both the substandard conditions of many cheap private apartments and the extreme disrepair of many units owned by the San Antonio Housing Authority. Some of the San Antonio projects were among the oldest in the Southeast and had never been renovated; consequently, problems with outdated plumbing, heating, electrical systems, and roofs were frequent. In addition, most of San Antonio's project residents complained of insect infestation.

Although public housing was in better shape in the other three cities, some of the low-cost private apartments had substantial problems. This was particularly true in Charleston, but they also occurred in Chicago and the Boston area. In the two northern cities, roofs sometimes leaked, plaster was falling from the walls, and winter winds whistled through large cracks between windows and frames. One Chicago mother lived in a shelter during the winter months because her landlord would not fix the boiler. She still paid her rent, however, because she could not find another place to live for the amount she could afford to pay. Another family's building burned, but they remained in the fire-damaged structure for several months paying full rent, because they could not afford to move. Gunfire had shattered another mother's living room window in January 1991, and the Chicago Housing Authority did not repair the window for several weeks. Meanwhile, she taped cardboard over the hole and kept her young children in their winter coats all day to ward off the cold. In Chicago and Boston's less expensive private apartments, heat, electricity, or hot water sometimes quit working, and as in the southern cities, most mothers complained of roach and rat infestation, which was not surprising since garbage accumulated in the alleys of these buildings for weeks, or even months. Ironically, to add to the housing problems faced by mothers in private dwellings, many of these dwellings were located in neighborhoods nearly as dangerous as those in which one finds public housing projects.

### Evicted or Homeless

Finally, we asked, "Have you been evicted from your home in the past two years for not being able to pay your rent?" Nine percent said their landlords had evicted them because of nonpayment of rent (as opposed to 1 percent of the Cook and Jencks group). We also asked, "Was there a time in the past two years when you actually went homeless?" Sixteen percent said they had experienced some form of homelessness during the preceding twenty-four months. (This figure includes not only mothers who had stayed in shelters or other public places but also those who had lived in abandoned buildings or who had moved from one relative's home to another's with no long-term place to stay.) Only one of Cook and Jencks's respondents had stayed in a shelter or public place during the previous two years. In all of the cases we found, the children shared their mother's homeless status. If our numbers were nationally representative, 1.3 million American children whose mothers relied on welfare were evicted over a two-year period, and 2.3 million experienced some form of homelessness during the early 1990s.[31]

Rates of eviction and homelessness varied substantially by site. Evictions were somewhat more common in low-benefit sites. Charleston rates were unusually high because the median rent there was more than twice the maximum benefit for a family of three—the result of South Carolina's low-benefit levels and Hurricane Hugo's destruction of large segments of the city's low-rent housing stock. Rates of homelessness over the past two years ran about 10 percent in Boston and San Antonio but were substantially higher in Chicago.[32]

## Doubling Up and Living in the Projects

Mothers also spoke of two other hardships related to housing: being doubled up or living in a large inner-city housing project. Cook and Jencks did not code these conditions as hardships (although they collected these data), but both were significantly and negatively correlated with their respondents' overall satisfaction with their standard of living, a point to which we will return below (also see appendix B). Overall, about one-fourth of our mothers had doubled up with a friend or relative for financial reasons (compared with 6 percent of Cook and Jencks's respondents). However, doubled-up families were smaller than the average family relying on welfare, so this hardship only affected 16 percent of children.[33]

Such housing situations were usually unstable. Relatives and friends often threatened to put single mothers and their children out when they had trouble getting along, and they sometimes made good on these threats. One welfare-reliant mother in Charleston told us,

> I tried living out on my own for a while, but then the bills just got to be too much. I ended up homeless. My sister finally took pity on us and we moved into her condominium. But she was used to living on her own, and couldn't understand why I couldn't always pay for my half of things. When I got behind on the electric, she kicked us out. Then, after another stay in the shelter, we had to move in with my alcoholic mother. She's a bad role model for the kids, right? Well, she made us all stay in one room because her condo is too small. Two teenagers and a mother in one 10-by 12-foot room? Well, that's where we are now.

A Chicago mother shared a similar story. After getting behind on her bills and having her gas (the main heat source in Chicago) cut off, the January weather forced her out of her apartment and into her grandmother's house. Her grandmother, accustomed to living alone, found the presence of several young children exhausting and when conflict ensued she asked the family to leave. This family then found a shelter, waited for the tensions with the grandmother to ease, and moved back in again. During the months we were in contact with her, this pattern reoccurred several times.

Another mother had lived with her mother in a dilapidated section of Chicago for several years. When her mother's arthritis made it nearly impossible for her to walk up the three flights to their apartment, she applied for a unit in a federally subsidized complex for the elderly that had a bank of elevators. After her mother moved, her daughter managed to cover the rent for a while, but she eventually fell behind and her landlord evicted her. Although the mother was again willing to take her daughter and grandchildren into her apartment, the complex for the elderly forbade it, and the grandmother did not want to risk her subsidy. The mother and children stayed at the bus station each night and went to her mother's house to wash and eat their meals during the day. After several months of this transient existence, this mother was able to save enough of her welfare benefits to put down a security deposit on a one-bedroom apartment. Despite the instability of shared-housing arrangements, we found that welfare-reliant mothers who doubled up felt better off than those mothers who lived in the projects.

Thirty-one percent of the welfare-reliant mothers we interviewed and 40 percent of the children in our sample lived in large public housing projects and had to cope with their well-publicized dangers. In one case, children had to walk to school across a tarmac that separated the territories of two opposing gangs, occasionally having to flee if gunfire broke out. The danger of violence and death was so real to residents of these communities that local morticians were able to sell what neighborhood residents called "burial insurance" for $10 to $20 per person per month. Police statistics suggest these fears, while exaggerated, were not groundless. The Chicago Metropolitan Planning Council (1985) found that 9 percent of the homicides, 8 percent of the rapes, and 9 percent of the aggravated assaults occurred on property owned by the Chicago Housing Authority—property that housed only 5 percent of the city's population. Chicago's planning council has not updated these figures, but local experts feel that the situation was possibly worse in the early 1990s than in the mid-1980s. In one project neighborhood, several respondents claimed that the school principal had been hit by random gunfire while standing in the school yard. In the projects, units are cheaper, however, than comparable private units, and most public housing projects had waiting lists despite their problems.

## Overall Hardship Measures

A good way to judge the relative importance of different hardships is to see how they influence people's overall satisfaction with their standard of living. Mayer and Jencks (1989) took this approach and analyzed how well each one of the hardship measures was able to predict the Cook and Jencks respondents' answers to the following question:[34]

> [QUESTION:] Could you tell me how you feel about your standard of living—your food, housing, medical care, furniture, recreation, and things like that? Would you say that you feel delighted, pleased, mostly satisfied, mixed, mostly dissatisfied, unhappy, or terrible?

Each hardship was significantly correlated with respondents' answers to this question. Then to assess the relative importance of each hardship in the standard-of-living responses, Mayer and Jencks assigned weights to each hardship and combined them into a single scale.

We took the same approach when formulating our own hardship scale. It is based on two questions about food (food shortage and hunger), two about health care (medical care and insurance), two about utilities (utility or phone disconnection), three about housing (housing quality, eviction, and homelessness), and one question about adequate winter clothing. We used some of these variables to construct several hardship scales that can tell us something about how welfare-reliant mothers viewed their overall standard of living.

Mothers did not rank these hardships in immediately obvious ways. For example, many of us would assume that sufficient food is more important than telephone service (this is why we have food stamps and not phone stamps), but some mothers from our sample who had children with asthma saw the lack of a phone as potentially life threatening and considered a few missed meals at the end of the month as less serious. Other mothers were willing to risk having a utility shut off or a food hardship in order to maintain a telephone so that a prospective employer could reach them to schedule an interview. Telephone service was also crucial for mothers who had to leave their children home alone while they worked at reported or unreported jobs so that they could check on their children or be reached in an emergency.

How mothers viewed the relative importance of housing hardships is also illuminating. While many readers might assume that homelessness is far more serious than doubling up or living in the projects, respondents did not always think so. Some mothers told us they had chosen a shelter over public housing because they were afraid to raise their children in the projects. Three mothers left doubled-up situations for shelters because they knew that homeless families jumped to the front of the queue for subsidized housing units.

Despite some unexpected variations in the mothers' rankings, our analysis of the Cook and Jencks data showed that some hardships correlate more closely than others with how people feel about their standard of living. We therefore constructed our core hardship index by adding together only those hardships that we found strongly predicted the Cook and Jencks respondents' satisfaction with their living standard: the food hardships, health care hardships, one of the utility hardships (utility shutoffs), and the housing-quality hardship.[35] We call this index our core hardship scale. We used the data on Chicago households to construct a weighted version of the core hardship index. The unweighted and weighted core hardship measures tell very similar stories. In both cases, Charleston and San Antonio welfare recipients, who received very little cash welfare, had almost twice as much hardship as Chicago and Boston mothers (see table 2-8).

Next we added shared housing and public housing to the core measure to construct a second measure, hardship I.[36] Both the unweighted and weighted versions of this measure again show that mothers who lived in the low-benefit sites experienced far more hardship than mothers living in the high-benefit sites.[37] Using regression analysis, we also assessed how changes in a mother's budget affected the hardships her family faced (not shown in table). Each additional $100 a welfare recipient spent each month reduced her family's material hardship by roughly 10 percent using the unweighted indices. Using the weighted indices, an additional $100 reduced hardship by 12 to 14 percent. In order to eliminate her hardships altogether, a typical welfare-reliant mother would have had to nearly double her expenditures (to $1,700 monthly, or roughly $20,500 a year) using the 12 percent figure.[38] (Our measures of material well-being do not tell us much about mothers' psychological well-being. This is an issue we address in chapters 3 and 5.)

## SURVIVING ON WELFARE

Americans have long worried that welfare benefits are too generous. Many hear about high rates of out-of-wedlock births among the poor and conclude that welfare contributes to the problem. A more fundamental question is how individual welfare recipients actually use the government support they receive? What standard of living do welfare benefits afford single mothers?

We have attempted to answer this question by interviewing 214 welfare-reliant mothers about what they spent to keep their families together. We also examined the level of welfare benefits available to the mothers. We found that for most welfare-reliant mothers food and shelter alone cost almost as much as these mothers received from the government. For more than one-third, food and housing costs exceeded their cash benefits, leaving no extra money for uncovered medical care, clothing, and other household expenses. When we added the costs of other necessities to the mothers' budgets, it was evident that virtually all welfare-reliant mothers experienced a wide gap between what they could get from welfare and what they needed to support their families. In fact, with only one exception, we met no welfare mother who was making ends meet on her government check alone. Mothers filled the gap through reported and unreported work and through handouts from family, friends, and agencies, all of which we explore in greater depth in chapter 6. Finally, we asked the difficult question of whether welfare-reliant mothers' expenditures were truly necessary. We found that our mothers' budgets were far below the household budgets collected by the Consumer Expenditure Survey in 1991 for single-parent families. Our welfare-reliant mothers also spent less than the lowest income group the CES interviewed. Our conclusion is that the vast majority of our welfare-reliant mothers' expenses were at the very low end of widely shared national consumption norms.

Despite spending far more than their welfare benefits, many of the families we interviewed experienced serious material hardship. Variations in benefit levels had real consequences for welfare-reliant single mothers and their children. Lower benefits substantially increased material hardship as did having larger families. Life on welfare, it seems, was an exceedingly tenuous affair.[39] An articulate Chicago respondent put it this way:

> I don't understand why [Public Aid is] punishing people who are poor if you want to mainstream them. If indeed, the idea is to segregate, to be biased, to create a widening gap between the haves and the have-nots, then the welfare system is working. If it is to provide basic needs, not just the financial but psychological and social needs of every human being, then the system fails miserably.

# Chapter 3

# Why Don't Welfare-Reliant Mothers Go to Work?

Iᴺ 1990, Bʀɪᴀɴɴᴀ Kᴇʀʀʏ had graduated from high school and was learning $4.55 an hour as a clerk in a large discount chain store. Because she could not get full-time hours (only twenty-six to thirty-four hours a week), she grossed about $600 a month. She had looked for better jobs, but the San Antonio economy was depressed, and she could find none. When Kerry learned she was pregnant, she called several day care centers for information and learned that the fee for full-time infant care equaled her paycheck. Because she did not see her economic situation improving any time soon and since she had planned to have children eventually, Kerry decided to have the baby. Shortly before her daughter's birth in 1991, she quit her job and applied for AFDC, food stamps, and Medicaid.

When we spoke with Kerry in 1992, she had been on the welfare rolls for almost two years and had tried to make good use of her time on welfare. She had completed one training program (a year-long business course offered by a proprietary school) but felt that the program had been a waste: that "ripoff school," as she called it, had put her $1,300 in debt and had not led to a job. Now, she told us, she was nearly finished with a second training program. This time the Job Opportunities and Basic Skills (JOBS) training program had paid for the course.

Kerry was enthusiastic about leaving welfare for work. When she finished her training as a home health aide, she was told she could earn $6 an hour, a much higher wage than she had earned previously. In the first year of work, she thought she could make ends meet because her living expenses were low (she shared the rent with her father and another couple) and because she would have a day care subsidy and Medicaid. Under the welfare rules at the time, both were continued for the first year after a mother left welfare for work. She was worried, though, about what would happen in the second year when she would have to pay for day care and doctor visits on her own. In her optimistic moments, she thought her child's father might get a steady, well-paying job and marry her, solving her economic problems. When she felt less optimistic, she feared he would never make more than "chump change." In these moments, she predicted that when the day care subsidy ran out, economic exigencies would force her back on welfare and into yet another training program.

## THE DECISION TO STAY ON WELFARE

Social scientists often analyze individual decision making processes in terms of incentives and disincentives, or what social scientists call "rational choice" models (Bane and Ellwood 1994). These models assume that women like Brianna Kerry choose between welfare and work by calculating the costs and benefits of each option, and then determining which has the biggest payoff. When economists apply these models, they typically focus on the *economic* costs and benefits associated with welfare as opposed to work and assume that individuals consider the long-run as well as the short-run economic consequences of their choices. Sociologists usually concentrate on the short run and take into account a somewhat broader array of costs and benefits.

In his influential book *Losing Ground* (1984), Charles Murray put forward what was essentially a rational choice argument to explain the growth of welfare between 1960 and 1980. In the 1950s, he argued, relatively few women used the welfare system because it paid very low benefits, married women were not eligible, and the "man in the house" rule meant that single mothers could not live with a man to whom they were not married and retain their benefits. During the 1960s and 1970s, all this changed. Welfare benefits became more generous, food stamps and Medicaid were added, more families became eligible, and the Supreme Court struck down the "man in the house" rule.

Murray argued that these changes fundamentally altered the rules by which poor people lived, and that these rules were the reverse of those mainstream Americans lived by. First, because welfare benefits now came closer to what mothers could earn by working, there was little economic incentive to leave the welfare rolls for a job, according to Murray. Second, since unmarried mothers who cohabited with men could now get benefits, they had far less incentive to marry. Murray explicated the latter change rather dramatically with the story of a mythical couple, Harold and Phyllis, who chose to live together but not get married because Phyllis could then claim full benefits and combine them with Harold's wages. In short, the new rules rewarded non-work, nonmarriage, and out-of-wedlock childbearing. Murray claimed these behaviors, in turn, increased the likelihood that poor families would remain poor. The only way to mend this system, he concluded, was to abolish AFDC.

Along with conservatives like Murray, political moderates and liberals have also applied the language of incentives and disincentives to welfare policy. Until 1968, mothers who earned a dollar from work lost a dollar in AFDC benefits. In 1968, a Democratic Congress passed a law allowing welfare recipients who worked part time to keep more of their benefits. Under the law, caseworkers were required to disregard both the first $30 of earned income and one-third of a welfare recipient's additional earnings when calculating the reduction in her AFDC benefits. This was called the "$30 and one-third" rule. Liberal lawmakers assumed that decreasing the penalty (or "tax rate") on wage income would encourage work. Ironically, Ronald Reagan persuaded Congress to eliminate the rule in 1981, because he claimed it discouraged mothers from working full time. More recently, the Clinton administration employed the language of incentives to justify expanding the earned income tax credit, which the administration believes will increase single mothers' incentive to work.

Social scientists have little direct evidence of how single mothers themselves view the incentives and disincentives associated with welfare or work. Do mothers make their decisions using a cost-benefit approach? How do government policies influence these decisions? Could government policies do more to encourage work? In our 1992 interviews, we spoke to welfare-reliant mothers at length about their economic circumstances and how they chose to deal with them. This chapter records what mothers actually said about the incentives and disincentives of welfare and work in the early 1990s. These first-hand accounts of the factors that influenced their welfare/work decisions provide important insights to those who seek to formulate welfare policies that are effective in moving mothers from welfare to work for good.

Our data lend a good deal of support to the idea that mothers choose between welfare and work by weighing the costs and benefits of each. Most of the welfare-reliant mothers we interviewed had an accurate view of the benefits they would lose by going to work—although they did not always know the exact dollar amount—and they made reasonable assessments of how much they would need to earn to offset the added costs of work. Mothers' views of the incentives and disincentives of each, however, were quite different from those assumed by many social scientists, including Murray. For poor single mothers, the welfare/work choice was not merely a problem of maximizing income or consumption. Rather, each woman's choice was set against a backdrop of survival and serious potential material hardship. The mothers with whom we spoke were less interested in maximizing consumption than in minimizing the risk of economic disaster. We return to this point later in the chapter.

We interviewed 214 welfare-reliant women, most of whom said that their decision regarding whether to leave welfare was predicated on their past labor-market experiences. These experiences shaped their estimates of their current job prospects. Contrary to popular rhetoric, mothers did not choose welfare because of a *lack* of work experience or because they were ignorant of their job options. Most of the welfare-reliant mothers we interviewed had held a job in the formal sector of the labor market in the past: 83 percent had some work experience and 65 percent had worked within the last five years. National data, though not directly comparable, suggest an even higher rate of labor-market participation; 60 percent of all welfare recipients surveyed by the Panel Study of Income Dymanics (PSID) had worked during the previous two years (U.S. House of Representatives 1993, 718). On average, our welfare recipients had accumulated 5.6 years of work experience before their current spell on welfare.

Elsewhere, we have demonstrated that their experience in the low-wage labor market taught these mothers several lessons about their likely job prospects (Edin and Lein forthcoming). First, returning to the kinds of jobs they had held in the past would not make them better off—either financially or emotionally—than they were on welfare. Indeed, this was precisely why most mothers were receiving welfare rather than working. Second, most mothers believed that taking a low-wage job might well make them *worse* off, because the job might vanish and they might be without any income for a time, since it took months for the welfare department to redetermine welfare eligibility and cut the first check. Consequently, working might put them and their children at risk of serious hardship. Third, no matter how long they stayed at a job and no matter how diligently they worked, jobs in what some called "the five-dollar-an-hour ghetto" seldom led to better jobs over time. Fourth, since job clubs and other components of the federal JOBS program were designed to place mothers in the types of jobs they held in the past, they saw little reason to participate in these programs: JOBS training programs added little to mothers' earning power.[1] Finally, mothers took noneconomic as well as economic factors into account when deciding between welfare and work. Although most mothers felt that accepting welfare carried a social stigma, they also feared that work—and the time they would have to spend away from home—could jeopardize the safety and well-being of their children.

Given these realities, it was surprising to us that most mothers still had plans to leave welfare for work. Some planned to delay leaving welfare until their children were older and the cost of working was lower. Others like Brianna Kerry planned to use their time on welfare to improve their skills so they could get a better job when they reentered the labor force. In the long run, the goal of most mothers was to earn enough to eliminate the need for any government welfare program and to minimize their dependence on family, friends, boyfriends, side-jobs, and agencies.

As we saw in chapter 2, half the mothers in the welfare-reliant group were engaged in some form of work (formal or informal) to make ends meet. Most had also worked at a job in the formal sector at some time in the past, and the vast majority planned to do so in the future. Indeed, they all knew that they would have to work in due course, since their children would eventually reach adulthood, making the family ineligible for welfare. Only a tiny portion had no concrete plans to work in the formal sector.

When welfare-reliant mothers thought about welfare and work, the vast majority calculated not only how their prospective wages would compare with their cash welfare and food stamp benefits but how much they would lose in housing subsidies and other means-tested benefits. They also calculated how much more they would have to spend on child care, medical care, transportation, and suitable work clothing if they were to take a job. This mother's comment was typical:

> One day, I sat down and figured out the balance of everything that I got on welfare [including fuel assistance and Medicaid] and everything that I [earn] and have to spend working. And you know what? You're definitely better off on welfare! I mean absolutely every woman wants to work. I always want to work, but it's hard.

Because the costs and benefits associated with leaving welfare for work were constantly on their minds, many of the women we interviewed could do these calculations off the top of their heads, and some were able to show us the backs of envelopes and scraps of notebook paper on which they had scribbled such calculations in the last few weeks. Although respondents' estimates were seldom exact, most mothers were able to describe their prospective loss in benefits and potential increase in expenses. They were also able to calculate how holding a regular job would affect their ability to supplement their income in various ways—a topic we discuss in chapter 6. In addition, mothers considered a variety of noneconomic "costs" of working: whether full-time work would leave them enough time to be competent parents and whether they could manage to keep their children safe from the potentially lethal effects of their neighborhoods. Mothers' concerns about their children's welfare were often as important as purely economic gains or losses in their decisions.

## "A Total Trap"

One Boston woman had only recently gone on welfare after seven years of working as a police dispatcher. Her top wage at this job was $7 an hour—a relatively high wage compared with the other women in our sample. She made ends meet on this wage only because she had a housing subsidy and a live-in boyfriend who paid a lot of the expenses. Despite the fact that she worked full time, she could not afford to move out of the projects. After her boyfriend left her and stopped contributing to her budget, she could not pay her bills. Thus, after seven years, she returned to welfare and went back to school:

> There's nothing in a low salary job because . . . your rent be so high . . . you know, people don't believe that people who work and live in the projects be paying $400–$500 for rent. But that's true because you can't really afford—for three bedroom, you can't really afford to go out and be paying $1,000 for a private apartment. You go out and get a job and then they take your rent subsidy away from you. You pay that much rent and it's hard just trying to maintain the low standard of living you had on welfare. You're in the same position, so it don't matter if you're working or not.

For women living in subsidized housing, working meant a double tax on earnings because housing subsidies are determined on the basis of cash income. For welfare-reliant mothers, only the cash welfare payment (and not food stamp benefits or the value of Medicaid) is used in determining rent. This means that even if a mother took a job that paid the equivalent of her combined cash welfare, food stamp, and Medicaid benefits, she would have had to pay more rent.

Another mother spoke of the combined effect of losing medical coverage, food stamps, and part of her housing subsidy when she took her last job as a housekeeper for a cleaning service:

> They say that they want mothers to get off the aid and work, okay. There's a lot of mothers who want to work, okay, like me. I want to work. And then you work, they don't give you a medical card. And sometimes, it depends on how much you make, they cut off your medical card, and when you go out and get those jobs you don't make enough to pay rent, then medical coverage and bills. It's really not worth it to go out working when you think about it, you know. It's not worth it 'cause you have kids and then they gonna be sick and you gonna have to go to the doctor and you gonna have to pay hundreds of dollars and that's why—that's mainly why lots of mothers don't go out and get jobs, because they don't think it's worth it. . . . You're losing double.

Mothers also had to calculate the effect that work would have on their abilities to garner the additional income that allowed them to survive on welfare. Those mothers who relied exclusively on their social networks for extra help each month felt they could more easily afford the time spent working at a job in the formal sector; mothers who relied on side-jobs or agency handouts were far less sanguine about their ability to keep up these strategies while working a full-time job. One mother captured this sentiment particularly well:

> I'm going to have to lose a lot in terms of what I earn from under-the table housecleaning to gain anything from a job. I'm a workaholic. I'm so unhappy with welfare. But I can't leave welfare for work. I'm ready to move back home with my mother, tell welfare to screw—excuse my French—and try to get child support so I could live off of work. Even if I get a part-time job, though, they take so much from you. I'm very creative, I'm very smart, and I know that I could get my way out of this. But, now, I just feel like I'm all boxed in.

Apart from believing that working was a financial wash, women also felt they would gain little self-respect from the minimum-wage jobs they could get with their current skills. Nearly all of our welfare-reliant respondents said they would feel better about themselves if they could make it without welfare, but this boost to their self-esteem seemed to depend on a working life that offered somewhat higher wages and better prospects for advancement than most of the jobs they thought they could get with their current skills and job experience.

## Risking the Future

The cost-benefit calculations that mothers made about leaving welfare for work were colored by the economic and social contexts of these women's lives. As we mentioned earlier, the mothers we interviewed had to weigh the utility of work against the real possibility that a subsequent layoff or reduction in hours could lead to serious material hardship. The jobs these mothers could get were among the least reliable in the U.S. economy. Typically, they demanded work at irregular hours, did not guarantee how many hours a worker would be able to work in a given week, and were subject to frequent layoffs. Nowhere was this more true than in the fast food industry. When we asked "What's the problem with working at a place like a fast food restaurant?" one welfare-reliant Chicago mother with eight years of experience in fast food restaurants told us,

> They work you really hard and you can't even get full-time hours. Those jobs are for the kids. I wouldn't go back because there would be no money. There is not even enough money for the teenagers, let alone for an adult supporting a family. It's for teenagers I feel, and I'm beyond that.

Fast food chains typically impose unpredictable schedules on workers, sending them home when business is slow. As a result, women could not predict how many hours they would be able to work. One mother recounted,

> Like I was supposed to work until 11:00 today. They turned around and sent me home at 9:30 in the morning. I get so mad. They make you slave and [then] they don't give you regular hours.

Even worse, if the job failed, it usually took several months to get their benefits going again, leaving these mothers with no source of legal income in the interim. A Chicago respondent expressed the frustration with the lag in benefits this way:

> [Because of the way the system is set up] it's just really hard to get off of [welfare]. When you go get a job, you lose everything, just about. For every nickel you make, they take a dime from you. [I have been] on and off welfare. Like when I [tried] working at a nursing home, I was making $4.50 an hour [and] they felt like I ma[de] too much money. Then they cut me off. And I just couldn't make ends meet with $4.50 an hour, because I was paying for day care too. So I [had] to quit my job to get back on it. It took me forever to get back on, and meanwhile I had to starve and beg from friends.

Another woman commented,

> One thing they should change is not to wait three months for things to catch up with you. They're like three months behind so like, say if I worked in April [I wouldn't get any benefits] in June, [even though I had no work] income in June. That's where a lot of people can't make it. That's what threw me off. Because like in April I made so much money with my job, and I was expecting my check to go down, but by the time it caught up with me I no longer had a job.

Even women who had not yet risked leaving welfare themselves learned to be cautious based on the experiences of their friends, relatives, and neighbors:

> The friend I have . . . I could see being on aid was really bothering her, and I could understand where she was coming from because for a couple of months she tried to leave welfare for a job. She found out she couldn't make it working after a couple of months. And then she had to quit her job and wait three months . . . to get back on. It was hard. She had to come over here and borrow money from me! And I gave her food. She couldn't even pay her rent or anything. Her mother was paying her rent for her. So I was thinking about this. I want to work but this scares me.

To aggravate matters, a large proportion of those respondents who stayed at one job in order to work their way up were eventually laid off. Gottschalk and Danziger (1989) found that women working in low-wage jobs were three times more prone to job layoffs than other workers (see also Blank 1995). One might expect that unemployment insurance would provide a safety net for such workers, but this is seldom the case. The percentage of job losers who collected unemployment declined throughout the 1980s. At the end of the decade, less than one in three jobless workers reported receiving unemployment benefits (about 34 percent were eligible), and those in the low-wage sector were the least likely to have coverage (Burtless 1994, 69; U.S. House of Representatives 1987, 330). This is presumably because an increasing proportion of Americans are working at jobs that are not covered by these benefits. Roberta Spalter-Roth, Heidi Hartmann, and Beverly Burr (1994) found that only 11 percent of welfare recipients with substantial work hours were eligible for unemployment insurance.

## Dead-End Jobs

The vast majority of those who had worked also found that hard work rarely led to anything better. Their past jobs had seldom produced the type of "human capital" (training, experience, or education) that they could parley into better jobs. Nor did they produce the "social capital" (professional contacts and links with

other jobs or employers) that might improve their career
prospects, since they worked with other women in equally low
level jobs. In short, these women were unable to build careers;
if they chose to work, they were much more likely to move from
one dead-end job to another.[2] Thus, women learned that the
kinds of jobs available to them were not avenues to success or
even to bare-bones self-sufficiency; they were dead ends.

One respondent from the low-wage worker group, an African
American woman in her late thirties with a high school diploma,
had spent twenty years working for a large regional grocery
chain. She worked the first fifteen years as a cashier, earning the
minimum wage. In 1986, management promoted her to the service counter and raised her hourly wage from $3.35 to $4.00 an
hour. In 1991, after five years in her new position, she had
worked her way up to $5 an hour, the highest wage she had ever
received. She had virtually never been late or taken a sick day,
and her boss told her she was one of his most competent employees, yet her hourly salary over the past twenty years had risen by
a total of $1.65.

Nonetheless, this mother was able to make ends meet for
three reasons. First, her children were all in their teens and
needed no day care; their truancy rate, however, was so high that
she felt they would not finish high school. Second, she had a Section 8 housing subsidy, which allowed her to live in a private
apartment within walking distance of her job. Third, she had lived
with a succession of steadily employed boyfriends (three men
over the past twenty years) who paid a lot of her bills. Her
twenty-year-old daughter was raising her two-year-old twins on
welfare and was a part of our welfare-reliant sample. Although
her daughter also lived in a Section 8 apartment close to the central business district, she had two children who would have
required day care if she went to work, and she did not have a
boyfriend who could pay her bills. Because of this, she turned
down a job where her mother worked.

Most of the welfare-reliant mothers we interviewed felt they
could get a job if they were willing to do minimum-wage work.
Even in Boston and San Antonio, where the labor market was
slack, most mothers thought they could get work. At a minimum,
however, they wanted a job that would leave them slightly bet-

ter off than they had been on welfare. The mothers' most common dream was to earn enough to move out of project housing
and into a better neighborhood. Other mothers wanted to buy
better clothing for their children so their peers would not ridicule
them. Yet, few mothers had had work experiences that led them
to expect such rewards from work; they knew first-hand that a
minimum-wage job would get them nowhere.

Most mothers told us they had originally entered the labor
market with high hopes. They believed that if they could manage to stay at one job long enough or, alternatively, use each job
as a stepping stone to a better one, they could make ends meet
through work. After a few years in the low-wage job sector, they
saw that instead of achieving their goals they were getting further
and further behind in their bills.[3] Not surprisingly, mothers concluded that the future they were building through low-wage work
was a house of cards.

Iris, a Chicago welfare-reliant mother with twelve years of
low-wage work experience, had spent her last seven working
years as head housekeeper at a large hotel. Although this job
gave her benefits and a two-week paid vacation, after seven
years she had gone from $4.90 to only $5.15 an hour. Two years
prior to our interviews, she had left this job for welfare with the
hope that she could use the time off to search full-time for a better job. After months of persistent searching, she concluded that
better jobs were simply not available for someone with her skills
and experience.

One displaced housewife, Bonnie Jones, applied for AFDC
when her husband deserted her and her savings ran dry. Because
she had substantial secretarial experience, she found a job
quickly. Her persistently low earnings, however, meant that she
was back on welfare after two years.

> I went on Public Aid when my ex left [1987]. He just up and poof, that
> was it. My daughter was four. And I was like "Oh God." I hadn't worked
> in five years. I lived on my savings until it ran out and then I went on
> welfare. After a few months on AFDC I went on an interview and I was
> hired at a computer supply store . . . for $5.50. I took it because I was liv-
> ing free with my mother and I figured it was a foot in the door. I already
> had office experience, but I had a five-year gap in my work history
> because of my child. I figured I would get in as a switchboard operator

and push my way up as high as I could. [But] there's no ladder. It's un-
believable. I just quit there in September. They drilled me to the ground.
My top wage there was $6.90 in two years when I quit.

National data echo these mothers' experiences. First, a large
body of research has shown that low-wage work does not pay a
living or family wage. Charles Michalopoulos and Irwin Garfinkel
(1989) estimate that workers with demographic profiles resembling those of typical welfare-reliant mothers could expect to earn
only $5.15 an hour (in 1991 dollars) if they left welfare for work.
Diana Pearce's (1991) analysis of PSID data also shows that for 70
percent of welfare-reliant mothers in the 1980s, spells of low-
wage employment left them no better off than they had been
before. The kinds of jobs that are available to these women more
often end up being "chutes" not ladders.

Second, there is growing evidence that low-wage jobs provide little or no access to better future jobs. In their book *Working but Poor*, Sar Levitan and Isaac Shapiro (1987) write that,

> Evidence of mobility among the working poor should not obscure the
> serious and enduring labor-market problems that this group faces. Their
> prospects may be better than those of the non-working poor, but many
> of the working poor have long-term earnings' problems. More than any
> other indicator, including demographic characteristics such as education
> or race, the best predictor of future status in a low-wage job is whether
> or not a worker is currently in a low-wage job. A core group of the work-
> ing poor remains impoverished for many years. . . . [Furthermore], the
> deteriorating conditions of the 1980s may have exacerbated the labor-mar-
> ket difficulties of the working poor and extended the duration of their
> poverty spells. (p. 25)

Unless the typical unskilled or semiskilled single mother finds
an unusually well-paying job or has medical benefits, a child care
subsidy, and very low housing and transportation costs, she cannot work her way from dependency to self-sufficiency. Despite
this reality, many single mothers remained committed to the work
ethic and tried to leave welfare again and again. Many had such
varied job histories that their employment records sounded like
the newspaper's "help wanted" advertisements. Most mothers had
moved from one job to another, always looking for some slight
advantage—more hours, a better shift, a lower copayment on a
health plan, more convenient transportation, less strenuous man-

ual labor, or less monotonous work—without substantially improving their earnings over the long term.

Nonetheless, some researchers have criticized women workers in the low-wage sector both for not moving enough and for moving too much. Lawrence Mead (1992), for example, argues that,

> The notion of the dead-end job misrepresents the nature of mobility in the economy. Most jobs are dead-end in the sense that any given employer usually offers employees only limited chances for promotion. Most workers move up, not by rising within the organization, but by leav ing it and getting a better job elsewhere. Mobility comes not in a given job but from a work history that convinces each employer that the job seeker will be a reliable employee. Advancement is something workers must largely seek out for themselves, not something given to them by employers. (p. 96)

At the same time, Mead (1992) remonstrates that "These workers exhibit what Hall termed 'pathological instability' in holding jobs" (p. 96).

## PAST EXPERIENCE WITH JOB TRAINING

Ironically, the types of jobs our welfare-reliant mothers had held in the past were precisely those that the mothers' JOBS case-workers recommended that they work toward in their training programs, which is perhaps why mothers placed so little faith in them. Typically, these programs had several components. In the work-readiness or Job Club component, recipients learned to write a resume and practice their interviewing skills. The Job Search component required recipients to show proof that they had applied for a substantial number of jobs each month. A third component, the Community Work Experience Program (CWEP), required recipients to work half time for a nonprofit agency in exchange for their benefits. Finally, recipients judged to be in need of remedial training could exempt themselves from the other components of workfare while they were enrolled full time in school or in on-the-job training.

Participation in the component programs varied by state. In Illinois, two-thirds of JOBS participants were enrolled in educational or job skills programs in 1993, with smaller numbers in the

Job Club and Job Search components. Massachusetts also enrolled about two-thirds of JOBS participants in educational programs, but placed nearly one-quarter in Job Search. In South Carolina, placement in educational programs was somewhat less common (about one-third of JOBS participants were enrolled); the state opted instead for Job Club (30 percent) and Job Search (25 percent). In Texas, 64 percent were enrolled in Job Club, 43 percent in educational programs, and 6 percent in Job Search (some mothers are enrolled in multiple programs). None of the states we studied used either on-the-job training or the CWEP components to any great extent (U.S. House of Representatives 1993).

Among our mothers, the least popular components were Job Club and Job Search. Women who had been through them believed the jobs that the caseworkers recommended were not a realistic alternative to welfare. They knew from their own experience and that of their friends that these jobs were "stupid" jobs—little better than the ones they could have acquired on their own. One Chicago-area mother who attended several Job Club meetings commented,

> It was disgusting. Here were these women getting jobs at a fast food restaurant for minimum wage, and people were clapping and cheering. And then they would find out that they couldn't make it on that amount, so they would just come right back on welfare a month or so later. And that was the best they seemed to do. They didn't offer any real good jobs to anyone.

This recipient was white, had been married when each of her children was born, and lived in a wealthy suburb. Our data show these so-called "mainstream" mothers were even more likely than mothers from less-advantaged backgrounds to express disdain toward Job Club and Job Search activities. On both ends of this spectrum, mothers' skepticism regarding JOBS programs extended to JOBS-sponsored training programs. Typically, women who received training through JOBS were enrolled in nurse's or teacher's aide courses, housekeeping courses, or low-level secretarial and word processing courses. One woman explained,

> They have training programs and I've called to find out how to get into them. I don't know how good they're going to be. I know that they don't

give you enough training to get a really good job, but they give you enough to get a stupid job and then you won't be any better off anyway. I want to go to technical college and get a two-year degree, but they just put you in some six-month computer course. I don't think those jobs will pay enough to make it worth getting off welfare.

Evaluations at the national level show rather convincingly that these mothers' assessments of low-cost, short-term job training are accurate: the wage rates of trainees increased very little or not at all (Blank 1994; Friedlander and Gueron 1992). The seeming futility of welfare-sponsored job training programs was another factor causing some women to choose welfare over work while they sought out better quality educational programs on their own.

## NONECONOMIC COSTS OF WORK

The chance to get ahead through work is what welfare-reliant women wanted and believed they deserved, particularly when they considered the added strain that work would bring to their lives. The single mothers we interviewed were therefore skeptical about working a job for years on end if they were just going to scrape by month after month. Indeed, they reported to us that the endless strain left them worn down and depressed. Nor were they willing to go continually to friends or relatives for substantial handouts. Thus, most mothers, while they wanted to trade welfare for work, were unwilling to do so unless that job held a reasonable promise of helping them to become self-sufficient.

One mother with more than ten years of work experience told us,

There were many days where I got my paycheck and I just looked at it and cried. It was not enough to pay my rent, and I had to work almost the full month to pay the rent. It never was enough that I could go buy groceries. And I had the two kids and they had to watch one another and I didn't want welfare. And it is just one up and down after another.

Suppose you have to go up to the school. You've got to be a full-time mother, then you've got to be a breadwinner, then you've got to be a nursemaid and you've just got to always be there. It's like you're being stretched so many different ways. Maybe your child is having behavioral or learning problems at the same time in school.

I know from my experience, I've had to deal with it. I would get depressed and I would withdraw. Somehow, you can even feel like you're not even a part of society because you're standing there looking at the American Dream and you feel like it's passing you over. Just the basics. To pay rent, to buy the food and to make sure your kids have decent clothing so they can go to school and look like they belong to somebody. You don't always have that when you're working.

The majority of American families still have two parents to share childrearing responsibilities and most can afford some form of child care for their children, but many poor families have only one parent and can hardly afford any child care. Faced with a job that does not pay the bills, some have argued that the poor should surmount their difficulties by working more hours (Mead 1992). For parents who have sole responsibility for their children, this solution may work in the short term but not in the long run. Every hour spent in the workplace is an hour children must spend without their parent (and often without any other adult supervision). Lack of supervision is clearly bad for younger children, but it can also have serious repercussions for older children. A mother's absence usually means that the influence of the peer group expands. Eventually, many single parents lose control. While they work, their adolescent children may stop doing their homework, stop attending school, drift into sexual activity, or get in trouble with the law.

Our respondents convinced us that they had one overriding concern in their lives—to provide for their children. That is why they turned to welfare in the first place, why they "worked" the system, why they cycled between welfare and low-wage reported work, and why they left the low-wage labor market for welfare and school.

## WELFARE-RELIANT MOTHERS AS
## LONG-TERM STRATEGISTS

In the face of the welfare/work dilemma, one might assume welfare-reliant mothers would simply resign themselves to welfare or look for a husband with a good job. Although a small number of the women we interviewed had clearly settled for one of these alternatives, most had not. Not only did most mothers plan to get out of their current situations, but these plans reflected their belief that they might never be able (or, in some cases, willing) to rely on a man to solve their economic problems. Although few were averse to the possibility of marriage, they were not counting on it. Rather, these women saw the responsibility of providing for their families as their own.

Although some women were either too sick, too deeply involved in the underground economy, or experiencing too much personal turmoil to believe that their circumstances would change, the vast majority of mothers we interviewed had spent a good deal of time thinking about how to make their lives better in the future. These mothers were making plans to leave welfare for work as soon as their skills or their health care and child care arrangements allowed them to make ends meet on their earnings.

Table 3-1 shows that only 14 percent of the welfare-reliant mothers we interviewed (twenty-nine mothers) had no clear plans to leave welfare for work. Of them, more than one-third (ten mothers) were receiving disability payments for themselves or a child because of a permanent disability. Although a child's disability might not preclude a mother's working, disabled children

**TABLE 3-1. Plans of 214 Welfare-Reliant Mothers**

|  | Number | Percent |
|---|---|---|
| *N =* | *214* | *100%* |
| No plans to leave welfare for work | 29 | 14 |
|   Permanently disabled | 10 | 5 |
|   Plan to marry | 5 | 2 |
|   Situations too unstable | 4 | 2 |
|   Prefer to combine welfare with unreported work | 10 | 5 |
| Plan to leave welfare for work | 185 | 86 |
|   Plan to leave now | 27 | 13 |
|   Plan to leave in the future | 158 | 73 |
|     Child's age only | 16 | 7 |
|     Need for training only | 13 | 6 |
|     Child's age and need for training | 105 | 49 |
|     Temporary disability | 24 | 11 |

*Source:* Authors' calculations using Edin and Lein survival strategies data.

typically missed a lot of school and had to be taken to a lot of medical specialists. These mothers received welfare because their disability payments did not cover their nondisabled family members. That left nineteen mothers who had no plans to leave welfare for a job. About half of these (ten mothers) believed they were better off combining welfare with unreported work in the informal or underground economy. That way they could keep their housing subsidies and medical benefits.[4] Of the nine mothers remaining, five planned to marry to get off welfare, and four claimed their current situations were simply too unstable to allow them to think about the future.

This means that the vast majority of our sample—86 percent (or 185 mothers)—was planning to leave welfare for work. This is not surprising: survey researchers have repeatedly found highly favorable attitudes toward work among the welfare poor (Goodwin 1972; Tienda and Stier 1991). Yet only 13 percent of all those in the sample who wanted to work (twenty-seven mothers) believed they could afford to leave welfare at the time we interviewed them. Seventy-three percent of the total (158 mothers) said that, while they both wanted and planned to leave welfare for work, they could not afford to take the kind of job they thought they could get at the time.

## Want to Work Now

The twenty-seven mothers who wanted to work immediately had more education and work experience than other mothers in the sample. The work-ready group was significantly more likely to have earned a high school diploma or General Equivalency Diploma (GED) (89 percent versus 68 percent of all the welfare recipients), and more than one-third had participated in post–high school training (37 percent versus 12 percent). Furthermore, nearly all had worked during the previous five years, versus three-fifths of all recipients. The work-ready group also had significantly more years of work experience (6.6 years versus 4.4 years) than the other mothers in the sample. Finally, only one-third of these mothers had preschool children compared with 93 percent of the others, and all work-ready mothers with young children told us they had a friend or relative who could watch their child while they worked.

These work-ready welfare-reliant mothers were not willing to take a minimum-wage job. Without exception, mothers in this group were holding out for jobs that paid above the minimum wage, had the potential for advancement, and offered benefits. Mothers in this group cited hourly reservation wages in the $8 to $10 range, which translated into $16,000 to $20,000 a year. But most were willing to take less initially if they could work their way up to these levels in a relatively short period of time (less than two years). Unfortunately, the U.S. economy does not produce nearly enough of these jobs to go around, particularly for unskilled and semiskilled women (Reskin 1993).

National data show that white mothers have a greater chance of commanding wages in this range than nonwhites. In 1989, white women who worked full time and year round earned an average of $19,880. Their African American counterparts earned only $17,680 a year. White full-time female workers whose earnings fell in the bottom quintile earned $13,920 a year, while their African American counterparts earned an average of $12,250 (U.S. House of Representatives 1993, 592). To make matters even worse, many women who wanted to work full time could not get the hours. This is not likely to change very soon, since part-time, temporary, or subcontracted employees are now the fastest-growing category of workers in the United States (Heclo 1994, 420–21).

## Want to Work, but Not Now

Seventy-three percent of our welfare-reliant mothers said they wanted to work but could not afford to do so now because of the gap between what they needed to pay their monthly bills and expenses and their present earning potential. Mothers told us that although some work-related costs were constant (transportation, clothing, medical care, and loss of some of their housing subsidy), some varied according to their current situations (the cost of day care and health care) and could be reduced when their situations changed.

Twenty-four of the mothers who did not think they could afford to work at present were experiencing a temporary disability (such as an injury sustained in an accident or a high-risk pregnancy) or were caring for a temporarily disabled family member (a child with a serious illness or a parent who was critically ill and needed constant care).[5] These women remained on welfare partly because their disability (or that of their family member) prevented them from working and partly because they needed to maintain their family's Medicaid eligibility to cover the cost of treatment. Most had worked in the past and planned to return to work once the health crisis had abated.

Another obstacle to work was a lack of child care. A total of 121 mothers said they could not afford to work at least in part because they had no access to low-cost child care. All these women had children under the age of six, and half had children under the age of three. One Boston mother commented,

> The babysitting up here is expensive . . . it almost doesn't pay to work. So, that's why I'm not working right now. I want to work, because I hate not working. I hate sitting home. They offered me a job at a fast food restaurant, but . . . if you figure out the babysitting expense and stuff like that . . . that was more than I was making.

Under the federal rules the welfare system subsidized the costs of day care for a year. But mothers doubted that their incomes would increase fast enough to assume the full costs once the subsidies lapsed. Mothers felt it would be a waste of time to take a job only to quit a year later and return to welfare, especially because of the time it would take to get their benefits going again.

Although child care concerns posed a significant barrier to work, only 16 of the 121 mothers in this group felt that a day care subsidy alone would make work affordable. The other mothers believed a significant gap would remain between what they could earn and what they would need to pay their bills. For these 105 women, the answer was twofold: wait until their children no longer needed day care and, in the interim, pursue further education. The following quotation is typical of what mothers in this group told us,

> If I got a job where I made $200 every week, day care would cost me $180! They won't help you with day care when you get a job. But you know, it's still better to work because then it's my money. I can't wait to get away from welfare. I'm going to start a job training program. I want

to go to business school. I have a cousin who went to business school and makes $10 an hour. Good, huh? Three years from now, I hope to be working and to have finished school. I love school.

An additional thirteen mothers did not have day care problems, but still believed their educational deficiencies prevented them from leaving welfare.

Altogether, 118 mothers believed they needed to improve their skills before they could afford to leave welfare for work. One San Antonio welfare-reliant mother with twelve years of work experience left her low-wage factory job in 1985 and began to combine welfare with part-time schooling. At the time of our 1991 interviews, she was a few months away from completing a four-year degree in elementary education. She told us that she viewed the strategy of combining welfare with schooling as the best way of "looking out for the future." We asked one Charleston woman, "When do you see yourself getting off public aid?" She responded,

> This is what I call restructuring myself. Because really I worked for seven years and didn't accomplish anything. Living over here in the projects they took more away from me when I worked. As I was trying to struggle to get out, they was taking away from me, and I was losing. And I worked seven years and it didn't benefit me. My goal was to make enough money through work to move out of the projects and make life a little better than what it was on welfare, but it didn't work out that way. So this time I said I was going to sit down and feel like I'm making a plan for myself, thinking about how I'm going to find some funds to go back to school. This time, when I go out and work I plan on going for the dollars. No more pennies, no more penny jobs. And I'm setting goals. I believe that if I could have stayed in school and gone to [technical] college, I would be better off working. But for now, and since I couldn't do that, I am happy to stay on welfare until I can get into a skills-training program.

Most other mothers also believed that combining welfare with quality training was the best way to achieve self-sufficiency. Almost half (42 percent) who told us they could not afford to leave welfare without further training were already enrolled in an educational program.[6] We should note, however, that only 12.5 percent of the total U.S. caseload in 1991 was enrolled in school or training, whereas 23 percent of our sample told us they were in school (U.S. House of Representatives 1993, 699). We doubt our sample is as unrepresentative as this contrast implies, because many of our mothers told us they were hiding their schooling for fear that their caseworkers would disapprove and force them to trade their current educational pursuits for an immediate job search or short-term training.

Mothers told us that the first question they asked regarding a training program was how much they could earn when they completed it. The vast majority wanted to enroll in programs that led to "meal-ticket jobs" rather than four-year college programs in the liberal arts that had no immediate application to a specific career. The most common four-year educational goals were nursing and teaching—jobs that have traditionally offered moderate wages and flexible schedules to women. Mothers who did not feel they could spend that much time in school typically wanted to pursue high-quality training in vocational and technical colleges. Although the women with whom we spoke were not enthusiastic about JOBS training, they showed tremendous excitement about pursuing two-year degrees in pharmaceutical, dental, and medical technology and in accounting, business, and cosmetology.[7]

Women with high school degrees entered directly into training programs and qualified for substantial financial aid. High school dropouts began by enrolling in GED programs, but most knew that a GED was not enough. Typically, they planned to use their high school equivalency diplomas as a stepping stone to postsecondary vocational and technical training. One woman told us,

> In June I'll be done with my GED program and then in September I'm going to college for nursing. It's a three-year program. By the time I finish, Troy will be in school and I won't have to worry about day care. When I'm finished, I will be able to make enough money to pay all of my bills.

Both this woman and the one to follow spoke with confidence of education as a way to improve their economic positions:

> I just tell my kids to stay in school and get as much as they can, because the way things are going you need more and more education. Otherwise

they'll be losers. My son and daughter will go to college. I'm in training with computers. I already know how to type, so I'm learning how to work computers. That's a $10 an hour job. I think the jobs are out there; I just think the people are not qualified for them. That's why I'm in college.

The women with whom we spoke also believed that it was nearly impossible to combine childrearing, full-time work, and full-time schooling; they felt it was possible to combine welfare with schooling and still take care of their children. Just as important, women on welfare had full access to Pell grants and other tuition remission, whereas they would have received less assistance if they were working and their countable incomes were higher.

## WHAT MUST A SINGLE MOTHER EARN
## TO LEAVE WELFARE?

We asked each welfare-reliant mother what she felt she would need to earn in order to leave welfare for work. Roughly 70 percent of mothers cited what economists call a "reservation wage" between $8 to $10 an hour. Mothers with only one child gave slightly lower estimates—averaging roughly $7.50 an hour—while mothers with more than three children and mothers whose children would need full-time child care tended to give slightly higher estimates.

The loss of health benefits so often associated with leaving welfare for work pushed reservation wages toward the upper end of this $8 to $10 range. We asked one work-ready Boston-area mother, "What is a decent wage? What could you support your family with?" She told us, "at least $8 an hour and with benefits." We then asked, "What would you do if you were offered a job for $8 an hour with no benefits and without possibility for advancement?" She answered, "I wouldn't take it. I would go into training or back to school, but I wouldn't take it."

This respondent's children had experienced serious health problems in the past, making it necessary for her to retain her medical benefits. Mothers whose families had no history of medical problems were more willing to risk their health benefits, but even these mothers believed that a job without benefits would have to pay more. Mothers' estimates of how much more varied, depending mostly on a family's health history and current health status.

How much did these mothers need to earn to maintain the same standard of living that welfare afforded? As we saw in chapter 2, the average welfare-reliant mother in 1991 needed $876 a month to pay her expenses; those who paid market rent needed over $1,000 a month. It seems reasonable to argue that if welfare-reliant mothers needed to spend an average of $876 a month to meet their expenses, working mothers would need to spend even more, because working adds extra costs to the monthly budget. Working mothers usually spend substantially more on medical care because they lose Medicaid, because few low-wage employers offer health care benefits, and because those employers that do usually require copayments and have deductibles. Most working mothers also pay more for transportation because of commuting costs and travel to and from their day care provider. In addition, working mothers probably need to spend more for child care than welfare-reliant mothers. Finally, some working mothers need to purchase more and better clothing than they had on welfare.

In previous work, Edin and Jencks (1992) used the 1984–85 Consumer Expenditure Survey to provide rough estimates of how much more working single mothers spent on these items than their welfare-reliant counterparts. They found that single mothers who worked spent $2,800 more each year on these four items—medical care, transportation, child care, and clothing—than their welfare-reliant counterparts. If we inflate these numbers to 1991 levels, the figure is roughly $3,500. We also looked at a group of 165 working mothers—their stories are told in chapters 4 and 5—who earned about what our welfare-reliant mothers reported having earned in the past. These mothers spent about $37 a month more for health care, $67 a month more for transportation, $58 a month more for child care, and $27 a month more for clothing than welfare-reliant mothers did. Taken together, these additional expenses total $189 a month, or $2,268 a year.[8]

By adding the extra costs of working to the average amount privately-housed welfare recipients spent each month ($1,077 + $189), we calculate what the average mother would need to take home each month from a job if she were to maintain the standard of living she had on welfare—roughly $1,300 in take-home pay. On an annual basis, she would have to gross roughly $16,000, or between $8 and $9 an hour depending on how many hours she could be expected to work.[9] Yet, Michalopoulos and Garfinkel (1989) have shown that a full-time, year-round worker with characteristics similar to the average welfare-reliant single mother in the 1980s could expect to earn only $5.15 an hour.[10] Kathleen Mullan Harris (1996) has made comparable estimates using PSID data for all women who left welfare for work during the 1980s. On average, during this ten-year period, she found that women who left welfare for work were paid $6.11 an hour in 1991 dollars.[11] The difference between Michalopoulos and Garfinkel's predictions and Harris's results reflects the fact that women who actually leave welfare for work have greater earning power than those who remain on welfare (or leave the rolls for other reasons).

If a single mother worked forty hours a week for fifty weeks of the year at $5.15 an hour, she would earn $858 a month, or about $10,000 a year after subtracting taxes and adding the EITC.[12] If she worked thirty-five hours a week for fifty weeks—the average number of hours our low-wage sample reported working—she would earn only $751 a month, or about $9,000 after taxes and the EITC. These figures mean that the average mother who left welfare for full-time work would experience, at minimum, a 33 percent gap between what she could expect to earn and what she would need to maintain her standard of living.

The break-even point—using our own data and national-level expenditure data—thus ranges from $8 to $9 an hour. Recall that our mothers' reservation wages ranged from about $8 to $10 an hour. Because most mothers in our sample knew they could not expect to earn this much given their current skills, it seems reasonable that they chose to delay work until their potential work-related costs decreased or until they had enhanced their education and training to a point where they could earn more.

## THE "WELFARE TRAP"

The Omnibus Budget Reconciliation Act of 1981, the Family Support Act of 1988, and the welfare reform law of 1996 all tried to push the welfare poor into low-wage employment. All evolved from two related assumptions:

1. Most welfare-reliant mothers have little or no work experience;
2. Employment at a low-wage job will provide access to better jobs in the future.

In other words, the welfare problem has been defined as an issue of labor force participation—once a mother gets a job, any job, policymakers assume she can move up. For this reason, welfare reform has focused on pushing unskilled and semiskilled mothers "out of the nest" as soon as possible. The astoundingly high rates of welfare recidivism show, however, that while such tactics may marginally reduce costs, fledgling working mothers more often crash than fly. Using longitudinal data from the PSID, Harris (1993, table 4) estimates that nearly one-quarter of all mothers who exit welfare for work return within one year, 35 percent within two years, and 54 percent within six years. Subsequent exits from welfare are also rapid: within twelve months of their return, half leave welfare again. Some of them then return to welfare yet again (Harris 1993, table 2).

The Institute for Women's Policy Research (IWPR) has studied the work behavior of welfare-reliant mothers using data from the Survey of Income and Program Participation (SIPP). IWPR found that seven of ten mothers reported some participation in the formal sector of the U.S. labor market during the two-year period of its study. However, their jobs were unstable (averaging only forty-six weeks), seldom provided health coverage (workers were covered in only one-third of the months they worked), paid poorly (an average of $4.29 an hour in 1990 dollars), and were concentrated in the lowest rungs of the occupational ladder (39 percent worked as maids, cashiers, nurse's aides, child care workers, or waitresses) (Spalter-Roth et al. 1995).

This chapter, too, has shown that many single mothers spend much of their adult lives cycling between welfare and work. The essence of this "welfare trap" is not that public aid warps women's personalities or makes them pathologically dependent, although that may occasionally happen. Rather, it is that low-wage jobs usually make single mothers even worse off than they were on welfare.

Because our data represent a snapshot rather than a longitudinal portrait of how welfare-reliant mothers were living in the early 1990s, we cannot fully describe how single mothers moved between the federal welfare system and work over time. Our data do allow us, however, to present monthly budgets (ones that balance) for poor persons—something that no national survey of low-income families has managed to accomplish. These budgets provide a clear picture of the cost that welfare-reliant mothers must take into account when making the decision between welfare and work. Our open-ended interviews with mothers also offered insights into how many women viewed the trade-off between welfare and work, and how they thought these trade-offs might affect their children.

What is interesting, then, is the continuing attraction of work for these women. Like mothers everywhere, these women dreamed of moving to a better neighborhood, making it a month without running out of food, regularly giving their children and loved ones birthday and Christmas gifts, taking their children down South to meet their kinfolk, buying their children good enough clothing that they would not be ridiculed at school, and maybe having a little nest egg for emergencies. Faced with the reality that welfare would never get them any of these things, and with the deadening knowledge that welfare receipt was daily eating away at their own and their children's self-respect, mothers planned ways in which they could make work more profitable for themselves and less of a threat to their children's well-being.

# Chapter 4

# Making Ends Meet at a
# Low-Wage Job

I N 1992, ALEXANDRIA GONZALEZ—a white woman of twenty-three who lived in San Antonio with her three preschool-aged children—had been off welfare and working for over a year. Of her job as a receptionist she said,

> I really like my work, but the money is not enough. People work me really hard, and there's nowhere to be promoted to unless I get more school. So sometimes it's depressing. I feel like I do a good job though, and I like to have contact with all these people.

Gonzalez's budget was tight. Although she made more from working than she had gotten from the state of Texas in welfare payments, some of her expenses rose when she went to work: she spent $110 a month more for child care (with a federal subsidy covering most of the cost) and $125 more a month to insure and maintain an older car. Her welfare benefits were also reduced: she lost her AFDC and Medicaid eligibility; the housing authority increased her rent from about $50 to $230 a month; and the food stamp program reduced her allotment from $274 to $175 a month. She took home roughly $800 a month from her job, but spent just over $1,000. Her mother, who lived nearby, provided the money she needed to bridge the gap between her income and expenses. If her children were not in subsidized child care or if she had lost her subsidized apartment, her expenses would have more than doubled, leaving a shortfall she could not have covered even with the support of her mother.

Meanwhile, Gonzalez worried about how her busy schedule was affecting her children. She worked forty hours a week and commuted one hour each way, for a total of fifty hours away from home. She brought the children to day care at 8:00 A.M. and picked them up at 6:00 P.M. After arriving home, she had just enough time to feed and bathe her children before she put them to bed. Not surprisingly, Gonzalez worried that her children were spending too much time away from her.

Some readers might wonder why the fathers of her children did not help out.[1] Gonzalez told us that she conceived her first child as a result of rape, and the father was incarcerated as a result. The second child's father was a military man stationed in Hawaii, who had threatened to sue for custody if she attempted to get a child support order:

> I'm going to tell you something you should write down about single mothers. They are afraid to try to make the fathers pay support sometimes because they might decide they want custody and try to take them away. I talked to the father of my two-year-old girl. He is in Hawaii, in the service. He didn't care or help or anything, until [I tried to get child support]. All of a sudden, he tells me he wants her. I said no. I told him he couldn't have her. I stopped trying to get him to pay support, but I still worry he might try to get her, and I'd just die.

The father of her third child had broken up with her as soon as he found out she was pregnant. She was planning to take him to court for child support but did not think she would get much as he was only episodically employed.

Based on our analysis in chapter 3, we would expect mothers like Alexandria Gonzalez, who traded their federal welfare benefits for low-wage work in the early 1990s, to be disadvantaged in three ways. First, full-time work would bring them no closer to balancing their budgets than federal welfare benefits would have, because they would have to spend more in order to work. Second, they would have less time in which to generate supplemental income. (This was not a problem for Gonzalez, since her only source of supplementary income was her mother.) Finally, their children would have less parental contact and supervision after school and during the summer.

When one considers how much these mothers could lose by taking a job, it is easy to understand why mothers choose welfare over work. Yet, as we have seen, national data amply illustrate that many single mothers have chosen to work rather than to take government money and that even single mothers who accept welfare at a given point in time typically leave the program for a low-wage job within two years. Most of them return to welfare, but a majority then cycle back into the low-wage labor market. Kathleen Harris's (1997) tabulations using PSID data show that among all mothers who received any public assistance between 1968 and 1988, the typical mother in the late 1980s reported receiving welfare in only four of these twenty years. The median number of years mothers reported labor-market earnings was over ten years. In other words, over time single mothers who received federal welfare benefits spent over two-and-a-half times more years in the low-wage workforce than they did on welfare.[2] That most welfare recipients receive benefits for relatively brief periods suggests they prefer low-wage work over welfare when they can manage it.

In order to fully understand how mothers choose between welfare and work, we must know more about how mothers with low-wage jobs get by. We interviewed 165 single mothers who did not get any cash welfare but chose to work instead at low-wage jobs, those paying less than $8 an hour. As with our chapters on welfare-reliant mothers, we show how much low-wage working mothers in the early 1990s spent each month to pay their bills and keep their families together. We also discuss how much they earned from their wages, the earned income tax credit, and the benefits available from various government programs including food stamps, Medicaid, and housing subsidies. We then compare earnings with expenditures and show that a mother's wages from a low-wage job typically covered only two-thirds of her expenditures. As with welfare-reliant mothers, we show that working mothers relied on various strategies for bridging the gap between their incomes and necessary expenditures. Finally, we attempt to assess whether the expenditures working mothers reported were necessary for their families' well-being.[3]

## HOW MUCH MUST WORKING MOTHERS SPEND?

Table 4-1 shows that the 165 wage-reliant mothers we interviewed spent nearly 50 percent more than our welfare-reliant mothers in a typical month. However, they did not spend substantially more on food, telephone bills, toiletries, appliances and furniture, cig-

**TABLE 4-1. Average Monthly Expenses of 214 Welfare- and 165 Wage-Reliant Mothers**

| | 214 Welfare-Reliant Mothers | 165 Wage-Reliant Mothers | Sig. |
|---|---|---|---|
| Housing costs | $213 | $341 | *** |
| Food costs | 262 | 249 | |
| | | | |
| Other necessities | 336 | 569 | *** |
| Medical | 18 | 56 | *** |
| Clothing | 69 | 95 | *** |
| Transportation | 62 | 129 | *** |
| Child care | 7 | 66 | *** |
| Phone | 31 | 35 | |
| Laundry/toiletries/ cleaning supplies | 52 | 53 | |
| Baby care | 18 | 10 | ** |
| School supplies and fees | 14 | 25 | * |
| Appliance and furniture | 17 | 22 | |
| Miscellaneous | 47 | 78 | *** |
| | | | |
| Nonessentials | 64 | 84 | *** |
| Entertainment | 20 | 27 | ** |
| Cable TV | 6 | 9 | ** |
| Cigarettes and alcohol | 22 | 22 | |
| Eat out | 13 | 25 | *** |
| Lottery costs | 3 | 1 | * |
| | | | |
| TOTAL EXPENSES | 876 | 1,243 | *** |

*Source:* Authors' calculations using Edin and Lein survival strategies data.
*Note:* Two-tailed tests for significance of differences in means between welfare- and wage-reliant mothers given by * > .10; ** > .05; *** > .01.

arettes and alcohol, or the lottery—which suggests that in these areas the working mothers practiced the same frugal consumption patterns and money-saving strategies as the welfare-reliant mothers we interviewed. Working mothers did spend significantly more, however, on housing, medical care, clothing, transportation, child care, school supplies, and miscellaneous expenses, and a little more on some nonessentials.

The similarities and differences in spending between the groups make a good deal of sense. We would expect wage-reliant mothers to have more work-related expenses—that is, higher costs for transportation, child care, medical care, and clothing. Moreover, we would expect housing costs to increase for working mothers living in subsidized housing because their higher cash incomes would reduce their rent subsidies. In another area—miscellaneous items—working mothers' added expenses were largely for haircuts and cosmetics, which could also be construed as work-related. Finally, working mothers tended to have older children than welfare-reliant mothers, so they spent more on school supplies, but less on baby care.

To this point, the differences in the budgets of welfare- and wage-reliant mothers largely offset one another. This leaves only one area, nonessentials, in which working mothers actually enjoyed additional consumption of goods and services that were not related to working. Working mothers spent about $20 more a month on entertainment, cable television, and eating out than welfare-reliant mothers did.

## Housing Expenses

Overall, our wage-reliant mothers spent $128 more on housing each month than our welfare-reliant mothers. As with the welfare recipients, the amount of rent each mother paid depended heavily on whether she paid market rent, had a housing subsidy in either a public housing project or a private complex, or shared housing with a relative or friend.

Wage-reliant families with project-based subsidies had the lowest rents. Because the Department of Housing and Urban Development (HUD) requires local housing authorities to set rents at 30 percent of all cash income, these families spent an average of $243 for rent or mortgage payments, utilities, taxes, water and sewer, and garbage collection each month—twice as much as our welfare-reliant mothers paid for such housing. Families who received Section 8 subsidies also had low housing expenses ($292 a month, on average), again nearly twice what welfare recipients spent for similar housing. Since cash income makes up a higher proportion of working mothers' total budgets and food stamps make up a smaller proportion, working mothers' rents are higher.

Wage-reliant mothers who shared housing with a relative or friend spent an average of $247 a month for rent and utilities, $100 more than our welfare-reliant mothers paid for shared housing. Two factors explain this difference. First, working mothers who were doubled up told us that their relatives expected them to pay more when they took a full-time job than when they were on welfare. Second, some of the doubled-up working mothers we interviewed were actually better off than their roommates (who were sometimes on welfare, SSI, or living off meager social security pensions). Because of this, they felt they could not ask these roommates to contribute their full share of the housing expenses.

Of all the mothers we interviewed, privately-housed wage-reliant mothers spent the most for housing—$446 a month. This amount was nearly identical to what the welfare-reliant group spent when they paid market rent. Although this rent still could seldom buy housing in a "good" neighborhood, these wage-reliant mothers—like their welfare-reliant counterparts in private housing  thought they were better off than those families living in the projects.

## Transportation Expenses

Monthly transportation costs averaged $129 for wage-reliant families, more than twice what our welfare group paid. Yet transportation expenses were rather low when one considers that mothers who owned cars had to cover car payments, insurance, taxes, licensing and registration, gasoline, maintenance and repairs, and parking. For those who did not own a car, we included all expenditures for public transportation and taxi cabs, as well as what mothers chipped in for car pools.

All the states we studied had mandatory insurance laws, and even the least expensive liability insurance cost families roughly $50 each month. South Carolina and Texas also taxed the value of a family's automobile, while Chicago and Boston residents had to purchase city stickers each year. Like their welfare-reliant counterparts, wage-reliant mothers living in Charleston spent the most on transportation because they had less access to public transportation and had to maintain automobiles. Mothers living on the outskirts of each city also paid more because of a lack of public transit services.

### Child Care Expenses

Although the working mothers we interviewed spent far more on child care than welfare-reliant mothers ($66 versus $7), they spent less than one might expect. This was partly because most mothers who worked had both fewer children and older children than their welfare-reliant counterparts and partly because they seldom paid market rate for child care. In our wage-reliant group, 5 percent of the mothers told us they paid market rate for child care, 23 percent received child care subsidies or had found an unlicensed provider who accepted less than the market rate, 18 percent had a friend or relative who watched their children for little or no cash, and the rest worked at home, worked only during their children's school hours, or felt their children were responsible enough to be left home alone. It was their ability to find low-cost child care that allowed our wage-reliant mothers to remain at their jobs. (Conversely, as we showed in chapter 2, the absence of such low-cost care was one of several factors that kept mothers in our welfare-reliant group out of the workforce.)

Mothers who paid market rates reported child care expenditures averaging $331 a month. Mothers with subsidies, however, paid only $83 in a typical month. Estimates drawn from the Survey of Income and Program Participation show that U.S. mothers who made any cash payments for child care services in 1991 (35 percent of all mothers) paid about $270 a month.[4] Interestingly, the SIPP data show that when poor mothers pay for child care they have to spend as much as nonpoor mothers do for care, so that child care ends up constituting a much larger portion of a poor mother's total monthly budget (27 percent versus 7 percent of a nonpoor mother's budget).[5]

Child care not only makes working more expensive; the limited hours offered by most child care providers can interfere with a mother's ability to move up in her job. One of our respondents worked evenings and weekends at a fast food restaurant because her mother, who worked a full-time day job, was able to care for her infant son during those hours. She told us,

> I don't think [I could accept a promotion]. I mean, they have talked to me before about being a manager, but I need the availability. See, I can only work weekday nights and weekends. They need someone to be there [whenever they need them]. If I could get her into a [subsidized] day care I would take a promotion.

In addition, concerns about child care can interfere with mothers' plans to advance professionally through increased education and training. One mother planned to return to school to obtain certification as a licensed practical nurse. She would not enroll, however, unless she could find someone who was willing to keep an eye on her children after school. In her words, "They're [school-age], but they still need someone to keep an eye on them, you know." In sum, working mothers often found that childrearing and jobholding conflicted in ways that limited their ability to get ahead.

## Medical Care Expenses

Health care premiums, prescription drugs, over-the-counter medicines, and other medical services constituted another $56 of an average wage-reliant mother's monthly budget. Although some of these mothers received Medicaid for their children, most had no insurance for either their children or themselves. Their employers seldom offered health benefits, and those that did usually required large copayments. National data show that 15 percent of all Americans went without any health insurance in 1993. Among the officially poor, the figure was 29 percent, despite the existence of Medicaid and Medicare. Among poor workers only, this figure rises to nearly 50 percent. The figure is also higher for persons living in southern states like South Carolina and Texas (states with weak labor unions and few unionized workers) than in northern states like Illinois and Massachusetts (U.S. Bureau of the Census 1994c).[6] One mother told us,

> We don't have any health insurance except for the baby. He's on his father's plan. When someone gets sick we go to the doctor and pay for it. Christmas day, my daughter had a high fever, so I took her to the doctor. I had to pay $175 and she was in there only fifteen minutes. Health insurance would cost $250 to $300 a month for the whole family.

The copayment problem was particularly salient for mothers whose children were not covered by Medicaid. Although employers sometimes covered all or part of an employee's health care premiums, they almost always required the mother to pay the additional premiums for the children. Not surprisingly, this meant that some children of insured wage-reliant mothers had no health insurance. One mother said,

> I'm not making that much. I started at $4.50. I've been working there almost a year now and I make $5. I have good benefits, . . . insurance, but it's just basically for me. I can't really afford to get the family insured. It would be $100 a month for my kids too.

Mothers' concerns about going without health benefits were so powerful that a few mothers we interviewed actually left jobs paying between $6 and $7 an hour for jobs that paid less but had better benefits. One mother left a job as a bookkeeper at a neighborhood health clinic for a minimum-wage job at a retail chain store for precisely this reason. Although she had worked at the clinic for seven years and had gotten several promotions, she had never been eligible for individual or family health benefits. One year prior to our interviews, an emergency appendectomy had left her deeply in debt. After she returned to work, she immediately began looking for a job that offered benefits. When she switched jobs, she had to take a $1 an hour cut in pay. In her own words, "I rely on my benefits. I don't know what I would do without my benefits."

Another mother worked for several years at a "letter shop" (a business that specializes in preparing bulk mailings) and had worked her way up to an hourly wage of $7. She told us, "I'm leaving that job because my employer can no longer afford to insure me. I'm taking a new job housecleaning. It pays only $6 but has some health benefits, and I get $2 for gas between houses."

Women without health benefits can get into serious debt if a health emergency occurs. Melinda Brown, a working mother in San Antonio, told us that over the last year she had run up nearly $1,000 in unpaid medical bills: "I am paying off various doctor bills at the rate of $5 or $10 a month. I owe the dentist $440 and a pediatrician $353. Then I owe another $68 for a doctor visit." Over time, unpaid medical debt can damage credit ratings, making it harder for mothers to obtain credit cards, automobiles, or homes.

## Clothing Expenses

Working mothers spent an average of $95 a month on clothing (or $26 more than the average welfare-reliant mother). Most of this increase was in mothers' expenditures for work clothes. Mothers in the fast food and health care industries had to purchase uniforms for work, and others, particularly those in clerical jobs, had to meet dress codes. Even so, these women shopped at discount stores, bought used clothing at garage sales and thrift stores, wore hand-me-downs from sisters and friends, and sometimes sewed their own clothing.

## Miscellaneous

Miscellaneous items in the working mothers' budgets included checking account fees, credit card fees, burial or life insurance (which we discussed in chapter 3), haircuts and cosmetics, and payments on existing debt. These items totaled $78 in the average month. Most of the difference between working and welfare-reliant mothers' expenditures in this catch-all category were for haircuts and cosmetics. Mothers explained that they needed to maintain a professional image at work to keep their jobs and to be considered, if a chance ever arose, for promotion.

## Nonessentials

As was true with our welfare-reliant group, entertainment for wage-reliant families—which cost them $27 each month—was usually limited to video rentals and an occasional movie.[7] Wage-reliant mothers spent an additional $22 for cigarettes, $25 to eat out, $9 for cable television, and $1 for the lottery in a typical month. All told, the typical wage-reliant family spent $84 a month on these nonessential items, or about 7 percent of their total budget.

## Variations in Expenditures by Site

As with our welfare-reliant sample, the averages given in the preceding section mask some variation across the four cities in our study. Housing cost Charleston and Boston mothers roughly $400 a month. Although Charleston rents were cheaper, more Boston wage-reliant mothers had doubled up, so their average rent payments were similar. In Chicago, where working mothers were even more likely to be doubled up than in Boston, mothers' rent averaged $328 a month. In San Antonio, where housing was least expensive, mothers who worked paid less than $250 in an average month for rent and utilities (see table 4-2).

Food expenses did not vary much by site, but expenses for other necessity items did, including medical care and child care. Overall, mothers' expenditures for nonfood necessities in Charleston, Chicago, and Boston averaged around $600 a month, while San Antonio mothers spent less than $500 a month for these items. San Antonians spent significantly less on medical care and child care than mothers in other sites. They were able to economize because their hourly wages, weekly working hours, and opportunities for overtime work were far lower than in any other site. As a result, their children more often qualified for Medicaid and child care subsidies. The working mothers in this site made ends meet because they received more noncash benefits, not because they were better at managing their money.

Half of the wage-reliant mothers interviewed in Charleston, San Antonio, and Boston, and one-third of those in Chicago, lived

TABLE 4-2. **Average Monthly Expenses of 165 Low-Wage Workers by Site**

| | Charleston | San Antonio | Chicago | Boston | Sig. |
|---|---|---|---|---|---|
| Family size | 2.83 | 3.27 | 2.56 | 2.94 | *** |
| Housing costs | $404 | $241 | $328 | $388 | *** |
| % paying market rent | 60% | 44% | 44% | 18% | *** |
| Food costs | $235 | $236 | $257 | $272 | |
| Food per person | 88 | 72 | 106 | 96 | *** |
| | | | | | |
| Other necessities | 615 | 476 | 572 | 615 | ** |
| Medical | 72 | 39 | 63 | 44 | |
| Clothing | 84 | 97 | 103 | 98 | |
| Transportation | 192 | 100 | 101 | 110 | *** |
| Child care | 76 | 33 | 90 | 63 | |
| Phone[a] | 39 | 28 | 32 | 45 | * |
| Laundry/toiletries/ cleaning supplies | 47 | 50 | 60 | 58 | |
| Baby care | 4 | 16 | 19 | 2 | *** |
| School supplies | 24 | 15 | 8 | 61 | *** |
| Appliances/furniture | 20 | 26 | 16 | 28 | |
| Miscellaneous[b] | 58 | 73 | 82 | 106 | ** |
| | | | | | |
| Nonessentials | 76 | 73 | 85 | 107 | |
| Entertainment | 32 | 20 | 25 | 32 | |
| Cable TV | 8 | 12 | 2 | 19 | *** |
| Cigarettes and alcohol | 17 | 16 | 36 | 18 | * |
| Eat out | 19 | 25 | 21 | 38 | ** |
| Lottery costs | 0 | 1 | 2 | 1 | |
| | | | | | |
| TOTAL EXPENSES | 1,330 | 1,027 | 1,243 | 1,383 | *** |

*Source:* Authors' calculations using Edin and Lein survival strategies data.
[a]Basic line charges varied from about $12 in San Antonio to $20 in Chicago, and more than $25 in Charleston and the Boston area.
[b]Includes monthly payments for burial insurance, haircuts, unspecified credit payments, and check-cashing fees.
*Note:* Two-tailed tests for significance of differences in means between cities given by * > .10; ** > .05; *** > .01.

in subsidized housing. Since most of this housing was federally funded, these mothers usually paid about 30 percent of their declared incomes for rent. The remaining wage-reliant mothers lived in private housing, either on their own or with another family. As we showed in chapter 2, private housing costs varied dramatically by site in the early 1990s, with Boston being the most expensive, followed by Chicago, Charleston, and San Antonio. San Antonio residents paid about half as much as Boston-area residents for a market-rent apartment.

Transportation costs also varied by city. Because public transportation was relatively good in Chicago and Boston, most working mothers in those two cities were able to limit their transportation expenses to about $100 each month. Like their welfare counterparts, Charleston workers spent the most on transportation, averaging $192 a month, because they were more likely to have cars. San Antonio mothers were also ill-served by public transportation, but the labor market was so slack and wages for women so low that few mothers could afford to take jobs that required commuting by car. San Antonio mothers were usually restricted to jobs within or near their immediate neighborhoods, often in light manufacturing or to jobs within the central city, which they could reach by bus if they were willing to walk a significant distance to a bus stop.

Finally, Boston mothers, who earned the highest wages on average, spent roughly $25 more each month for nonessential items than mothers in other sites, although this difference was not statistically significant.

## HOW MUCH MONEY CAN LOW-WAGE
## WORKING MOTHERS EARN?

In order to make our wage-reliant group as comparable as possible to our welfare-reliant group, we selected a sample of working mothers whose wages reflected the range of wages that welfare-reliant mothers had reported earning in past jobs. Following this rule, we only interviewed mothers earning less than $7.00 an hour in San Antonio, $7.50 in Charleston and Chicago, and $8.00 in Boston. On average, San Antonio respondents earned $4.50 an hour, Charleston and Chicago respondents earned just over $5.75 an hour, and Boston respondents earned $6.50 an hour. In Charleston, Chicago, and Boston, mothers worked roughly thirty-five hours a week. In San Antonio, full-time work was harder to get and layoffs more common, so wage-reliant mothers averaged only thirty-one hours. As a result, their average monthly earnings were much lower ($667 a month) than in Charleston ($799), Chicago ($767), or Boston ($892).

Just over a third of our wage-reliant mothers worked at technical and skilled jobs—as secretaries, receptionists, licensed practical nurses, cosmetologists, maintenance workers, licensed health care workers, restaurant cooks, and teacher's aides.[8] About two-fifths of these mothers described their jobs as secretarial, and most of them had qualified for their positions by completing a secretarial course. The rest of the mothers in this category were fairly evenly spread across the other occupations listed above.

Two-thirds of our wage-reliant mothers worked at unskilled or semiskilled jobs. The most common jobs in this sector were cashiers, stock clerks, general office clerks, nurse's aides, and child care workers.[9] These mothers were less likely to have completed a training program, although a surprising number had trained for skilled jobs but had been forced to take less-skilled jobs when they could not find full-time employment in the field for which they had trained. We talked to a number of cosmetologists and women with secretarial and business training, for example, who had had to take jobs as cashiers or child care workers.

Because our data were gathered between 1988 and 1992, the effects of the EITC on working mothers' net incomes were somewhat smaller than they have since become. In Chicago, where we interviewed between 1988 and 1990, we saw the smallest effects. The effects were somewhat more noticeable in the other sites, where we interviewed between 1990 and 1992. San Antonio mothers, whose wages were far below those of the other mothers, were the most likely to receive EITC benefits. This was because more of them qualified for the credit and because more of them told us they knew how to apply. (We are not sure how this local knowledge was circulated in San Antonio neighborhoods.) When mothers did receive the EITC, it generally made up for what they had paid into social security during the year but not what they owed to their respective states (except for Texas, which has no state income tax).

## HOW MUCH MONEY CAN WORKING MOTHERS RECEIVE FROM WELFARE?

If we count wage income alone, working mothers faced worse financial problems than welfare-reliant mothers, but working mothers also had recourse to some government benefits. In this section, we discuss these benefits, including cash welfare, food stamps, housing, and Medicaid. It is important to note that because of the way we constructed our study, our working mothers did not get any cash welfare. But a good number of our working mothers did get other benefits, and these proved crucial to their families' well-being.

### AFDC

No workers in our sample received anything from the AFDC program. Nonetheless, the interaction between AFDC and earnings is important to very low-wage working mothers across the nation. Table 4-3 shows how much money working mothers could earn in various states and still receive any payments from AFDC. The figures in column one are simply the maximum 1993 benefit for a family of three in various states. The standard deduction of $90 is added.[10]

The vast majority of states excluded even minimum-wage workers with average size families if they worked full time (two thousand or more hours a year); in the South, virtually all minimum-wage part-time workers were excluded as well. Mothers with larger families were allowed more earnings before they were excluded. This was particularly true in Boston, where benefits varied a lot by family size.

San Antonio mothers with average-size families were excluded from the welfare rolls if they grossed more than $264 a month, and in Charleston, the cutoff was $280. In Chicago and Boston (our median- and high-benefit sites), mothers could earn up to $477 and $619 a month, respectively, before being cut off. These thresholds meant that benefits were available to poorly paid part-time workers, but none to full-time workers.[11]

TABLE 4-3. **Income Levels at which AFDC Eligibility Ends for a Family of Three after 12 Months of Work in Four States**

| | Illinois | Massachusetts | South Carolina | Texas |
|---|---|---|---|---|
| Monthly earnings level at which mothers with two children could receive at least $10 in AFDC payments in 1993[a] | $447 | $619 | $280 | $264 |
| Mothers with three children | 494 | 708 | 332 | 301 |
| Mothers with four children | 565 | 800 | 375 | 326 |
| Monthly earnings level for a mother with two children as a percent of poverty level for a family of three in 1993 | 49% | 67% | 31% | 29% |
| Monthly earnings level for a mother with two children as a percent of gross earnings from a minimum wage job (assuming the mother works 2,000 hours per year) | 63% | 86% | 40% | 37% |

*Source:* U.S. House of Representatives (1993).
[a]We calculated these levels simply by adding the standard work-expenses deduction available to AFDC mothers after twelve months on the job ($90). We then subtracted $10 to take into account the fact that mothers must be eligible for at least $10 in benefits to receive anything.

## Food Stamps

Because the Food Stamp Program was federally funded, there were no state-by-state variations in eligibility criteria. Because the program had a relatively high cutoff (185 percent of the poverty line), virtually all low-wage working mothers were eligible for some benefits. This was particularly true because food stamps were adjusted upward for mothers who paid more than 30 percent of their reported income for rent, as many low-wage mothers did. A mother who worked full time for $4.25 an hour would have earned an average of $708 each month before taxes. From this, she could have deducted 20 percent of all her earnings, in recognition of her work-related expenses, leaving her with $566. She could then have applied the $127 standard food stamp deduction to this amount, to be left with $439 in countable income (U.S. House of Representatives 1993, 1613). The food stamp program then assumed that she would spend 30 percent of her countable income ($132) on food and determined her benefits by subtracting that amount from the maximum benefit for her family size—$292 for a family of three in 1993.[12] If she had two children, her benefits would therefore have totaled $160 a month.

By applying this formula, we can estimate that a full-time worker with two children who earned $5 an hour would have been eligible for $130 a month in food stamps. A mother who earned $6 an hour could have gotten $90 a month in food stamps; a mother working for $7 received $50; and a mother earning $8 would have been eligible for $10 a month. If a mother had substantial child care costs or paid market rent, her deductions would have increased and she would have been eligible for a somewhat larger benefit. Income and housing costs alone, however, did not determine food stamp eligibility. If a family had $1,000 or more in assets (excluding a mother's home and car), that family was ineligible. Although few wage-reliant mothers with whom we spoke had substantial assets, most had automobiles, which, according to food stamp rules, could not exceed $1,500 in value. Mothers with more expensive cars sometimes evaded the automobile asset rule by asking a family member to hold title to the car.

Eligibility was also threatened if a family doubled up to reduce housing costs, because food stamp benefit levels were usually based on total household income rather than the income of the mother and her children. Thus, when low-wage mothers shared housing with better-off friends or relatives, they generally lost their food stamps. Some savvy women who lived with their mothers convinced them to sign affidavits stating their daughter paid rent and kept her expenditures separate, but most were not aware that they could circumvent the rules in this way.

## Housing

Low-income working mothers were often eligible for housing assistance. In 1991, a full-time worker earning $4.25 an hour would have paid $212 a month for federally subsidized housing. For each extra $1 in wages, rent rose 30 cents, so by the time wages reached $6 an hour, the rent was $300 a month. Since private housing in those neighborhoods surrounding public housing cost about the same, the mothers we interviewed who earned more than the minimum wage often felt that a housing subsidy was not much of a bargain. Indeed, most former welfare mothers who entered the labor force while still living in subsidized apartments expressed dismay at having to pay so much more for the same housing unit while their earnings amounted to only a little more than their welfare benefits.

## Medicaid

Wage-reliant mothers and their children were sometimes eligible for Medicaid. States were required to cover three groups: pregnant mothers in their third trimester with incomes below 133 percent of the poverty threshold; children under age six in families with incomes below 133 percent of the poverty threshold; and children born after September 30, 1983, in families with incomes below 100 percent of the poverty threshold. Table 4-4 shows what these rules meant to full-time working mothers with two children. Most wage-reliant mothers we interviewed who were not covered by other plans and had applied for Medicaid were surprised to hear that they "made too much money" to enter the program.

## THE SHORTFALL

Before we began our interviews, we expected to find that the mothers in our study who chose work over welfare would need substantial income from other sources—such as overtime; second jobs; jobs in the informal or underground economy; contributions from friends, boyfriends, and absent fathers; contributions from

TABLE 4-4. **Medicaid Eligibility for a Mother and Two Children at Various Hourly Wage Levels**

|  | $4.25 | $5.00 | $6.00 | $7.00 | $8.00 |
|---|---|---|---|---|---|
| Mothers who are not pregnant or pregnant mothers in their first or second trimester | No | No | No | No | No |
| Pregnant mothers in their third trimester | Yes | Yes | Yes | Yes | No |
| Children born after 9/30/83 | Yes | Yes | No | No | No |
| Children under six | Yes | Yes | Yes | Yes | No |

*Source:* Authors' calculations using data drawn from U.S. House of Representatives, 1994.

agencies; and student loans or grants—in order to make ends meet. These suppositions were strongly supported by our data: no mother in our sample met all her expenses with her earnings at a low-wage job; all had supplemental income.

More specifically, like their welfare counterparts, all 165 wage-reliant mothers told us that their regular earnings ran out well before their next paycheck. After paying for shelter and food each month, the typical wage-reliant mother had $187 left. After paying for transportation and child care, she was $8 in the hole. Money for her family's clothing, laundry, cleaning supplies, toiletries, school supplies, furniture and appliances, health care premiums, over-the-counter medicines, haircuts, telephone bills, diapers, and dental care had to come from some other source.

Although every mother in our sample experienced a shortfall each month, that gap differed substantially within the sample, largely because of housing costs. As table 4-5 shows, wage-reliant mothers receiving a project-based housing subsidy came closest to meeting their expenses with their regular earnings. They earned $812 a month while spending $1,107, so their expenses exceeded their income by $295. The mothers who shared housing with a friend or relative came the next closest to living on their earnings—mainly because they shared many household expenses with their housemates—and experienced a monthly shortfall of $396. These families were small since large families could rarely double up.

TABLE 4-5. **Main Job Income and Expenses of 165 Wage-Reliant Mothers by Housing Category**

|  | Project-Based Subsidy | Shared Housing | Section 8 Subsidy | Private Housing | Sig. |
|---|---|---|---|---|---|
| Number of families | 23 | 40 | 31 | 71 | N/A |
| Family size | 3.04 | 2.58 | 3.10 | 2.93 | * |
| Main job income | $ 812 | $ 716 | $ 703 | $ 833 | ** |
| Total expenses | 1,107 | 1,113 | 1,236 | 1,364 | *** |
| Housing | 243 | 247 | 293 | 446 | *** |
| Food | 262 | 212 | 263 | 259 | * |
| Transportation | 84 | 106 | 147 | 148 | ** |
| Other | 518 | 548 | 533 | 511 | |
| Main-job wages minus housing and food expenses | 308 | 257 | 146 | 129 | *** |
| Main-job wages minus total expenses | −295 | −396 | −533 | −530 | *** |

*Source:* Authors' calculations using Edin and Lein survival strategies data.
*Note:* Two-tailed tests for significance of differences in means between housing types given by * > .10; ** > .05; *** > .01.

The budgets of privately-housed Section 8 families were tighter than the first two groups because they had to pay more for transportation than publicly-housed mothers and had higher household expenses than mothers in shared housing. Their monthly gap was $533, the highest of the four groups in table 4-5. The wage-reliant mothers living in unsubsidized private housing faced a similarly large shortfall. In a typical month, these mothers earned $833, but spent $1,364, leaving them $530 short. The financial situations of privately-housed mothers probably come the closest to the national norm for poor families, since only a small fraction of low-income wage-reliant families receive housing subsidies.

## HOW DO WAGE-RELIANT MOTHERS MAKE ENDS MEET?

We found during our interviews that many low-wage working mothers were able to keep their families afloat because they had an unusually generous parent or boyfriend, worked substantial overtime, took a second job, or got a lot of help from an agency. Although we reserve a detailed discussion of these strategies for chapter 6, table 4-6 shows that, on average, mothers' earnings from their main jobs covered only 63 percent of their monthly expenses. Another 7 percent came from food stamps, SSI, and the EITC. Earnings from other legal and illegal work made up 7 percent of their total monthly income. The remainder came from family and friends (5 percent), boyfriends (5 percent), absent fathers (10 per-

**TABLE 4-6. Survival Strategies of 165 Wage-Reliant Mothers**

| Variable | Amount of Income Generated Through Each Survival Strategy | Percentage of Total Budget | Percent of Mothers Engaging in Each Survival Strategy |
|---|---|---|---|
| TOTAL EXPENSES | $1,243 | 100% | N/A |
| Housing costs | 341 | 24 | N/A |
| Food costs | 249 | 30 | N/A |
| Other necessities | 569 | 39 | N/A |
| Nonessentials | 84 | 7 | N/A |
| | | | |
| TOTAL INCOME | 1,226 | 100 | N/A |
| Main job | 777 | 63 | 100 |
| Food stamps | 57 | 5 | 28 |
| SSI | 3 | 0 | 2 |
| EITC | 25 | 2 | 28 |
| | | | |
| Work-based strategies | 88 | 7 | 39 |
| Reported work | 27 | 2 | 12 |
| Unreported work | 59 | 5 | 28 |
| Underground work | 2 | 0 | 1 |
| | | | |
| Network-based strategies | 253 | 21 | 82 |
| Family and friends | 65 | 5 | 47 |
| Boyfriends | 60 | 5 | 27 |
| Absent fathers | 127 | 10 | 42 |
| | | | |
| Agency-based strategies | 36 | 3 | 22 |

*Source:* Authors' calculations using Edin and Lein survival strategies data.

cent), and cash or vouchers from public or private agencies (3 percent).[13] Like their welfare counterparts, wage-reliant mothers made up the remaining gap in three ways: generating cash, garnering in-kind contributions, and purchasing stolen goods at below market value. Table 4-6 shows only cash income and expenditures, so it is quite conservative in estimating working mothers' total needs.

We can get a clearer sense of working mothers' income-generating strategies by looking at the percentage of workers who relied on each source of income in a typical month. By definition, none of these mothers received anything from AFDC. However, table 4-6 shows that 28 percent received food stamps, 2 percent received SSI for a disabled child, and 28 percent reported benefits from the EITC during the previous year. Two-fifths worked at second jobs, and four-fifths got help from family and friends, boyfriends, or absent fathers. When we compare welfare- and wage-reliant mothers' strategies (table 4-7), we see that working mothers were more likely to get large contributions from members of their personal networks.

Some readers may still suspect that single mothers could get by on a low-wage job alone if they managed their money more carefully. Yet when we compare our respondents' reported expenses with the poorest income group interviewed by the CES, we see that the expenses these mothers reported were, in virtually all cases, substantially lower than those reported by other very poor families. Table 4-8 divides our mothers' expenditures into categories that are roughly comparable with those the CES uses. Columns 1 and 2 show what our two groups of mothers spent; columns 3 and 4 show how much the CES's very low-income families spent in these same categories. As with the welfare-reliant mothers, our wage-reliant families spent far less than the CES families for both necessary and nonnecessary items. This again suggests that our working mothers' expenses reflect the very low end of national consumption norms.

## Work and Material Hardship

Despite their higher monthly incomes, the working mothers we interviewed were having a very difficult time coping financially. Indeed, they reported experiencing somewhat more material

TABLE 4-7. **Income Generated Through Each Survival Strategy, Percent of Total Budget, and Percent of Welfare-Reliant and Wage-Reliant Mothers Engaging in Each Survival Strategy**

|  | % of Welfare-Reliant Mothers Engaging in Strategy | % of Wage-Reliant Mothers Engaging in Strategy | Sig. of F. | Average Amount — Welfare-Reliant Mothers | Average Amount — Wage-Reliant Mothers | Sig. |
|---|---|---|---|---|---|---|
| N | 214 | 165 | N/A | 214 | 165 | N/A |
| Total % work-based strategies | 46% | 39% |  | $128 | $ 88 | ** |
| Total network-based strategies | 77 | 82 |  | 157 | 253 | *** |
| Total agency-based strategies | 31 | 22 | ** | 37 | 36 |  |
| Food Stamps | 95 | 28 | *** | 222 | 57 | *** |
| SSI | 9 | 2 | *** | 36 | 3 | *** |
| EITC | 7 | 28 | *** | 3 | 25 | *** |

*Source:* Authors' calculations using Edin and Lein survival strategies data.
*Note:* Two-tailed tests for significance of differences in means between welfare recipients and workers given by * > .10; ** > .05; *** > .01.

hardships than our welfare-reliant mothers. One woman who had left welfare for work said,

> I received welfare for a few years in the '80s, but once I got off I wasn't going back. But since I have been working I have gone to work in the winter without a coat because I had to give it to my daughter to wear, and we have lit candles because we didn't have any lights. I have even gone a full year without a phone.

TABLE 4-8. **Average Expenses of Welfare-Reliant and Wage-Reliant Mothers Compared with Those of Poor Households in the Consumer Expenditure Survey**

| | Mean for 214 Welfare-Reliant Mothers | Mean for 165 Wage-Reliant Mothers | CES 90-91 One-Parent Households with at Least One Child Under 18 | CES 90-91 Two or More Person Households with Very Low Incomes (less than $5,000 per year) |
|---|---|---|---|---|
| TOTAL EXPENSES | $876 | $1,243 | $1,804 | $1,563 |
| Size | 3.17 | 2.9 | 2.9 | 3.0 |
| Housing | 213 | 341 | 469 | 394 |
| Food | 275 | 274 | 303 | 289 |
| Food (at home) | 262 | 249 | 217 | 193 |
| Food (eat out) | 13 | 25 | 88 | 97 |
| Medical | 18 | 56 | 65 | 97 |
| Clothing | 69 | 95 | 147 | 103 |
| Transportation | 62 | 129 | 260 | 247 |
| Phone | 31 | 35 | 51 | 44 |
| Laundry/toiletries/ cleaning | 52 | 53 | 45 | 42 |
| School supplies | 14 | 25 | 22 | 23 |
| Appliances/furniture | 17 | 22 | 61 | 64 |
| Entertainment | 26 | 36 | 81 | 86 |
| Cigarettes/alcohol | 22 | 22 | 32 | 42 |
| Miscellaneous | 47 | 78 | 259 | 130 |

*Sources:* Column 1, Edin and Lein survival strategies data. Column 2, extracted from U.S. Bureau of Labor Statistics (1993), pp. 146–47, table 34. Column 3, extracted from U.S. Bureau of Labor Statistics (1993), pp. 30–33, table 5. Although we include child care, baby care, and lottery expenses in the total, we do not itemize them, because they were not included in CES categories. The family size is rounded to match the CES figures.

Another woman told us,

[Although I go to work every day] I have had to have the telephone turned off at different times. Before I qualified for Section 8, I lived without electricity for a week or two. I did get emergency assistance to help, but without that help, we would have a lot of hardship.

Yet another woman recounted,

> Since I have been on the job, there was a couple [of] times where I really thought I was going to have a nervous breakdown. It was just really hard. I mean, because you worry about your children, you care about them, and you see all these other children, and there's these times where they need new shoes, well I don't even have the extra $20 to go to the store and buy a pair of shoes. I have to try to go to the thrift shop and hope that I can find a decent pair for three dollars, and my son just went down there and he found a decent pair for $4. He had a [pair of shoes] that he had worn so long that the soles had a hole in them. And I'm not talking money to party with or anything like that, because that's not where my money goes. I just don't have it. I didn't have any money to buy any Christmas [presents] for my children. This Christmas, that was another time I thought I was getting out of control. I just knew that they weren't going to get anything. Nothing.

To elicit more specific information about their family's hardships, we asked wage-reliant mothers the same questions about material hardship that we asked welfare-reliant mothers (see chapter 2). Again, we focused on deprivation in several broad areas: food, housing, clothing, medical care, and utilities.

## Food and Hunger

With regard to food and hunger, we asked whether the family had run out of food or gone hungry at some point in the previous year. Table 4-9 shows that 24 percent of wage-reliant mothers had experienced a food shortage, and 8 percent had actually gone hungry. Many of these mothers told us that their worst problems had occurred when they first began to work. Mothers who moved into the labor force from the welfare rolls usually experienced substantial reductions in their food stamps. One mother told us,

> Food is always a problem, since bills consume most of [my] cash income. The kids always get fed, but I don't. [In fact], I have lost fifty pounds in the last four months [since I went to work and my food stamps were reduced].

Most mothers who ran out of food, however, were not able to shield their children from food hardship.

TABLE 4-9. **Individual and Summary Measures of Material Hardship for 214 Welfare-Reliant and 165 Wage-Reliant Mothers**

| Hardship | 214 Welfare-Reliant Mothers | 164 Wage-Reliant Mothers | Sig. |
|---|---|---|---|
| *N* | *214* | *165* | *N/A* |
| 1. No Food | 31% | 24% | * |
| 2. Hungry | 15 | 8 | * |
| 3. Doctor | 7 | 39 | *** |
| 4. No | 0 | 42 | *** |
| 5. Utilities off | 17 | 17 | |
| 6. At least two housing-quality problems | 25 | 25 | |
| 7. Public housing | 39 | 14 | *** |
| 8. Shared housing | 22 | 24 | |
| Evicted | 9 | 8 | |
| Homeless | 16 | 12 | |
| Winter clothes | 12 | 15 | |
| Phone off or no phone | 34 | 36 | |
| Core hardships (1 to 6)[a] | 1.06 | 1.63 | *** |
| Weighted core hardships | .66 | .86 | ** |
| Hardship I (1 to 8) | 1.58 | 2.01 | *** |
| Weighted hardship I | .00 | .99 | |

*Source:* Authors' calculations using Edin and Lein survival strategies data.
*Note:* Two-tailed tests for significance of differences between welfare- and wage-reliant mothers given by * > .10; ** > .05; *** > .01.
[a] Unweighted scores are the sum of the individual hardships.

## Winter Clothing

When we asked working mothers whether their families had gone without winter clothing that they felt they or their children had needed, 15 percent said yes. The rate in Boston was nearly twice that of other sites, probably because a local group that had long been providing vouchers for winter clothing had just closed its doors.

## Telephone and Utilities

More than one-third of welfare-reliant mothers had either had their telephone disconnected or had gone without any phone service at all during the past year. Telephone hardships did not vary significantly by site. Seventeen percent also said their electricity or gas had been shut off during the past year for lack of payment.

Utility-related hardships were most common in the two southern sites, where mothers had sometimes run up large electric bills by using air conditioners. The southern cities also relied mainly on electricity for heat, so winter heating bills were almost as high as in Boston and Chicago.

## Medical Hardship

Between one-third and one-half of working respondents in each site said they had needed to see a doctor during the previous year but could not afford it. One out of five mothers had no insurance for their children, and an equal number had no insurance for themselves even though they worked full time and full year.[14] This made mothers feel their employment situations were precarious: "The thing I am lacking now is medical. I don't have any insurance at the job I'm at. If I or one of my kids were to go get sick, we would have to go to [the] county [hospital or] go on public aid."

Although the proportion of mothers who had insurance did not vary much by site, children of San Antonio working mothers were more likely to be insured than children in other sites. This was because mothers' wages in San Antonio were usually low, leaving more of their children eligible for Medicaid. Chicago children whose mothers worked at low-wage jobs were the least likely to be insured, partly because we interviewed them before the 1990 legislative changes in Medicaid took effect. But even when children received Medicaid, mothers had to worry about their own health bills. One mother said,

I don't have any insurance. I had bronchitis about five months ago really bad. And then I've had bladder infections on and off for the last year. Some doctors want their payment right away, so I don't go. It's really hard for me and I don't go unless I am in a lot of pain. I just got done paying my doctor bills off. It was like $200 and something. I used to have insurance with my employer, but she cut it off.

## Housing-Quality Hardships

One-quarter of working mothers said they had at least two housing-quality problems. This was about the same rate at which welfare-reliant mothers experienced them. We found more housing-quality hardship in San Antonio and Boston than in Chicago or Charleston. These differences were almost entirely due to Boston's high living costs and the very poor condition of some of San Antonio's public housing, as described in chapter 2.

## Evicted or Homeless

One in twelve working mothers (8 percent) said their landlord had evicted them for nonpayment of rent, and 12 percent said they had been homeless for some period during the past twelve months. These hardships varied substantially by site. Evictions were more common in Charleston, where market rents at the 25th percentile were nearly as high as in Chicago but where wages were nearly as low as in San Antonio. In Boston, the eviction rates were lowest because rent control made evictions very difficult and because so many families were doubled up and paying only half of the rent. Rates of homelessness ran between 6 and 7 percent in Boston and San Antonio, but were substantially higher in Chicago and Charleston. Based on our case records, the higher Charleston rates were due mostly to Hurricane Hugo: some mothers' homes had been destroyed, and the subsequent rapid rise in rents had driven other families out of their apartments.

## Doubling Up and Living in the Projects

Working mothers also spoke of two other housing problems. Overall, about 24 percent of our sample doubled up with a friend or relative because they could not afford their own apartment. The rates were higher in Chicago because fewer families there received a housing subsidy. Still, those who doubled up did not think they were as badly off as those who lived in public housing, a perception shared by our welfare-reliant mothers.

Working mothers who lived in the projects felt its disadvantages as keenly as they felt most other hardships. One mother told us,

> I live in a housing project. It is a housing project filled with low-income families, welfare families and working families, who don't make enough to get out. There are too many people here selling drugs and trying to destroy what little we have, and no one seems to care. . . . The community is trying to work together on things like watching the children while they are outside so that nothing happens to them, but that doesn't help much. Some of the parents just don't care what their kids are doing. Too many people have given up hope of having a good life. . . . Some gang members have started hanging out right in front of this building. It's getting real bad around here. I wish that I could afford to move. I wish that I could raise my kids in the house I was raised in, but I can't.

Another woman reported,

> Living in the projects is not good for me or my children. It does not feel safe around here at all. I would prefer it if we could live in an old house with nice neighbors all around. Over here, so much garbage happens that I can hardly stand being here. The buildings are in disrepair, and every time something gets fixed the gangs just break it again.

Some of the wage-reliant mothers with whom we spoke felt such a repugnance for public housing—or, alternatively, for living near African Americans—that they chose homelessness over an apartment in the projects:

> I was working in a bar full time last year. Social services got involved because we didn't have a place to live. I was moving my children from place to place. And I was washing my hair out in the back of the bar, in the wintertime, trying to get clean. And then someone says "Go down and apply for housing, you'll get a house." I said "Okay," so I went down to housing; the one lady I talked to said, "Okay, these are your three choices." And I'm sorry but I'm not gonna live in these areas, because I have lived in this town all my life and I know what they are like. They are very bad neighborhoods. These were all black projects. How many white people live there? And I said, "Well, I'm trying to stay in the same school district because my children are in school; they've been moved to seven different schools because I have no home. Could I try to stay in this area?" "No. We don't care. These are your choices. You take them or you get nothing."

Eventually, this woman was able to double up with her sister, which she felt was less of a hardship than living in the projects. She continued,

> Anyway, I couldn't get into anything that was halfway decent. I wasn't looking for a mansion or anything that was real—with a lot of luxury—just something decent and safe for my children. I couldn't get it. So I ended up moving from place to place for a while and I had to give up both of my children [to foster care]. So finally, my sister says "Well, you can take the two children and come stay here." [Social services] didn't give me a choice. "Either you find them a home that they can stay in or we're gonna take them."

Overall, 14 percent of our wage-reliant mothers lived in public housing projects.

## HARDSHIP MEASURES

When we compare the material well-being of welfare- and wage-reliant mothers, we find that, on balance, working mothers were worse off than those who received welfare, although they did do better on some individual measures (see table 4-9).[15] Of course, mothers' assessments of which hardships were the worst varied. Although no one wanted to run out of food at the end of the month, some mothers believed it preferable to going without needed medical attention. Others were willing to go without medical coverage if they could avoid living in the projects. These rankings often played a key role in a given mother's choice of whether to work or receive welfare, as we argued in chapter 2.

Table 4-9 compares working and welfare-reliant mothers' hardships using the various indices we introduced in chapter 2. No matter which hardship index we use, wage-reliant mothers had more hardships than welfare-reliant mothers. Yet even these indices underestimate the differences between the two groups because the wage-reliant mothers had fewer children than the welfare-reliant group: theoretically, smaller families should have fewer hardships than larger families. If we control for differences in family size and for our sample selection criteria, working mothers had 1.5 times more hardship than comparable welfare recipients using the unweighted core hardship scale and 1.3 times more hardship using the weighted version of this scale. These differences were due entirely to differences in health care. The third scale (hardship I) shows that the fact that working mothers lived in slightly more desirable housing partly offset their health care disadvantage.

Using the weighted core hardship scale, working mothers would have needed to spend roughly $9,000 more a year than their welfare counterparts to be equally well off in the early 1990s. Using the weighted hardship I scale lowers the figure to roughly $6,500. In both cases, using the unweighted scales yields even higher estimates.

We also used these summary measures to assess whether there were differences among wage-reliant mothers by site (see table 4-10). Using the unweighted core hardship scale, site differences are not statistically reliable. The weighted version of this measure does show variations, but they are due almost entirely to the differences in housing quality discussed previously. The hardship I measure again shows no important differences among sites, but adding weights reveals that the differences are due to a combination of housing quality and the number of mothers living in the projects. Again, it seems that San Antonio and Boston working mothers were the least able to purchase adequate housing in the early 1990s.

## IS WORK WORTH IT?

The lives of wage-reliant mothers paralleled those of welfare-reliant ones in some important ways. Low-wage working mothers did not make ends meet with the wages from their main job: all had to take on extra work, accept government help when eligible, or receive cash assistance from family and friends. A nearly equal number experienced food, housing, clothing, and utilities hardships. Because nearly two in five working mothers lacked health insurance, they experienced substantially more medical hardship than welfare-reliant families. Working did not protect these women from the deprivation and financial insecurity one normally associates with welfare-reliant families. In fact, working often increased a family's financial pressures, by raising the costs of child care, health care, commuting, and clothing.

In this chapter we examined the monthly budgets of 165 low-wage working mothers and found that in most ways their expe-

TABLE 4-10. **Measures of Material Hardship for 165 Wage-Reliant Mothers by Site**

| Hardship | Charleston | San Antonio | Chicago | Boston | Sig. |
|---|---|---|---|---|---|
| N | 47 | 41 | 43 | 34 | |
| 1. No food | 15% | 27% | 28% | 26% | |
| 2. Hungry | 9 | 5 | 5 | 18 | |
| 3. Doctor[a] | 40 | 39 | 33 | 47 | |
| 4. No health benefits | 55 | 41 | 65 | 44 | |
| 5. Utilities off | 21 | 12 | 21 | 12 | |
| 6. At least two housing-quality problems | 19 | 39 | 7 | 38 | ** |
| 7. Public housing | 6 | 22 | 5 | 26 | *** |
| 8. Shared housing | 15 | 22 | 43 | 18 | ** |
| Phone off or no phone | 30 | 42 | 40 | 29 | |
| Winter clothes | 13 | 12 | 14 | 24 | |
| Evicted | 15 | 7 | 7 | 0 | |
| Homeless | 15 | 7 | 19 | 6 | |
| Core hardships (1 to 6)[b] | 1.57 | 1.78 | 1.37 | 1.85 | |
| Weighted core hardships | .82 | 1.04 | .56 | 1.08 | ** |
| Hardship I (1 to 8) | 1.79 | 2.22 | 1.84 | 2.29 | |
| Weighted hardship I | .88 | 1.89 | .72 | 1.22 | *** |

*Source:* Authors' calculations using Edin and Lein survival strategies data.
[a]Includes medical and eye doctors, but does not include dentists or mental health professionals.
[b]Unweighted scores are the sum of individual hardships.
*Note:* Two-tailed tests for significance of differences in means between cities given by
\* > .10; \*\* > .05; \*\*\* > .01.

riences paralleled those of the welfare recipients we examined in chapter 2. Moreover, our conclusions held up when we compared the spending patterns of our sample with those of a national sample, the 1991 CES. The budgets of the mothers in our sample fell at the very low end of national consumption norms, which suggests that our data capture well the experience of low-income mothers who have chosen work over welfare. Why they decide to work despite the financial difficulties involved is the subject of our next chapter.

# Chapter 5

# Why Some Single Mothers Choose to Work

TERRI BLACKWELL, a twenty-four-year-old African American mother with one child, had worked steadily since she graduated from high school. In the year between high school graduation and her daughter's birth, she combined part-time work with full-time training at a local community college. Just before the birth, Blackwell left her job and applied for Medicaid and welfare. Medicaid covered the cost of her daughter's birth, for which she had been uninsured. Receiving welfare made her eligible for an apartment in a housing project. After securing this apartment, she left welfare for full-time work as a cashier at a convenience store. Her grandmother, who was disabled and receiving SSI, watched the child when Blackwell was at work. Though Blackwell earned only minimum wage at first, her live-in boyfriend also worked and contributed to the household expenses.

When we interviewed her, Terri Blackwell had worked at this job for two years. She had gotten a promotion to manager and was earning $8 an hour. Even with her raise, she was having difficulty making ends meet because her boyfriend, now "into selling drugs," had moved out and stopped contributing:

> [For a while], I just didn't notice what he was into. You just notice they're having [a little] more money, more shopping, leather jackets, fixing up the car. . . . But then his behavior started to deteriorate and I found out what he was into. Eventually I just completely broke away from him.

The boyfriend took his car with him, leaving Blackwell without transportation to her suburban place of work. She bought a used car and had to make payments of $200 a month, as well as buy gas and insurance. Thus, a third of her regular earnings (which were roughly $1,200 a month) went for transportation. The housing authority took nearly another third because her rent was set at 30 percent of cash income. This left her with $400 to buy food, clothing, and other items that she and her daughter needed. Fortunately, Blackwell still had the help of her grandmother: "If I didn't have Grandma [I couldn't afford to work]. I have to be at work at 6:00 A.M. [and no day care opens that early]." Because her grandmother was willing to watch her child for free, she was able to adjust to these increased financial pressures by taking on a lot of overtime hours.

In chapter 3, we saw that many welfare-reliant mothers had worked at low-wage jobs in the past but had found that employment entailed greater costs than remaining on welfare. We argued in chapter 4 that single mothers who worked at low-wage jobs were seldom much better off than those receiving welfare. Like Terri Blackwell, some had to supplement their regular earnings with overtime work. Others worked a second job or convinced a family member, friend, or agency to help them out financially.

Given this state of affairs, several questions present themselves. First, with the higher costs of child care, clothing, and transportation, how could these women afford to work? Second, did the working mothers experience the same hardships, uncertainties, and limitations on their advancement that had driven other single mothers back to welfare? Third, if the wage-reliant mothers did experience these same problems, how did they plan to surmount them? Did they think about turning to welfare (or, for the 60 percent of our sample who had previously been recipients, returning to welfare)? If not, what other plans were they considering?

## SPECIAL CIRCUMSTANCES

Most wage-reliant mothers were able to work only because they enjoyed a special set of circumstances that lowered the costs of working. These circumstances included having only school-aged children; receiving substantial and regular child support payments; paying very little for rent, child care, or transportation costs; and enjoying access to full health care coverage for themselves and their children. Nine of ten working mothers reported at least one of these special circumstances; two-thirds reported two or more; and nearly one-half reported three or more.

## Child Support

Of the working mothers we interviewed, 21 percent said they received regular and substantial child support payments from their children's fathers. This figure is lower than the national average of 38 percent for all mothers, but quite close to the rates for all never-married mothers and nonwhite mothers (U.S. Bureau of the Census 1991). For many of our mothers, child support was the single most important factor allowing them to work at a low-wage job. One woman described to us how she had first worked as a cashier for $5 an hour, then as a truck driver for $4.25 an hour. She quit this job after her second divorce, went back to school, and applied for welfare and a housing subsidy. She stayed on welfare only for a short while before she began working as a legal secretary for $7 an hour, a job she had had for three years when we interviewed her. Although she budgeted carefully, she depended on substantial and regular child support payments in order to make ends meet.

## Free or Reduced Rent

Fifty-eight percent of our employed mothers received a housing subsidy, lived with friends or relatives, or lived in housing owned by a friend or relative who charged them little or no rent. One woman with whom we spoke had held a bookkeeping job for nine years, put in at least ten hours of overtime each week, and had worked her way up to $6 an hour. She was satisfied with this job until she delivered her first child at the age of thirty. Because she needed money to pay for child care during the day and someone to watch the baby while she worked evenings and weekends, she moved in with her mother and grandmother. In this way, she saved enough on rent to pay for child care, and her mother and grandmother (both of whom worked full time during the day) were able to watch her child when she worked overtime.

We asked another mother who doubled up with family members and shared expenses with them whether she could survive at a low-wage job if she lived on her own. She answered,

> No other help? Well, I'd have to cut down on a lot of things. On clothes—I wouldn't buy no clothes. Any money I would get would go toward the necessities: the rent, phone, utilities. As it is now, going to work everyday and checking my money and making sure I have enough, I'm just [doubling up] so that I can pay my bills.

Another mother told us,

> I come from the middle class. My husband wouldn't let me work. I knew nothing about the world of work. When he left I moved in with my mother. I got a job at a fast food restaurant at night and went to [a local business college] during the day. I got a two-year degree but couldn't get a job in business, so I went to work for a dry cleaner for minimum-wage pay. I had a friend who told me that I could get training as a nurse's aide so I went to a nurse's aide training school for a six-month program. I got a job at a dialysis clinic for the minimum wage, then a job at a hospital for $4.75 an hour, and then finally at the medical center for $6 an hour. In all this time I have never been able to move out of my mother's house and take care of my family by myself.

## Low-Cost Child Care

Like Terri Blackwell, most of our working mothers had a child care arrangement that costs less than the market rate.

One striking difference between our working and welfare mothers was that only 41 percent of the working mothers had preschool-aged children, compared with 61 percent of the welfare mothers. Many mothers felt that working would not pay economically or be manageable logistically until their children were in school and old enough to take care of themselves after school and during summer vacation. However, these mothers also recognized the risks they took in leaving their children alone, a point we will return to in the next section. Some received a child care subsidy; some received free or inexpensive care from friends, relatives, or other unlicensed providers; some worked at home or had flexible hours; and some of those with school-aged children left them alone at home after school and in the summer. Overall, 72 percent of our sample of workers paid nothing for child care, and only 5 percent paid market rates for all-day or after-school care. Nationwide, about 18 percent of poor working families received a direct subsidy for child care (Hofferth 1995), and only 65 percent of all working mothers paid no child care fees in the fall of 1991 (U.S. Bureau of the Census 1994b). (The discrepancy between our numbers and the national estimates is likely due to the fact that the national figures are not limited to low-wage or to single mothers, who are likely to have greater difficulty in paying for care.)

Mothers who managed to get day care subsidies were fortunate indeed. But even when mothers could get their children into subsidized day care, the center's hours and the mother's work hours did not always coincide. One mother found a subsidized slot for her four-year-old son, but the center closed at 5 P.M. and her shift ended at six. She resolved the dilemma by drawing on a strategy others in her community employed: she hired a neighborhood taxi driver to pick up her child from the center at 5 P.M. and bring him home. The cab driver provided this service to the families of several other children in the neighborhood, and the mother arranged to have her son dropped off last, so he spent only a few minutes home alone. Neighborhood taxi drivers who provided this service in the sites we studied charged mothers between $15 and $20 a week for transporting each child to and from school or day care.

Mothers with young children who could not get a subsidy were hard-pressed to stay at their jobs unless they could find someone who charged substantially less than the market rate. One mother told us,

> I pay the woman down the street $100 a month to watch my son. She is not licensed so I don't have to pay her much. Besides he is in school and she only watches him for a few hours each day during the week so she doesn't feel like it's worth it to get a license.

Some mothers had connections with welfare-reliant mothers who watched their children in return for a carton of cigarettes or a couple of bags of groceries every month. One mother described her situation this way:

> My kids stay with a friend of mine who is at home because she gets welfare. If she is not available, then I try to find someone who doesn't need to be paid, but will accept a favor in return.

Cheap providers were often hard to find. A substantial minority of our working mothers did not know anyone who was both suitable and available. A small number of mothers told us they had managed to find unlicensed providers in the past but that the arrangements were generally short-lived and unreliable. Inexpensive providers were usually receiving welfare and feared that neighbors or acquaintances with a grudge might report them to the welfare department for working off the books and without a license.

Family members and members of mothers' personal networks were widely preferred to unlicensed strangers. Though mothers seldom paid cash for a relative's or friend's help, almost all of these situations involved some kind of exchange and thus were not strictly free. Terri Blackwell's grandmother expected Terri to take her shopping and to accompany her on other errands. Other people's relatives and friends expected more. For example, Barbara Church's daughter was six years old and attended the first grade. Though her daughter's school day ended at 3:00 P.M., her work shift ended at 7:00 P.M. Since Church felt her child was too young to stay home alone, she recruited a neighbor to watch her daughter after school and feed her dinner. The neighbor then went to work the graveyard shift, so her children slept at Church's apartment; she also agreed to feed her neighbor's children breakfast and get them ready for school.

As this case illustrates, the use of family members and friends as child care providers often required mothers to find work that accommodated their child care schedule. This sometimes limited a mother's ability to take a better job. One mother took the graveyard shift at a restaurant because her children's grandmother, who was willing to watch them for free, worked the day shift. This mother had wanted the morning or evening shift because waitresses working those shifts made more in tips, but she did not think the increase in her prospective earnings from the day shift would be enough to offset the cost of day care.

Summers were a particularly troublesome time for arranging child care. One mother had managed to find a relative who would watch her children between the time the children arrived home from school and the time she returned from work. During the summer, however, she could not find anyone who could watch her children all day. To resolve her dilemma, this mother left a twelve-month clerical job for a nine-month job at her local Head Start center because she would not have to work in the summers. She told us,

> Now my pay is lower but my hours are about the same as my children's. That's one reason Head Start came in handy, because you don't work in the summer. And I'm able to be home with my kids.

Still other mothers resolved the child care problem by taking jobs that allowed them to work primarily at home or to take their children with them:

> I had a better job, an office job, but I left it for a job as a salesperson for a chemical manufacturer's rep—it was a perfect job because I didn't have [supervision]. My boss was in Atlanta, and I was here. So when the kids were real sick, I would stay home with them. If they were medium sick, I could take them with me in the car and drive around. When they started school, I was here to meet their bus everyday. Whatever paperwork or anything, I did at night. It didn't pay well, about $5, but it gave me an opportunity not to have my kids feel abandoned.

Jobs such as cosmetic or Tupperware sales also paid poorly but offered the flexibility a mother with young children needed. One such mother told us, "I have worked for Tupperware for ten years. I like it because I can work out of home and be there for my kids."

## Health Care Benefits

Although more than a third of the wage-reliant mothers had no health insurance at all, 47 percent had medical insurance for both themselves and their children. Though not directly comparable, data from the Current Population Survey (CPS) show that only 50 percent of all persons aged fifteen and over who worked full time received any public or private coverage during 1993 (U.S. Bureau of the Census 1994a). For the mothers we interviewed, employers provided some of this coverage, absent fathers insured some of the children, and Medicaid covered others. Except for Medicaid, the policies tended to have high deductibles and limited coverage, so even mothers with full family coverage had some out-of-pocket medical costs each year. Mothers with insurance felt more secure and less worried, however, about running up serious medical debt. On a more practical level, having private insurance meant that when someone in the family became ill, mothers did not have to take a day off to wait for hours in the hospital emergency room.

### Free Transportation

As we showed in chapter 4, the average working mother spent $129 a month for transportation (twice what the average welfare-reliant mother spent). However, 7 percent of the wage-reliant mothers spent nothing on transportation. These fortunate few either could ride to work free or were close enough to walk.

## LIABILITIES OF WORKING

Despite the special circumstances that made it possible for these mothers to work, many of the wage-reliant women said that they were no better off financially than they would have been on welfare, that there was little prospect of promotion in their jobs, that they worked in industries characterized by unstable employment, and that working full time placed substantial strains on their ability to be a good parent. These were the same concerns that welfare-reliant mothers had about trading work for welfare.

### No Better Off

One mother summed up the experiences of the majority of our wage-reliant mothers when she told us,

> Five dollars an hour is nothing to live on. When I was on AFDC I was really scraping. Even with my job now, if I told people my income now, people would look at me and say, "How come you can't budget your money better?" Even though I pay [market] rent, they say I should still have enough money [to make ends meet every month]. I don't mind working, but I feel bad [when I have to go to my relatives for money]. They feel that I shouldn't need it because I'm working now. I [need] to make $10 an hour because I have to pay rent, clothes, food. . . . [Now that] I'm working for $5 an hour, people tell me that I am doing better for myself [than I was on welfare]. But I'm not. I'm not getting anything more than when I was on aid.

Another mother expressed similar frustrations. When she ran out of money for food at the end of the month, she had to rely on an upstairs neighbor to feed her children. In addition, her landlady let her clean the apartment building and grounds in exchange for a reduction in rent. She also employed other money-saving strategies:

> We have a lot of beans and rice. I make a lot of bread. We don't have any luxuries. My sister cuts my son's and my hair for free. We can't afford real milk so we drink powdered. I mean, I am on a very strict budget. By the time I get that lousy check and pay rent, electricity, and gas, I have to make that last dollar stretch across the street. I usually do [laundry] by hand. I keep things washed out in the sink. For [my clothes] I go to the thrift store. For cigarettes, sometimes I roll my own.

National data suggest that the financial hardships our wage-reliant mothers reported were the rule rather than the exception. Longitudinal data on mothers who leave welfare for a job suggest that one in three will remain below the official poverty threshold after one year. In the second year, these mothers' chances of falling below the official threshold *increase* to about 46 percent. Moreover, most of the other mothers are only slightly above the official threshold and far below the amount mothers really need to achieve self-sufficiency (U.S. House of Representatives 1994, 724).[1]

## No Long-Term Payoff

Not only were wage-reliant women struggling to make ends meet in the present, they saw little prospect for improvement in the future. The types of positions these women held offered little opportunity for promotion and few rewards for job experience, and their employers seldom offered any training or education.

One Charleston woman who had just started working in a factory told us, "There have been people who have been there like two or three years, and they're not making very much. They're making like fifty or seventy-five cents [more per hour than I am]." Another wage-reliant mother told us that she had fourteen years of low-wage work experience and had never received assistance from a government welfare program. Even though she had worked virtually every day of her adult life, she had never made more than she was earning at her current job—$5 an hour. She told our interviewers,

> I always worked—the longest was maybe four months I'd stay at home. I kept us going. . . . I worked in a shoe factory. I took care of an old lady that had a stroke. I worked in a circuit place, where you hook up circuit [boards]. When I lived in Philadelphia I worked in a luncheonette. I was a short-order cook. I worked in a sewing factory to make leather jackets that the police wear in Philadelphia. I ended up getting laid off because I worked too fast. I worked in a factory that made curtains. Worked in another factory that made [neck braces]. I worked for a home supply store [as a stock clerk]. I worked in day care for two years [while my daughter was an infant, because I could take her with me for free].

QUESTION: HAVE YOU EVER EARNED MORE THAN $5 AN HOUR?
    All lower, everything has been lower. This is the best-paying job I ever had.

One wage-reliant mother told us that no matter how many times she had switched jobs, she could never seem to escape the $5-an-hour ghetto. When we met her in 1991, she had been working steadily at a variety of low-wage jobs for more than a decade. Her first job was in a clerical position at a military contracting firm, where she made $4.75 an hour. When cuts in the federal defense budget forced the company to lay her off, she took another clerical position at a law office, where she was paid $5 an hour. When her boss at the law office told her she could not get promoted without training as a legal secretary or a paralegal, she took a clerical job with a large teaching hospital that offered its employees assistance with tuition. She never managed to enroll in school, however, because she could not find an affordable babysitter to take care of her children while she was away at evening classes.

Frustrated by the lack of opportunity for promotion at the hospital, she quit that job for yet another clerical job at the county courthouse that paid the same hourly wage but included benefits. When the county budget was tightened, she was laid off again. When we spoke with her one year later, she had signed up with a temporary agency and had managed to get work for nine of the last twelve months. She said she would have been satisfied with any of the jobs she had held during that time, but none of the employers could afford to take her on year-round.

One of our Chicago respondents had a work history illustrating the same constraints:

> My first job I had, I worked at a hamburger place. . . . I didn't like it there much because there wasn't a chance for advancement, and they didn't want to give you raises. If they did, it was like five and ten cents, and it wasn't very often. At the restaurant place, I got paid every week. It was like $4 an hour and I made like $175 to $200 a week. So I stopped working there, and I got a job at the Cookie Factory. I really liked that because I made a little more money. But they really didn't give me benefits there. I made like $4.25 an hour. . . . Then my girlfriend, she was waitressing at this restaurant [and I went there to work]. I liked it a lot because I made like $50 [on a good day] in tips beside my regular paycheck. [But they didn't have any benefits either]. And the tips varied, you know. [In a good week], I made almost $400, [but in a bad week I made less than $200]. I couldn't take the uncertainty.
>
> Then I was a receptionist for a guy for a year, but then he went out of business. I really liked that [job]. I got to talk to people. He had benefits and everything. When he went out of business it really hurt me. I made $5 when I first started. Then while I was there I got up to $7 an hour. So that was like $300 a week [plus the benefits].
>
> So then I was on AFDC for a while after I stopped working there [because I couldn't find a job].
>
> Right now, I'm a sandwich maker for [a college] food service. I make like $350 every two weeks plus $50 a week for [the babysitting I do on weekends]. I'll get a $1 raise in another six months. No promotion though. They really don't give promotions too much. They'll give you a raise before they'll give you a promotion, because the next promotion up is like the assistant director or the director, and you have to go back to school for that.

This mother's experience typifies the problems faced by low-wage single mothers in the late 1980s and early 1990s. They frequently moved from one position to another as one job evaporated and another appeared. These were primarily lateral moves, and wage-reliant single mothers rarely saw much improvement in their wages, benefits, or career prospects as a result. For these working mothers the labor market was not a ladder leading upward to better wages and opportunities but a carousel on which they went around and around in circles, with an occasional change of horses.

Of course, we only interviewed low-wage workers, so those mothers who had attained promotions to higher-level positions were excluded from our sample. We must turn to national data on unskilled and semiskilled women workers to get the full picture. Gary Burtless (1995) has studied what happens to welfare-reliant respondents participating in the National Longitudinal Survey of Youth (NLSY) as they age. Burtless's tabulations are based on a large, nationally representative group of young women who were first interviewed in 1979, when they were between fourteen and twenty-two years old, and were reinterviewed each subsequent year. His data cover the years from 1979 to 1991; in the latter year, respondents were between twenty-six and thirty-four years old. All the subjects received AFDC at some point during this twelve-year interim.

Burtless's tabulations show that unskilled and semiskilled women's wages have fallen sharply in real terms since 1979. Almost half of all welfare-reliant women have fewer than twelve years of education. Young female dropouts earned nearly 20 percent less in 1989 than their counterparts had earned ten years earlier. Nor did these young women's prospects improve as they grew older. Among female high school dropouts, wages grew by only 1.2 percent a year between the ages of twenty-one and twenty-nine (or about 7 cents an hour). Among all those who had received AFDC at some point between 1979 and 1981—wage growth was even slower—6 cents per hour per year between 1979 and 1989.

Burtless's calculations of potential annual earnings for all welfare recipients (including the half who have a high school diploma or more) show that women who received welfare at least some of the time between 1979 and 1981 and who worked at least some of the time in 1979 commanded hourly wages that would have yielded roughly $12,000 a year for a full-time, year-round worker (in 1990 dollars). In 1989, these women reported hourly wage rates that translated into approximately $13,700 for a full-time, year-round worker. Though these figures most likely overestimate the potential earnings of all welfare-reliant women, either in the present or over time, (because not all could work full-time or year-round) both estimates are well below our break-even threshold of $16,000 a year, which we calculated using the monthly expenses that mothers reported to us (see chapter 2).[2]

### Precarious Nature of Work

Not only does low-wage work pay as badly as welfare without much opportunity for advancement, it is much less reliable. First, labor markets in many cities contain a large number of seasonal jobs. In order to remain employed full-time, year-round, our mothers who worked in seasonal occupations had to move among three or four jobs. Even jobs that were not seasonal were often unstable, either in hours or in tenure. Some industries such as fast food restaurants and retail sales rarely offered incumbents enough hours to make ends meet, and many workers could not predict how many hours they would be assigned in a given week. Other industries were subject to frequent layoffs, mergers, or other shake-ups. One wage-reliant mother had been laid off three times between April 1990 and October 1991. She collected unemployment between these jobs and expected to continue this cycle. Another mother in a similar situation commented,

> Before I had [my baby], I worked at a stockbroker firm. [After I got off welfare,] I work[ed] putting computers together. I worked there off and on for a while before they hired me full time. Then I got laid off. Now I am working part time doing telemarketing. I was recently upgraded to full-time temporarily [but they say that won't necessarily last].

Like this mother, many of our low-wage mothers were employed fewer hours than they wished. One mother tried to resolve this problem by combining informal babysitting with work at a fast food restaurant. Although she doubled up with friends to save rent, and her roommates watched her child for free while she was working, she still could not make ends meet. She told us she planned to go back on welfare and babysit "under the table" until she could find a better job.

Corporate buyouts, mergers, and takeovers can affect the earning power of low-wage workers as well. One of our Charleston respondents had worked at a large hotel chain for ten years, where she was initially hired as a receptionist. During her first year of employment, she proved herself by showing up early, staying late, and never missing a day of work. As a result, she was promoted to the payroll division and then to a supervisory position in the payroll department, where she earned $8 an hour.

Three years before our interviews began, a large corporation bought the hotel chain. The new parent company decided to move the payroll operation to their corporate headquarters and demoted her to general receptionist, stripped her of her benefits, and reduced her pay to $6 an hour. This demotion had a disastrous effect on her budget. She had just bought a small house through a special HUD program for single parents that allowed her to forgo closing costs and finance her down payment. To her, home-ownership represented everything she had accomplished during her last seven years of hard work. She believed that owning her home represented new status and respectability. Because her new wage of $6 an hour would not allow her to keep up with her mortgage payments, she was forced to take a second job waitressing in the evenings and on weekends.

## Placing Children at Risk

Along with the financial risks these mothers faced, they also worried that full-time work placed their children in jeopardy because they could not provide adequate supervision. The mothers we interviewed viewed a lack of supervision as especially detrimental in bad neighborhoods, since they feared that their older children would make friends who would lead them into drugs, crime, or early sexual activity. SIPP data show that only a small portion of all working mothers admit to survey researchers that they leave their children home alone while they work. Among parents with children ages five to eleven, for example, only 5 percent admitted to leaving their children alone while they worked. This percentage steadily increases with age. By the time their children are fourteen, one in five mothers report leaving their child home alone. Overall, survey data show that 8 percent of the children of working mothers were "latchkey kids" in 1991 (U.S. Bureau of the Census 1994b). No doubt, this ratio is much higher for working single mothers, particularly those who work at low-wage jobs.

Most mothers with whom we spoke seldom left their preschool children home alone. Some mothers, however, felt they had no choice but to leave children alone for at least a couple of hours during the work week. One mother commented,

> I trained my kids when they were young to take care of themselves. They really know how to take care of themselves. They have been doing that . . . my son, he [has] been trained basically to take care of himself, basically since he was four.

One mother said of her six-year-old daughter, "When my daughter was younger, I paid for babysitters, but now she no longer needs a babysitter." Another mother told us that when she was at work her eight-year-old daughter took care of her younger siblings. She commented, "I don't know what I would do if I didn't have her. She is very mature for her age."

This dilemma was particularly acute in the more dangerous neighborhoods, where many poor Mexican and African American mothers lived. An African American mother with an eight-year-old son who lived in a high-rise housing project told us,

> I am ashamed to say it, but I have a latchkey child. When he comes home from school, he locks himself in the house and waits for me to come home. In the summertime, he can go outside, but only if he calls me to check in every hour. I had to get him a little watch with a timer so that he would remember to check in with me. If I don't get that call, I leave work to go find him.

Another mother felt it was simply too dangerous to leave her children home alone after school and in the evening. This mother lived in a notorious Chicago neighborhood, across the street from a row of abandoned two-flats; one of which was used as a crack house. During the afternoon and evening hours, the street filled with young men who were either high or wanting to get high. Fights and drive-by shootings were common. Because of her concerns about leaving her children alone in this environment, the mother worked the graveyard shift at a local twenty-four-hour drugstore. Before she left for work at 11 P.M., she made sure the children had completed their homework and gone to bed. The children, ages five and seven, had her work number posted on a telephone between their beds. Because there had been three fires on their block that winter, she and her children would stage a fire drill each night after supper. She had also arranged for an upstairs neighbor to allow the children to come upstairs in case of an emergency she had not foreseen. Mothers who did have to leave their children alone when they went to work often avoided leaving their children for any other reason. As one mother commented,

> My kids are in school while I am at work, and they come home and stay inside until I get home. If my mother can't watch them for me on the weekend or if I want a night out, I don't go.

As single parents, the working mothers we interviewed felt acutely the tension between their roles as mothers and employees. One mother, whose job at a discount store required that she work from noon to 8 P.M., felt she was losing control of her eight- and eleven-year-old children. She commented,

> With the one job, I'm not here with my children, so how can I control. . . . I mean, you can say, "You're not allowed to do this and you're not allowed to do that." But when you're not here, they're at an age where they're going [to] do what they want to. I was a child and I know how it is. You can threaten them, but they're going [to] do what they want to do [unless I'm there to stop them].

Sickness was also a major problem. As any parent of a young child knows, children who go to day care or school are exposed to more infectious diseases than children who stay at home. Most day care centers and schools, moreover, will not admit a child with the sniffles, much less a child with a fever. Thus, mothers of sick children often find that their only responsible option is to remain home. Not surprisingly, employers lose patience with employees who repeatedly miss work to nurse their sick children. One mother said,

> When Jay started at day care, he came home every week sick. One week it's an ear infection, the next week it's a cold. The doctor gives him ten days of medicine and when the ten days are up, he is sick again. But that was when he first went. He's pretty healthy now. We'll have to see how the winter goes.

Some mothers even told us that they had quit better paying jobs for jobs with employers who were more sympathetic to their child-minding responsibilities. One mother explained why she had left a $6 an hour job for a job paying only $5.50, "I have had better paying jobs than I have now, but none of them understood that my kids come first. At least this job understands that if my kids are sick, I just won't be in that day."

The same mother who had to take two jobs in the wake of a corporate takeover found that although this strategy allowed her to keep her newly purchased home, it had a deleterious effect on her fourteen-year-old daughter. With her mother away so much, the daughter began to have promiscuous and unprotected sex. The mother was caught in a difficult dilemma. On the one hand, she was convinced that if she did not decrease her hours, her daughter would end up pregnant. On the other, if she were to quit either of her jobs—even temporarily—she would be unable to keep up with her mortgage payments. Her solution was to dedicate what little spare time she had to looking for a new job that paid better wages—a strategy that took her away from home even more. Six months later, she had sent out over a hundred resumes, had gone on several dozen interviews, and still could not find a job that paid more than the one she already had. Though her daughter was not yet pregnant, she was in trouble with the law for repeated school truancy and shoplifting. When we followed up on this situation two years later, the daughter had just delivered her first child and had dropped out of high school.

Wage-reliant mothers also worried about how their absence affected their children's performance in school. One mother who worked a second job at night was notified by her child's teacher that her ten-year-old was failing. Alarmed, this mother quit her second job and began spending her evenings helping the child with homework and the extra reading and math exercises his teacher had assigned. She did not think she could live without the extra income for long, but she was determined to wait until summer recess before going back to her night job.

## FUTURE PLANS

The enormous demands of combining solo parenthood and full-time low-wage work made it hard for a few of the women we interviewed even to think about the future. When we asked one mother about her future plans, she responded,

> I will just keep on pushing the way that I have been for a long time now. I don't have any choice. Plans? I don't have the energy to make any plans past tonight. I have to live in the "right now."

This type of response was atypical, however. Most women had given considerable thought as to how they could better their situations, and almost all of their plans involved going back to school. Indeed, some had already entered short-term programs to obtain extra skills. One mother who was currently enrolled in a secretarial program commented on her progress,

> I'm thinking about going back to school, getting a degree. I can't keep living like this. I'm taking a typing course now. I paid $60 for it. And I usually am taking some course.

However, many women found that these short-term courses did not lead to more opportunities, and most of them realized they would have to pursue two- or four-year degrees to make a difference in their employment prospects. This was a much more difficult proposition for work-reliant than for welfare-reliant mothers, as it meant adding the responsibilities of long-term schooling to the already overwhelming tasks of single parenting and full-time work.

One wage-reliant woman with whom we spoke worked sixty hours in a typical week hanging wallpaper for $5 an hour. When we spoke with her, she had just been notified of her acceptance into a highly competitive pharmacy technician program at a local two-year college. Though she managed to get a loan to cover her tuition and books, she found she could not possibly go to school full time and continue to work so many hours. When the program began, she cut her work down to forty hours a week and began attending classes. After a few months, it became evident that if she wanted to pass her courses, she would have to work even less. To make this option affordable, she moved in with her parents and shared a small bedroom with her fourteen-year-old son. Other wage-reliant mothers with whom we spoke managed

in similar ways, but many found the obstacles to completing their
education overwhelming and dropped out of school as a result.

Not only did wage-reliant mothers lack the time and energy
for continuing their educations, they also had less access to financial support. Welfare-reliant mothers who wanted to further their
education were more likely to get Pell grants or other need-based
student assistance, because their cash welfare grants were low
and because grant and loan programs did not count in-kind assistance, such as food stamps. If wage-reliant mothers wished to go
to school, they relied on loans rather than grants or paid the costs
out-of-pocket. One Boston mother told us,

> I went to [the local community college] for two years, and I would like
> to go back to school and graduate, but who can afford to pay all of that
> money for tuition? It costs too much to get adequately trained and edu-
> cated these days.

Another wage-reliant mother, who had recently left welfare
for a $5-an-hour job at a discount store, told us,

> I feel like, you know, [if you work] you can't get the welfare and you
> can't get the food stamps, the things you need to improve yourself. Like
> I would like to go to college. I would like to go and make something of
> myself, but with the little [income] I get I would never be able to do that.
> Never. I don't think of anything getting better. [Since I work from 1:00 to
> 9:00 P.M.] I could go to [technical] college if I had the assistance I needed
> to be able to go. [But they say I make too much money for a grant.]

Beyond the cost of tuition and books, mothers who attended
school while on welfare could, in some cases, qualify for subsidies to cover their child care costs while they were in class. Welfare-reliant mothers with school-age children also arranged to take
classes during the day, when their children were in school. Wage-
reliant mothers were less likely to qualify for child care subsidies.
Even if they could, most working mothers who worked during
the day had to go to school in the evening or on weekends, and
evening and weekend child care was hard to find at any price.
One mother planned to return to school to complete her practical nursing training. She told us she would not enroll, however,
unless she could find someone to keep an eye on her children
after they returned home from school.

Because of these obstacles, some working mothers found that continuing their education was simply not an option. One mother with whom we spoke had worked as a child care worker since the early 1980s. Her starting pay was the legal minimum at that time—$3.35 an hour. At the time of our interview in 1992 she earned the top salary she could get without a certificate in early childhood education—$5.85 an hour. Since she was not eligible for student aid, she could not afford to take the courses necessary for certification. Not surprisingly, she started looking for a new job that would pay more without requiring more schooling, even though her friends told her such a job did not exist.

Since mothers found it difficult to combine full-time work with schooling, it is not surprising that some of them contemplated leaving their jobs for welfare in order to go to school full time. In one mother's words, "I am going to continue working for now, although some days I can definitely see quitting and getting back on welfare. I would like to attend secretarial school." Despite these plans, leaving work for welfare was not always possible. Some women, particularly white women from middle-class origins, found that they were ineligible for welfare because they had assets (usually a car or some savings) that placed them over the asset limit. One of these respondents commented bitterly,

> The system is so screwed up. I thought that when you needed help, that you get it. That's what I was taught as a kid. I found out that the system wasn't all that I thought it was. There is no safety net. There just isn't any safety net for people like me.

For most of these women, however, turning to welfare was considered an absolute last resort. One mother told us that her current situation was so bad that she had considered "hustling men" to earn some extra money (a strategy she had used while on AFDC) because she thought it less stigmatizing than welfare:

> I get food stamps every month, but I refuse to use any other kind of government agency because they just don't know how to treat you when you walk in there. They treat you like an animal just because you need a little help getting back on your feet. I don't know anyone who likes getting welfare because of the [garbage] you have to deal with in the welfare office.

Another mother told us,

> This year I left welfare and took a job to get me on my feet. But it is not getting me on my feet; it is getting me down. But I will not go back on public aid. They make you feel like dirt in the street.

Still another quipped,

> Since I have gone off welfare, I have vowed never to go to any government agency for help again. You know that expression, "I'm from the government and I am here to help"? Well, that's the scariest thing a person can ever say to you.

These mothers realized that working did not necessarily leave them better off financially, but it made them feel better about themselves and their ability to be good role models for their children. As one mother remarked,

> The worst part of [working] is that you are no better off as far as your financial situation. It is just as bad as waiting on the mailman knocking on your door once a month bringing you $188. Once you get it, it's gone. The good part about working is that it makes you feel good to know you have a job. You don't get much, but then, I have a job.

Another told us,

> I'm ... happier now [that I'm working]. You know, [when I was on welfare] I was kind of upset because I had nothing to do; I had a lot of time on my hands, just thinking about the bad times, you know, of all the problems I was having. And now that I'm working, I go to bed early; I wake up, you know; I feel good because I have something to do. I have a job and then when I come home it's easier to be with my child, instead of sitting there at home all day so uptight.

Yet, despite their determination to stay off of welfare, the punitive conditions of low-wage work usually force mothers back onto the rolls for a time. National data show that after six years, nearly two-thirds of welfare recipients who had left welfare for work had returned to the government rolls for another spell (Edin and Harris forthcoming; Harris and Edin 1996). Though not all of our workers were past AFDC recipients, this figure suggests that a sizable majority of those mothers we interviewed would, at some point in the future, find work untenable.

## THE RISKS AND REWARDS OF WORK

The American public and many political leaders seem convinced that all poor mothers should get a job. But, as this chapter has shown, life on low wages is extremely difficult and unstable, posing significant risks to both single mothers and their children. Work entails extra costs; most mothers must pay more for child care, medical care, transportation, and clothing. In addition, the ability of full-time, year-round workers to command a living wage eroded at every skill level between 1979 and 1992.[3] As a result, most of the work-reliant mothers we interviewed—those whose primary source of monthly income was their wages from a low-wage job—enjoyed some special circumstance that made work affordable for their families: large child support payments, very low rent, few child care or commuting costs, or full family medical benefits. These conditions allowed mothers to spend less so they could afford to work.

Such circumstances did not spell any great improvement in a family's standard of living, however; they simply assured the family's survival. In the end, these mothers essentially broke even: the additional income they earned through their jobs was eaten up by their new work-related expenses. In addition, work exacted a toll on these mothers' families. Low-wage employment was often unstable, with frequent fluctuations in hours and occasional layoffs, and it offered little prospect for advancement.[4] Mothers also felt torn about leaving their children either in the care of others or unsupervised at home. When children became sick or ran into trouble, these mothers had a difficult decision to make—stay at home and risk losing their job, or go to work and risk their child's well-being. Almost all said they would choose the former, which meant that many expected to switch jobs or go back on welfare if an emergency hit. In short, working mothers had to take frightening risks.

Despite the trials of employment and the fact that few mothers did better financially on a paycheck than on a welfare check, most mothers reported a greater sense of self-esteem while working. Overall, they expressed great reluctance to return to welfare; in some cases, they went to extraordinary ends to ensure their family's independence from government handouts. Yet, the nature of low-wage work and the demands of raising a family placed these women's hopes of self-sufficiency in constant jeopardy. Only a minority were likely to be able to survive long-term on work alone.

— Chapter 6 —

# Survival Strategies

IN PRIOR CHAPTERS, we have focused on how the unskilled and semiskilled mothers we interviewed chose between welfare and work. Their choices were partly shaped by another set of decisions: each mother also had to choose among a range of survival strategies to scratch together enough supplementary income. These survival "choices" were not entirely up to the mother, since other factors, including her personal characteristics and the characteristics of the neighborhood and city she lived in, often limited the range of options available to her. Despite these constraints, however, most mothers said they still had a range of strategies to try.[1]

Some mothers relied on the father of their children or a boyfriend for help. Others relied mainly on their own mother or other family members.[2] In cases where neither a child's father, a boyfriend, nor a relative could help, mothers often relied on an off-the-books job. Some sold sex, drugs, and stolen goods. Still others moved between informal and illegal jobs. When these strategies failed, many went to churches or private charities to get help to pay the light bill or the rent.

Mothers who did not have supportive friends and relatives generally had to find some kind of side-work. But some mothers told us they could not do side-work because they had no one to watch their young children. Others could not get a side-job because they were disabled; still others did not have the know-how to get an off-the-books job without getting caught by their welfare caseworker; and others lived in small, tight-knit communities where a side-job would be hard to hide from authorities.

Mothers who could get neither network support nor side-work were the most dependent on churches and private charities. Not surprisingly, these mothers invested a lot of time learning about the range of public and private sources of help available in their communities. Some mothers had a relatively easy time finding out about agencies because members of their social networks offered them guidance or because such services were well publicized. Other mothers lived in neighborhoods or cities with poor service environments, making agency help more difficult to obtain.

Most women expressed clear preferences for some strategies over others. These preferences had two dimensions. First, most mothers thought some strategies compromised their self-respect more than others. Second, mothers felt that some strategies involved more blatant violations of the welfare rules—and could be more easily tracked by caseworkers—than others.[3]

Self-reliance through work remained most mothers' long-term goal. The vast majority said that they wanted to pay all their bills with what they earned. Full financial independence, allowing them to forgo any outside help, was the only strategy that, in these mothers' eyes, involved no loss of self-respect; yet, not one mother earned enough to make this possible. Instead, they turned to their second-, third-, and fourth-best alternatives to make ends meet. In general, both welfare- and wage-reliant mothers felt that their second-best alternative was to rely on cash help from members of their personal networks. Mothers thought this strategy was the most acceptable for a number of reasons (listed below), not the least of which was that network help was seen as the best bet for moving from welfare to work. But the quality and extent of mothers' networks varied a lot, and some had no one to whom they were able (or willing) to turn.

Mothers also had preferences for some types of network support over others. Many said they would rather get cash help from their children's father or from a boyfriend than from their relatives. Mothers almost always felt that the father of their children had an obligation to help. Yet, as we will show, welfare recipients had to break the reporting rules and evade the formal child support system to get any substantial help from the fathers of their children.

Though many mothers felt the rules governing fathers' contributions were unjust, they still felt uneasy about breaking them.

Mothers with live-in boyfriends believed strongly that their lovers were obligated to contribute. We will show that mothers seldom felt guilty about getting help from a live-in boyfriend, since they felt he got a lot in return. Neither did they feel very guilty about hiding such help from their caseworkers because the help was both intermittent and short-lived and because caseworkers had no way of tracking it. Even mothers who received a boyfriend's help consistently for many years did not feel obligated to report such help, since they still believed the man and his money might disappear at any moment. Their fears made sense, since many of the men had difficulty finding steady work in the regular economy and were tempted by work opportunities in the underground economy. (Several mothers told us they would marry their boyfriends if the men could find steady jobs in the formal sector.)

Many mothers also felt they had some claim on their relatives' income. The norms of reciprocity that existed among kin, however, made it difficult for mothers to rely on long-term help from relatives. Those receiving means-tested benefits said they almost never felt guilty about hiding such contributions from their caseworkers. Most had never even considered reporting these contributions because their caseworkers would deduct the entire amount from their welfare checks. Mothers told us that no family member in his or her "right mind" would continue to make contributions under these conditions. In addition, mothers knew that caseworkers had virtually no way of tracking such contributions, even if they suspected mothers were receiving them.

Mothers who could not get sufficient funds from men or kin generally took a side-job—most mothers' third-best alternative for generating extra income. They typically opted for cash work or jobs in the informal economy over a "real" job that required a false ID. Caseworkers could track income from a job in the formal sector unless the mother quit after a few months or unless she used a false social security number. While mothers did not generally feel guilty about hiding informal work, they did feel that having to lie about their identity to take a formal sector job was a "rip-off" because it robbed them of the self-respect that could have resulted if they could have gotten enough hours or enough pay to leave welfare behind.

Getting agency-based help ranked very low on mothers' lists because most felt that going to community groups and private charities was as humiliating as going to the welfare office. Though welfare caseworkers could not track such income, mothers had a hard time getting much help from any single agency. Most agencies had very few resources, so mothers often had to go from agency to agency if they needed a lot of help.

Finally, the option of selling sex, drugs, or stolen goods was generally at the bottom of most mothers' list of work preferences. This is because mothers generally believed that criminal activity would rob them of the self-respect they gained from trying to be good mothers. This is why most mothers who did underground work moved between crime and more "legitimate" strategies.

Notions of the relative acceptability of these income-generating strategies were widely (though by no means universally) shared, and they helped to shape mothers' survival repertoires at any given point in time. They also helped to determine how mothers moved between strategies over time. Movement between strategies was often necessary because most were unreliable. For example, many fathers paid child support intermittently because they could not find steady work. Similarly, some employers were willing to pay a mother cash for seasonal work but had no need for a year-round cash employee. When one strategy dried up, mothers had to find another.

Thus, mothers' survival strategies were dynamic rather than static. The best metaphor to describe the nature of strategies came from one of our Chicago mothers. She likened the efforts of welfare mothers to continually mending a worn patchwork quilt. For each mother, this quilt is constructed of a variety of strategies: welfare- and work-based income; cash and in-kind assistance garnered from family, friends, absent fathers, and boyfriends; and cash and in-kind help from private charities. For most mothers, the quilt needs constant mending as one patch wears out and others need to be added. Failure to mend one's quilt has harsh consequences, including material hardship and even the loss of one's children to the state. Mothers therefore spent a great deal of time and energy planning what they would do if their current set of strategies failed.

At the same time, many were afraid that the strategies they devised would get them in trouble with the welfare department, the housing authority, the IRS, or—in some cases—the law.

In the pages that follow, we describe each of the survival strategies mothers used to patch together supplemental income and explain why mothers preferred some strategies over others. We also discuss how mothers' personal characteristics and the cities in which they lived influenced their choice of survival strategies. In order to quantify the value of different strategies, we have taken all of the income-generating strategies that mothers reported using over the past twelve months, summed the income generated over the preceding year, and then divided by twelve. The exceptions to this rule are discussed in chapter 1. This technique provides some idea of how a typical low income mother generated her money each month. But no mother was really typical in this sense, since no mother used all the strategies we discuss.[4]

Just as no mother was typical, no month was typical, since few survival strategies were stable enough to provide a steady stream of income. Our tables therefore oversimplify what was actually a complex and dynamic process, making it appear that mothers were getting small amounts from each source each month, when in fact they were receiving a large fraction of their income from one source in one month and from another source in the next. Nonetheless, we decided to report averages because they are somewhat representative both of mothers' strategies over time and of the range of strategies available to mothers.

## HOW DO SINGLE MOTHERS SURVIVE ON
## WELFARE AND LOW-WAGE WORK?

As we showed in chapter 2, cash welfare and food stamps covered only three-fifths of welfare-reliant mothers' expenses, so that they typically experienced a substantial gap between their welfare income and her expenses. Obviously, no mother without substantial savings could run such a deficit for long. The women we interviewed had no savings accounts, no certificates of deposit, no individual retirement accounts, no stocks or bonds, and no other valuable assets; if they had, they would have been ineligible for welfare. In short, they had little to fall back on when they ran out of cash welfare and food stamps. As we have seen, welfare-reliant mothers obtained the extra income they needed through a generous friend or relative, through a side-job, or through agency contributions.

The complexity involved in assembling all of this support often meant that time as well as money was at a premium for these mothers. All had to invest at least some time in maintaining their welfare eligibility, which involved keeping appointments with caseworkers and other welfare professionals (child support enforcement officials, JOBS personnel, and the like), dealing with an inefficient Medicaid system, filling out paperwork, and keeping track of rent and utility bills, pay stubs, and other proofs of eligibility.

In addition, nearly three-quarters had family, friends, boyfriends, or absent fathers who gave them substantial cash assistance. Half were also working at jobs in the formal, informal, or underground economies, and some of the rest were trying to find such jobs. Finally, one in three was receiving some sort of cash or voucher assistance from private charities or from student loan or grant programs.

Working mothers' situations were often no better (and sometimes worse). Their main jobs covered only 63 percent of their expenses. Most of the working mothers' other income came from other individuals and agencies, but the EITC, food stamps, overtime pay, second-job earnings, and agency contributions also helped. Work in the underground economy (selling sex, drugs, or stolen goods) made up less than 1 percent of their total monthly budgets, on average.

Beyond these activities, both the working and welfare mothers were keeping house, raising children and protecting them from the fast and violent street life endemic to many of their neighborhoods, taking training courses, and hunting for a better job. Despite their efforts, most *welfare-reliant* families experienced periods of considerable financial difficulty, continuing economic insecurity, and regular episodes of material hardship. *Work-reliant* families earned only a little more than welfare recipients, and their slight gains were wiped out by the additional expenditures of working. This meant that workers typically suffered slightly more hardship than welfare mothers did, as we showed in chapter 4. One working mother voiced her frustration with her plight:

> Ask any politician to live off my budget. Live off my minimum-wage job and just a little bit of food stamps—how can he do it? I bet he couldn't. I'd like him to try it for one month. Come home from work, cook dinner, wash clothes, do everything, everything, get up and go to work the next day, and then find you don't have enough money to pay for everything you need.

## NETWORK STRATEGIES

Both groups of mothers were more likely to get cash contributions from friends and family than from side-jobs or agencies. Table 6-1 shows that about three-fourths of *welfare-reliant* mothers got cash help from members of their networks. Recipients who used network-based strategies netted an average of $208 a month. Table 6-2 shows that 82 percent of *wage-reliant* mothers reported that they relied on family or friends to make it through the month. Those workers who received this help generated $291 a month. Table 6-3 indicates that these differences are significant. For both groups of mothers, contributions came from three main sources: family members, boyfriends, and children's fathers (whom we refer to as "absent" even though one-quarter of them "stayed" with the mother at least occasionally).

### Cash Contributions from
### Family Members or Friends

Forty-six percent of the *welfare-reliant* mothers we interviewed received cash assistance from a family member or a friend who was neither a boyfriend nor the father of any of their children, netting an average $136 each month. A similar proportion of the *wage-reliant* mothers told us they had received money from a family member during the prior twelve months and averaged $140 a month.

For both groups, mothers' own mothers were the most prominent among their supporters and provided both cash and in-kind help. One wage-reliant mother recounted,

**TABLE 6-1. Survival Strategies for Welfare-Reliant Mothers**

| | Mothers Engaging in Strategy | Average Amount for Those Receiving Anything | Average Amount for All Mothers |
|---|---|---|---|
| *Number in sample* | *214* | *N/A* | *N/A* |
| Work-based strategies | 46% | $276 | $128 |
| Reported work | 5 | 399 | 19 |
| Unreported work | 39 | 229 | 90 |
| Underground work | 8 | 228 | 19 |
| Network-based strategies | 77% | $208 | $157 |
| Family/friends | 46 | 136 | 62 |
| Cash from men | 53 | 180 | 95 |
| Boyfriend | 29 | 195 | 56 |
| Absent father | 33 | 121 | 39 |
| Covert support | 23 | 141 | 33 |
| Formal support | 14 | 46 | 7 |
| Agency-based strategies | 31% | $117 | $ 37 |
| Food stamps | 95% | $233 | $222 |
| SSI | 9 | 384 | 36 |
| EITC | 7 | 49 | 3 |

*Source:* Authors' calculations using Edin and Lein survival strategies data.

> My mom helps me. She gives me money and buys Pampers and clothes for the baby and washes the baby's clothes. She babysits on Saturday when I work. She picks the baby up from day care during the week while I go to school. Sometimes she comes and picks me up from work.

Siblings and other maternal kin also contributed cash and in-kind assistance. Another mother described her situation this way:

> The kids give me a headache about clothes. Usually my mom, brother, or sister-in-law gives me money to buy them clothes. I can't afford it. I get clothes at church and other charitable clothes giveaways, or at garage sales. My kids haven't had any store-bought clothes paid for by me for eight or nine years. Mama buys them shoes when we visit her. It's cheaper where my mother lives.

## TABLE 6-2. **Survival Strategies for Wage-Reliant Mothers**

| | Mothers Engaging in Strategy | Average Amount for Those Receiving Anything | Average Amount for All Mothers |
|---|---|---|---|
| *Number in sample* | *165* | *N/A* | *N/A* |
| Work-based strategies | 39% | $227 | $ 88 |
| Supplemental reported work | 12 | 225 | 27 |
| Supplemental unreported work | 28 | 207 | 59 |
| Supplemental underground work | 1 | 170 | 2 |
| Network-based strategies | 82% | $291 | $253 |
| Family/friends | 47 | 140 | 65 |
| Cash from men | 61 | 309 | 187 |
| Boyfriend | 27 | 226 | 60 |
| Absent father | 42 | 300 | 127 |
| Agency-based strategies | 22% | $165 | $ 36 |
| Food stamps | 28% | $203 | $ 57 |
| SSI | 2 | 132 | 3 |
| EITC | 28 | 88 | 25 |

*Source:* Authors' calculations using Edin and Lein survival strategies data.

Absent fathers' kin also helped, especially among African Americans. One mother commented,

> His [paternal] grandmother do for him, buys him clothes. She bought both kids an Easter basket. She also got a stroller, a walker, and gives me money for Pampers and food.

Overreliance on one family member, however, often bred resentment. Because of this, most mothers developed as wide a range of family contacts as they could. Another woman told us,

> If I need something I can go to my sister. If she doesn't have it, by me having a large family, someone in the family will let me borrow until the next check comes in. Everyone in my family helps me even if it's just a small amount.

**TABLE 6-3. Amount of Income Generated Through Each Survival Strategy**

| | Welfare-Reliant Mothers Engaging in Strategy | Wage-Reliant Mothers Engaging in Strategy | Sig. | Average Amount for Welfare-Reliant Mothers | Average Amount for Wage-Reliant Mothers | Sig. |
|---|---|---|---|---|---|---|
| *Number in sample* | *214* | *165* | *N/A* | *214* | *165* | *N/A* |
| Work-based strategies | 46% | 39% | | $128 | $ 88 | ** |
| Reported work | 5 | 12 | *** | 19 | 27 | |
| Unreported work | 39 | 28 | ** | 90 | 59 | *** |
| Underground work | 8 | 1 | *** | 19 | 2 | ** |
| Network-based strategies | 77% | 82% | | $157 | $253 | *** |
| Family/friends | 46 | 47 | | 62 | 65 | |
| Cash from men | 53 | 61 | | 95 | 187 | *** |
| Boyfriend | 29 | 27 | | 56 | 60 | |
| Absent father | 33 | 42 | * | 39 | 127 | *** |
| Covert supp. | 23 | N/A | N/A | 33 | N/A | N/A |
| Formal supp. | 14 | N/A | N/A | 7 | N/A | N/A |
| Agency-based strategies | 31% | 22% | ** | $ 37 | $ 36 | |
| Food stamps | 95% | 28% | *** | $222 | $ 57 | *** |
| SSI | 9 | 2 | *** | 36 | 3 | *** |
| EITC | 7 | 28 | *** | 3 | 25 | *** |

*Source:* Authors' calculations using Edin and Lein survival strategies data.
*Note:* Two-tailed tests for significance of differences in means between welfare- and wage-reliant mothers given by * > .10; ** > .05; *** > .01.

Mothers who "borrowed" could seldom pay back their loans in a timely manner, if at all. Therefore, mothers with fewer contributing family members exhausted their relatives' goodwill sooner. Our data suggest wide variation in how long it took women to exhaust their network resources. Some mothers' relatives would help only in a crisis and refused to assist mothers on a regular basis. Other mothers' families had been helping for more than a decade.[5]

Even though network-based contributions were invaluable to many mothers, network membership involved obligations. This was especially true in poor communities where hardly anyone had many surplus resources. In these communities, mothers had to provide something in exchange for what they received. Though our mothers were almost never able to offer cash to other members of their network, they did invest time and energy in maintaining relationships and providing whatever in-kind assistance they could manage. A sister who paid the utility bill, for example, might expect free babysitting or house cleaning in exchange for her financial contribution. In other words, such contributions were not generally free.

For working mothers, kin often paid for specific items that allowed mothers to keep working (car payments, insurance, and day care payments were the most common items). For welfare mothers, kin made similar arrangements so mothers could work covertly or go to school. One mother told us,

> My one sister is very supportive financially—she helps me a little bit—she pays for day care while I work and go to school. That's a big help. She's divorced; that's why she's doing this—she knows how hard it is. My son goes to [an] after-school program which I have to pay for. Summer is even more difficult. He would be home alone if my sister did not pay. I can't do that to my child. She can afford to help because she's a data analyst and doesn't have any of her own kids.

By the time mothers had exhausted their relatives' goodwill, their children were sometimes old enough to contribute to the family budget. When one woman lost the support of her mother, her high school–aged son took an after-school job at McDonald's and gave virtually all his earnings to his mother. Though her thirteen-year-old daughter was too young to work legally, she began babysitting for neighbors on the weekends and earned "$10 here or there," which she contributed to the household budget. In some cases, mothers were not sure where their children were getting the money but suspected involvement in petty crime and drug sales.

## Cash Contributions from Men

Though family and friends were the most frequent contributors to the support of welfare- and wage-reliant families, tables 6-1 and 6-2 show that men also played a crucial role in balancing mothers' budgets. Over half of the *welfare-reliant* mothers in our study had received contributions from men during the previous twelve months, netting $180 in an average month. A similar proportion of our *wage-reliant* mothers had received cash assistance from men in the preceding year. But men's contributions to the typical working mother's budget were much larger than those to a welfare-reliant mother's budget ($309 versus $180). These contributions varied according to a mother's need, the state of the man's relationship with the family, and his own financial position. Although we discuss the contributions of boyfriends and absent fathers separately, the reader should be aware that boyfriends can, over time, become absent fathers, and nominally absent fathers can remain boyfriends.

### Boyfriends

For both groups of mothers, the men we call boyfriends were neither legally married to the mother nor the father of any of her children but did have an ongoing romantic relationship with her. While we use the term "boyfriend," the women themselves used a variety of terms including "friend," "husband," "common-law husband," "my man," "old man," and sometimes even "significant other." Boyfriends who contributed financially to the family usually lived with the family, at least part of the time.

Twenty-nine percent of the *welfare-reliant* mothers with whom we spoke told us that a man who was neither a relative nor the father of any of her children had helped out the family at some point during the past year. Welfare-reliant mothers who received such contributions got monthly amounts averaging $195. *Wage-reliant* mothers were about as likely as welfare mothers to get cash contributions from boyfriends, and they contributed similar amounts. Mothers who did not receive help from family members were particularly likely to get help from a boyfriend. This could have been because mothers without generous relatives sought out others who would help or because a mother's relatives chose not to contribute when a boyfriend was present because they expected him to help.

A mother seldom allowed her boyfriend to stay with her unless he contributed both cash and in-kind goods to the household. Boyfriends, in turn, typically expected to be able to "stay," at least occasionally, in return for their cash contributions. Because boyfriends had no legal obligation to contribute to the household, mothers created such an obligation by including boyfriends in family life.

The "friend" of a Chicago mother, for example, made half of the time payments on her furniture, paid half the family's phone bill, bought her cigarettes, and gave small presents to the children. During the past year, this same man had also given her $20 or $30 in cash each week for incidentals, as well as $250 to pay for the Christmas gifts she put on layaway. A Boston-area recipient with two older daughters who had recently married and gotten off the welfare rolls explained their survival strategies with a single sentence: "When they were on welfare, they had a boyfriend."

Mothers sharply criticized boyfriends who did not contribute. One mother told us,

> My last boyfriend was really disgusting. Didn't help at all with expenses, but wanted to be able to walk into the living room and have me give him a blow job. He was such a pig. I'm so glad he's gone. He would drop money for drugs, no problem, but after a while he wouldn't give me any money to pay bills.

Again and again, mothers told us that men who "don't pay, can't stay." Mothers were both unable and unwilling to sustain non-contributing boyfriends on their meager welfare checks. One mother told us, "I don't pay no bills if I can help it. I just let my boyfriends live in my house if they take care of my bills." Another said,

> While my boyfriend is in residence I am able to pay my bills. We split everything—rent, electricity. I had known him, and we had a relationship once before. He got married, then his wife left him. He needed somewhere to stay, and I needed someone to help me with those bills.

This pattern of "no pay, no stay" is in sharp contrast to media images of men who hang out on street corners and live off the welfare checks of naive women. One mother in Chicago had lived with her boyfriend on and off for nearly ten years. Though he found work easily, he also tended to lose these jobs. This mother told us,

> Kevin will get a job for three months. So he'll be bringing stuff home and paying his way. Then I let him stay over here. But Kevin doesn't always like to keep his jobs. Sometimes they lay him off, sometimes he just lays off the job. So when that happens, I kick him out. I tell him, "If you pay, you can stay."

Boyfriends contributed important in-kind assistance as well. Yet, when boyfriends spent cash on mothers or their children, the items they bought usually cost the men far more than they saved the mothers. A Chicago mother recounted, "He buy me this leather cap—paid $80 for it. Now what do I need an $80 hat for?" Another Charleston mother said, "He bought me that stereo. I don't listen to music much, so for me it's just decoration. But he had to buy it." Another boyfriend used his tax refund to make a down payment on a new car for his girlfriend. Infuriated by his foolishness, she told us she was relieved when it was finally repossessed nine months later. Because of situations like these, we did not try to include the cash value of boyfriends' in-kind contributions (or in-kind help from any source) in mothers' household budgets.

In spite of the concentration on nonessentials, a boyfriend's "gift" generally had a positive impact on a mother's budget. One mother recounted,

> I met him for lunch. He said, "Why don't you buy yourself something?" He gave me $100. It was eerie at first. He knew that I was having a hard time with the kids. I went to the mall and bought two pairs of tennis shoes for the kids, $45 each. I didn't buy anything for myself. He said, "I kind of like that in you." He gave me $150 the next time. So I bought some clothing for myself and the kids. He gave me $350 for Christmas. I was not planning to put a tree up. He asked, "Why not?" I said, "I'm not in the mood." He knew I had nothing to put under it. But when I brought it home the living room was full of things. It was a nice Christmas after all.

Our interview transcripts and field observations repeatedly demonstrated how a mother's need for steady income and the erratic earnings of boyfriends created a pattern of what some mothers called "serial boyfriends." The mercenary nature of these relationships occasionally made it difficult for mothers to distinguish between serial boyfriends and outright prostitution. One mother explained that her continuous use of live-in boyfriends "isn't for love, and it isn't just for money. I guess I'd call it social prostitution, or something like that." But this language was unusual among women who let boyfriends live with the family. Women who engaged in one-night stands were more likely to talk about "turning tricks," "street walking," or "selling my ass" when they had no ongoing relationship with the man and received cash in return for sex. We only coded such liaisons as underground work if women described them in this way.

Boyfriends who did "pay and stay" reaped considerable benefits. First, a typical boyfriend contributed a few hundred dollars each month—a substantial addition to a mother's monthly budget. This amount usually provided him with a place to stay and a few meals (although men usually ate out or at the homes of their own mothers, because their girlfriends could not afford to feed them). Boyfriends who paid were also more likely to be able to "play Daddy" to the mother's children. Since boyfriends were often cut off from biological children they had not supported, the opportunity to play Daddy to other men's children provided an important avenue for resurrecting their identities as fathers and responsible family men.[6]

One Chicago mother told us how her boyfriend played this role in the lives of her children. Before she met her boyfriend, she got by on the income from side-work. Her health deteriorated, however, and she could no longer work at those jobs. In exchange for his help, she allowed him to live with her:

DID YOU EVER DO ANY HOUSECLEANING OR BABYSITTING OR ANY ODD JOBS?:
    I used to, until I had an operation. 'Til I had that operation and had to quit.

DO YOU REMEMBER HOW MUCH YOU USED TO MAKE?:
    I don't remember. It was like $100 or something like that. I was doing maid work in about twenty-seven rooms a day. I made about $100 a week under the table for this.

My new boyfriend Bill, he helps. He lives in now. He works odd jobs around the neighborhood. He gives me as much as I was making cleaning motel rooms.

Bill is like a father to my children. They love him, and they know they can go to him with their problems. Their own father is deceased. His own children are all grown and he don't see them on a regular basis. And he also helps me with my grandchild who lives with me now since her mother is in drug treatment. We are like an old married couple.

The involvement of boyfriends in the lives of families was not always positive, however. Maintaining relationships with boyfriends demanded time and energy from women who were short of both. On occasion, women talked explicitly about the need to balance what they gained through their liaisons with men against the costs of such assistance. Sometimes boyfriends became violent, brought drugs, alcohol, or undesirable companions into the household, or used the household as the headquarters for their illegal activity.

Mothers who relied on boyfriends for income sometimes had to choose between danger and destitution. While not all boyfriends were involved in illegal activity, many mothers reported that they or their children had been physically or sexually abused by their domestic partners at some point in the past. When mothers discovered that a boyfriend was abusing their children, most immediately evicted him. A few told us, however, that they had ignored the evidence because they were so desperate for their boyfriend's money. Most did eventually evict the abuser, but the damage had already been done.

## Contributions from Absent Fathers

Even more prevalent than contributions from boyfriends were contributions from former boyfriends or husbands who had fathered a mother's children. (We refer to them as "absent" fathers, but one-quarter of them "stayed" with the mother at least occasionally.) One-third (33 percent) of the welfare-reliant mothers we interviewed reported receiving contributions from absent fathers during the previous twelve months (see Edin 1995 for a more detailed account), nearly three times what national data on child support show. The reasons for this discrepancy are easy to explain. Only a third of these contributions were made through the formal child support system; the rest went directly to the mother and were not reported to the authorities. We call these under-the-table contributions "covert support." Welfare recipients preferred covert support because federal rules made official payments more costly to families.

When a single mother applies for and receives AFDC, she must sign her rights to child support over to the state. Furthermore, she cannot receive AFDC unless she agrees to cooperate with the state in identifying and tracking down the father. These rules have been in place since 1975. Still, it is nearly impossible for the state to distinguish between those who pretend to cooperate and those who truly cooperate. Because fathers are hard to track down and making them pay is difficult, even mothers who cooperated fully seldom received child support through the formal system.

In our sample, 60 percent of *welfare-reliant* mothers fully cooperated with the child support authorities in the case of at least one of their children's fathers. Those who cooperated were not assured of payment because they often did not have all of the information the state needed and because the system was so overwhelmed with cases. As a result, the state was seldom successful in finding the father, proving paternity, getting a court order for child support, and enforcing that order. Even when child support officials accomplished all the necessary steps, the mother could receive only $50 of this amount each month (or less if he paid less than $50) in what was known as a "pass through" payment. Under the old welfare rules the state kept the rest as partial reimbursement for the cost of the mother's welfare.

Furthermore, while the federal AFDC program allowed a mother to keep the first $50 of what the absent father paid, both the food stamp program and federal housing programs counted this income when determining benefits. Thus, a mother who received food stamps and lived in subsidized housing found that if she got $50 in a "pass through" payments, she lost $15 in food stamps and paid an extra $15 in rent. As a result, her net income rose by only $20 a month, even though her child's father might have been paying hundreds of dollars each month to the state. One mother explained how these rules affected her other welfare benefits:

> My food stamps vary because they punish me if I get a child support payment. Occasionally, my ex-husband will give them $30 a month, in which case they then dock my food stamps and housing by $10 each.

Naturally, welfare-reliant mothers disliked these rules. So did fathers, who felt that their children received little or no benefit from their contributions. One woman from Chicago exclaimed, "If I turned him in to child support, I would only get $50 a month! What do they do with the rest of it? That is ridiculous! That's a rip-off! I would be steaming mad if that happened!" Therefore, mothers and fathers sometimes colluded to deceive both the child support authorities and the AFDC program.

Some mothers who cooperated with child support officials in the case of one father protected the identity of another. Thus, 60 percent of welfare-reliant mothers told our interviewers that they had either lied about the identity of a father or hidden crucial identifying information (social security number, address, or current employer) from the enforcement agency. Deception was common in all four sites that we studied, ranging from about half of the welfare-reliant mothers in Chicago to two-thirds in San Antonio.

The deception was quite easy—child support enforcement is largely a desk job, where workers compare fathers' social security numbers with those of workers provided by the Department of Labor, the IRS, or other databases. Mothers who wished to evade the formal system did not need to lie about the father's identity, or even about his whereabouts. All they had to do was withhold his social security number, if they had it (which some did not). Without this piece of information, child support enforcement officials seldom tracked down fathers or made them pay.

But while deception was easy, mothers had varying levels of knowledge about how other aspects of the Child Support Enforcement system worked. Some believed that they had to name another man as the father (and some took the opportunity to name someone they had a grudge against) or to claim they did not know who fathered their child. One Charleston mother told us,

The child support enforcement [official] took me in a little cubicle. He asked me who was the father of my child. I look at him and I say, "I have to confess, I have been having sex with men that I don't know. One night stands and such. I know it's wrong, but I cannot tell you the identity of my child's father. I do not know who he was, just one of many I have known." Of course, I was making all this up, but I had gotten very loud, carried away. So when I walked out of the cubicle everybody in the waiting room had heard me. They were all staring, like "look at that sinner!"

Other mothers knew they could be more truthful and still evade the system.[7]

Meanwhile, many mothers arranged for their child's father to pay them directly. In this way, mothers retained all of the money that fathers contributed. Mothers held fathers to these informal agreements by threatening to turn them over to the state if they failed to live up to their end of a bargain. Fathers profited as well, because mothers were usually more sympathetic than the state when the father could not pay due to unemployment or other financial crises.

Mothers preferred private bargains for several reasons. First, some received more money from the father than the $50 the system would have allowed them to keep. Second, many believed that fathers' economic situations were simply not stable enough to sustain a regular child support commitment. In these cases, they preferred getting at least a portion of the money to seeing the father harassed or jailed (in which case they would get no support at all). Third, some mothers believed that "direct" payment enhanced the relationship between the father and the child. For example, a father who maintained some contact would know when his child needed new shoes or clothing, or money for a school trip. It was also more difficult for fathers to deny birthday and Christmas gifts to children they visited regularly. According to mothers, arranging child support through the courts diminished the absent father's sense of parental pride and obliterated any feeling of gratification for doing his duty. A father who paid informally not only expected the mother's cooperation in evading the formal system but also wanted regular access to his children. Mothers, in turn, knew that receiving covert support meant that they had to grant visitation "rights" to the father and his kin.[8] Nonetheless, it should be emphasized that the existence of the formal system was crucial to mothers who evaded it because they used it as a negotiating tool, threatening to turn in a father if he failed to honor his informal agreement.[9] According to one of our respondents,

> Well, I don't get child support, but her father gives me at least . . . I'd say $1,500 last year. And I'm gonna tell you it's more than that. He does his share for his kids. If welfare find that out, they will probably try to cut off everything. He does his share. And I told him, "I'll make sure child support stays like that as long as you keep doing your share." As long as I got anything to do with it, that's how it gonna be.

Another of our respondents made good on her threat to turn her ex-boyfriend over to the enforcement authorities when he did not pay:

> Sometimes you have to put them on child support, 'cause these men don't realize that sugar is sweet [how good they have it]. Before I decided to give his name to child support, all I did was call him and say, "Can you help me out this week?" But he took advantage of the situation and kept telling me: "I don't have to do this and that." I said, "I need you to get a big box of Pampers to take to the babysitter." He said, "Yeah, all right." I found out that he didn't do it. So I said, "That's that. That's the end," and I put his papers in for the child support. And I said, "What do you want me to do? I don't want to embarrass you like this!" We went to court.

This woman's comments reflect a nearly universal sentiment among the welfare-reliant women we interviewed: fathers should pay voluntarily if possible, and mothers should only "put the law" on them as a last resort. They preferred to negotiate informal systems of support that matched their own assessments of the father's ability to pay. In large part, welfare-reliant mothers reported that their young, unemployed, or underemployed ex-partners saw "doing for the child" on a day-to-day basis as the mother's responsibility; an economically hard-up father could be expected to "help out" only occasionally. For the mothers we interviewed, covert payments meant that mothers and fathers negotiated the payments as their situations and the child's needs changed.

Although our data show that only about a third of recipients received *cash* from an absent father during the previous twelve months, another third reported regular in-kind assistance. For fathers with younger children, this usually consisted of a bag or two of diapers each month. In fact, our interviews with mothers of younger children revealed that buying "Pampers" (a generic term often used to describe all disposable diapers) was an accepted symbolic expression of fatherhood for many poor absentee fathers. Fathers of older children typically affirmed their paternal status by purchasing an occasional pair of shoes or school clothes. In addition, fathers (as well as boyfriends and the mother's and father's kin) often purchased birthday and Christmas gifts for children of all ages, taking the financial burden for these events off the mother.

Though boyfriends who contributed almost always took up part-time residence in single mothers' households, less than half the fathers who contributed lived with the family. Those fathers who did were generally required to "bring their money home" and contributed twice as much, on average, as fathers who lived elsewhere. Live-in fathers who could not pay because they were unemployed were more likely to be granted temporary reprieve from financial responsibility than boyfriends. This made sense both economically and emotionally; if mothers could manage to remain on good terms with an unemployed father, they could negotiate a deal and could potentially receive more from him over the long run once the father found work. This was not so relevant for boyfriends because they could be replaced, while a biological father could not.

Mothers were also more lenient on fathers because many felt that their children benefited from contact with them:

> Now he's out of work, so he has no money. So before, when he was in work, he'd help me with the car payments. He paid like one-half of the car payment for me for two months. And then he was giving me like $50 a week. But it's not like one big set thing that is done every time, because he cannot hold a job, so he doesn't always have money. But he's there for the children. That's important. I didn't have a father, so I know it's important.

If the father remained unemployed for a long period, however, he was almost always evicted from the mother's household. In some cases, he and his kin were also denied access to his children. One mother with whom we spoke had evicted her children's father because he could not or would not find work. He moved back in with his mother and began to work intermittently as a construction worker. He found little work, though, and his occasional token contributions were not enough. She told us,

> He sometimes give me money. When I sent her up there to his mother's house, he buy her Pampers and baby food, but all he puts into my hand is a $20 bill. I mean, what does he expect me to buy with $20? I can't even buy but two boxes of Pampers with $20. He's coming over here tonight to bring her back, and I said I needed $40 'cause she need so many things right now. But I don't think he gonna bring it. He always says he's gonna bring money, but he never does because he's never working steady. If he doesn't bring money this time, I am not gonna let her go up there to his mother's house to visit anymore.

In this mother's case, the absent father eventually began to sell drugs in the underground economy, both to meet his own living needs and to contribute more toward the care of his child. Like this absent father, chronically unemployed fathers who wanted to maintain their claim on their children were powerfully motivated to engage in any kind of work, including work in the underground economy. A detailed discussion of the employment problems of unskilled and semiskilled men is beyond the scope of this book, but longitudinal data suggest that these men's ability to get a regular job, much less one that pays a living wage, has declined dramatically over the past two decades (Wilson 1996). Yet, whatever the source, fathers learned that they had to contribute to maintain their role in the family and their right to reside in the mother's household.

Fathers also provided essential and nonessential in-kind assistance. Like boyfriends, absent fathers were prone to purchase nonessentials like videocassette recorders and electronic games for their children—items most mothers would not think of "wasting money" on. More often, however, they provided essential goods like disposable diapers, formula, and baby food. As important as these contributions were to mothers' budgets, most mothers knew that they could not count on fathers over the long term because fathers' incomes were too precarious.

Because they saw fathers as hard-pressed to provide regular assistance, our mothers did not generally feel guilty about hiding fathers' contributions from welfare or child support officials. One mother said of the father of her child,

> He says he can take care of me and the baby. But like I said, it won't be easy. I mean, I know I shouldn't plan on depending on him, because it can end at any time. I don't report it because I know I cannot count on it. If I'm learning anything, it's the fact that I'm going to have to do something where I can take care of us. You never know what's going to happen. Having this baby taught me a lot young. You do grow up fast.

Another mother told us that the father of her four-year-old boy lived nearby and had a job parking cars. She insisted that when he came over to see his child, he bring food and some money. The father of her oldest child had never contributed, she explained, because he became involved in drugs and went to prison while she was still carrying the child. She thought that low-income fathers often split from the women with whom they had children because they did not make enough to support a family.

Yet another mother's story illustrates how women's expectations depended on the father's situation and his willingness to be involved. The father of Betty Williams's first child had some contact with the child and paid covert support averaging $30 a week. Her second child's father was a disabled veteran of the Vietnam War who lived very near the edge of financial destitution. Williams agreed to let his brother take over his obligation of $100 a month. Williams was legally married to the father of her third child, and although she had a formal child support order, he did not give her any money. In retaliation, she was in the process of "putting in papers" on him.

Overall, *welfare-reliant mothers* who received contributions from fathers averaged $121 a month. Because the welfare system restricted the amount of support the mothers could keep to $50, mothers receiving contributions through the formal system averaged only $46 a month. Mothers who received covert support generated an average of $141 a month. Absent fathers contributed more to mothers who worked. Overall, 42 percent of the *wage-reliant mothers* with whom we spoke told us they had received contributions from absent fathers during the prior year, compared with only one-third of welfare-reliant mothers—a marginally significant difference. The big difference was that those working mothers who received such help averaged $300 a month.[10]

Some mothers told us that fathers were more willing to contribute when they felt mothers were trying to better themselves through work. One mother put it this way: "He see I'm trying to make things better by working, so he decide to throw a few dollars at me." In large part, however, the causal connection probably ran the other way. If the children's father provided regular and substantial support, mothers had more incentive to work since they could then legally keep all the money he gave them and could make ends meet without begging from family members and friends. In the mothers' view, a father's help was the fulfillment of an obligation rather than an act of charity (from a family member or agency), and therefore far preferable to dependence on other network members.

While fathers' contributions were a crucial piece in the patchwork quilt of survival for many wage-reliant mothers, those mothers seldom saw child support payments as an economic panacea.[11] Child support obligations, whether informal or formal, are very hard to enforce at any income level, and longitudinal data show that fathers' contributions decrease as their children age. Our wage-reliant mothers felt they could not count on fathers over the long term. Nonetheless, when fathers' contributions were late (or stopped coming), the economic stability of most working mothers was shaken. One respondent told us that the court had ordered her husband to pay $500 each month in child support, and $150 in spousal support. One month when his check bounced, she went without heat. Cheretta Stevens, an African American mother of four, told us her ex-husband stopped paying when he moved out of the state. Stevens, who had recently scraped together enough money to buy a modest home in a low-cost neighborhood, went first without electricity, then without heat and water. Finally, many months behind in her mortgage payments, she declared bankruptcy and moved with her four children back to her parents' three-bedroom home.

Still another mother told us that she had court orders for support from both of her children's fathers. Each father was supposed to pay $300 a month. One paid intermittently and the other paid nothing. She told us, "My first husband owes $3,000 in back support. He has no intention of paying it. [The second husband], he is two months behind right now." When we asked her how this

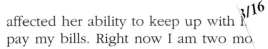

affected her ability to keep up with I can't
pay my bills. Right now I am two mo

Low-wage workers seldom had the                          yer to
sue the father. Some knew of law firms on a con-
tingency basis, but hiring such firms mean ing up a large portion of any future payments they might receive. (They would
probably have been more keen to approach such firms if their
lawyer's fees could have been added to the amount the father
had to pay.) All of them could have asked the state Child Support Enforcement agency for help at minimal cost, but state agencies were so overloaded that the mothers who used them seldom
saw results.

## USING SIDE-JOBS TO GET BY

Mothers who could not get enough cash help from their networks
generally took a side-job to fill the remaining gap between their
income and expenditures. Overall, 46 percent of the *welfare-
reliant* mothers with whom we spoke had relied on income from
some form of work during the past year to supplement their welfare checks (see table 6-1). Those *welfare-reliant* mothers who
worked made an average of $276 a month. Since *low-wage work-
ing mothers* could not earn enough from their regular jobs to support their families, they too often had to work overtime or take
a second job (see table 6-2). Indeed, 39 percent of working mothers took on extra work to help balance their budgets. Among
those workers who took on overtime hours or a second job, such
work added $227 to their monthly budgets.

For both groups of mothers, we divide work into three categories: work reported to the welfare department, the housing
authority, the IRS, WIC, Medicaid, and other relevant means-tested
government programs; work that was legal but not reported; and
work that was neither legal nor reported.

### Reported Work

Among our *welfare recipients,* 5 percent of mothers told us that
they had engaged in some reported work during the year (see
table 6-1). Most welfare recipients who reported their work did

so only after having been caught working by their caseworkers and subsequently forced to do so. Nationally, 7 percent of the welfare caseload told their AFDC caseworkers they were working in a given month during 1991 (U.S. House of Representatives 1993, 701-2).[12]

These welfare-reliant mothers generated an average of $399 a month, usually working part time as waitresses, domestics, store clerks during holidays or peak tourist seasons, child care workers in after-school or summer recreation programs, or line workers at fast food restaurants. These jobs offered welfare-reliant mothers limited, uncertain, and often seasonal hours. Most paid the minimum wage or (in the case of waitresses) less.

Despite the irregular hours, low pay, and the low regard most of their friends and relatives had for these jobs, many welfare-reliant mothers reported enjoying them. In time, however, most found that the "tax" that various means-tested welfare programs imposed on their earnings made it hard to stay at reported work. One welfare recipient told us,

> When I was working at a [reported] job, my rent was almost more than my paycheck and I was only getting paid twice a month. My rent was $173 and I get $225 every two weeks [from my job]. The next check was either the phone bill or whatever the children need. And I wasn't receiving hardly any AFDC or food stamps, so it's either food or the other things they need. So I was running into a thing where I had to make a choice and I was steadily getting behind.

Welfare-reliant mothers who could not get enough hours or command high enough wages to keep afloat financially often quit their reported jobs and found an unreported one in the informal sector, a point which we will expand upon in the next section. Other mothers found that their reported jobs conflicted with child care responsibilities and had to develop a set of nonwork-based survival routines. Some could not find reliable transportation to and from their reported jobs and lost them because of absenteeism or repeated tardiness. Others were only eighteen or nineteen and, like many adolescents, had not yet developed the self-discipline necessary to get to work on time each day, complete their work, and submit to their supervisors. Consequently, they did not keep these jobs. Finally, the kinds of jobs the welfare-reliant mothers were able to get were among the most unstable in the labor market. Thus, even those who wanted to keep their jobs and had no obstacles to employment were frequently laid off after a few months.

Welfare-reliant mothers who took jobs in the formal sector had three choices. First, they could use their own social security number and report the job at once to their caseworkers (as the welfare regulations required). Second, they could give their own social security number to the employer and wait to report the job until the welfare system's computer notified the caseworker that they were employed. Finally, they could use a false social security number, in which case their caseworker would not detect their earnings unless someone informed on them. Among the welfare-reliant mothers we interviewed, only a few chose the first option. Many more chose the second option, however.

In order to understand why welfare recipients chose simply to delay reporting their jobs, one must understand a bit about how these state welfare departments operated. In each of the states we studied, welfare caseworkers typically had several hundred families on their caseload. To identify recipients who worked, caseworkers compared the social security numbers of the women on their caseloads with those provided by the Department of Labor (collected quarterly from employers).[13] Therefore, while a woman who used her own social security number knew she eventually would be caught, most also knew that caseworkers worked with old data and it usually took six months or more for them to make the discovery.[14]

Thus, when welfare-reliant mothers took a formal sector job, they knew they could remain on the rolls for up to one year before their case was flagged. Most recipients also knew that if they were to report their work to their caseworkers sooner, their benefits would be reduced or eliminated immediately. If their job subsequently failed to provide enough hours, if they experienced difficulty with child care or transportation, or if they were laid off, reporting meant that they courted economic disaster because it would take the welfare department at least two months to get their benefits going again, leaving them with no income in the interim.

This trial period that welfare-reliant mothers imposed on their jobs before reporting them minimized the risks involved in taking a job. If the job did work out or if the mother saw hope for rapid advancement, she would generally stick with the job long enough for her caseworker to discover her work activity. When caseworkers flagged such a case, they usually filed what welfare bureaucrats called an "overpayment" and taxed the mother's subsequent benefits (if she remained eligible) by 10 percent. The welfare department continued to reduce her benefits by 10 percent until she made up the difference between the amount of AFDC and food stamps she received and the amount she was supposed to have gotten. If her earned income was too high for her to qualify for any benefit, she had to reimburse the welfare department in full. If she did not, the welfare department could garnishee her wages, EITC, tax return, or child support payments.

Technically, caseworkers could have charged welfare recipients who failed to report formal sector jobs with fraud. Caseworkers who wanted to pursue this strategy, however, had to prove that the recipient intended to defraud the welfare system. This was difficult to do, since mothers could easily claim (sometimes correctly) they did not understand the reporting rules. In addition, the practice of hiding work activity for the first few months was widespread. Caseworkers simply did not have the time and energy to pursue any but the most outrageous violations of the income reporting rules.[15]

Nor would it have been cost-effective to bring criminal charges against these mothers. Jailed mothers could not reimburse the state for overpayments, and the state would often have to take responsibility for the children. For these reasons, most caseworkers viewed violations of this type as minor (see Edin 1993). Mothers shared this view, since they knew that if they stayed at the job, they would eventually be forced to reimburse the welfare department for the excess benefits they had received. In the meantime, they could assess whether the job would last, give them enough hours, allow them to fulfill their mothering roles, and involve a realistic commute. If these conditions were not met, mothers could withdraw from the labor market without endangering their family's economic survival. Even if their employer reported them to the Department of Labor, the most the welfare department could deduct from subsequent welfare checks was 10 percent of the total (provided there was no prosecution for fraud).

Table 6-2 shows that *wage-reliant* mothers also engaged in supplemental reported work. Overall, 12 percent of wage-reliant mothers took on additional reported work to bolster their income. Mothers who reported additional earnings to authorities in charge of the food stamp, Medicaid, or housing program were almost always working overtime at their main job rather than at a second job, and these overtime earnings reduced their eligibility for these means-tested benefits. Overtime work is hard to hide, since employers must include it on an employee's W-2 form, and means-tested programs like food stamps require pay stubs as evidence of income.

Those who worked overtime generated an average of $225 a month. This work generally paid time-and-a-half and presented less hassle than a second job. One mother told us,

> I work as a nurse's aide at a nursing home. It's all right. I like working with patients. I've been working there two years. Sometimes I work to fill in at night. The job pays $4.56 an hour, and I get paid every two weeks. If I only work my regular hours, I take home about $283 after they deduct my health care premium from my check. It's not a lot, but it's better than nothing. To make a fuller check, I work on my days off so I can keep the check up to $320.

We asked another mother what she did to survive each month. She answered,

> Working overtime if I have to, anything to get a few extra dollars. I try to get to work one-half hour early, and leave one-half hour late, that's an extra five hours worth of pay each week! It comes in handy.

Although mothers liked to work overtime because it paid relatively high hourly wages, they disliked the fact that their extra earnings were on the books and therefore led to a reduction in whatever means-tested benefits they received. For some, this "cost" outweighed the higher wages associated with overtime work. These mothers chose instead to take an unreported job, either using a false ID in a formal sector job or taking a job in the informal economy.

## Unreported Work

Because of the high tax the welfare system imposed on reported work, *welfare-reliant* mothers who chose to work seldom reported their jobs. The proportion of welfare-reliant mothers who told us they had engaged in some unreported work during the preceding twelve months to supplement their incomes was quite high, roughly four in ten (table 6-1). Those who did such work earned $229 in a typical month.

For welfare-reliant mothers who were busy piecing together enough money to keep their families together each month, choosing unreported over reported work made a great deal of sense. This is clear from a brief review of the federal welfare rules at the time, which applied to all the states we studied. During the first four months of a mother's employment, states were required to deduct or "disregard" the first $30 of her earnings, a standard monthly deduction of $120, and a third of all additional earnings when calculating a mother's cash welfare benefits. For the next eight months, states were supposed to disregard the $30 and the $120 deductions but subtract all other earnings from the mother's welfare check. After the first year, states disregarded only $90 of earned income each month.

To understand why these rules would make unreported work more attractive than reported work for welfare recipients, consider the following example. In Chicago, a welfare-reliant mother with two children could get a maximum of $367 in cash welfare and $285 in food stamps in 1993. If she decided to work twenty hours a week, earned the minimum wage ($4.25 an hour), and did not pay for child care, she would have earned $368 in a typical month. After four months, federal welfare rules would have limited the amount of income she could disregard to $150 monthly. Since the federal welfare program imposed a 100 percent tax on all income in excess of the disregard, her welfare benefit would have been reduced from $367 to $150—a $217 reduction. Therefore, her net monthly gain from working would have been $151 ($368 in earnings minus $217 in cash benefit reductions), less whatever expenses she incurred in order to work.

For food stamps, the rules governing earned income were more generous. In 1993, a welfare mother who worked initially could deduct 20 percent of her earnings plus an additional $127 each month in standard deductions. (The standard deduction decreased to $90 after twelve months on the job.) The food stamp program would have allowed a Chicago mother, for example, to deduct $201 a month (0.20 × $368 + $127). For the food stamp program, then, her taxable earned income would have totaled $167. The food stamp program taxed all nondisregarded income at a rate of 30 percent, so this mother's food stamp check would have been reduced by $50 each month.

With these rules in mind, we can calculate the net gains from reported and unreported work for welfare-reliant mothers under the then current rules. A mother who reported $368 in monthly earnings from her half-time job would lose $217 in cash welfare and $50 in food stamps each month. In contrast, a mother who did not report her earnings would get to keep them. Thus, the "costs" of reporting one's work in the early 1990s were substantial—about 70 percent of total earnings in this hypothetical case.[16]

Welfare recipients found unreported jobs in a variety of ways.[17] Some took a formal sector job under a false social security number, some worked only a short amount of time using their own social security number (to avoid being reported to the Department of Labor), and some simply reversed two numbers of their own social security number on their employee documentation—a trick that easily fooled employers.[18] Others colluded with employers to receive their pay in cash, an arrangement some employers liked because it saved them money too. Many employers requiring temporary, contract, or irregular labor preferred not to list these jobs on their official payrolls in order to avoid paying into unemployment and workers' compensation programs.[19]

Typically, employers who offered off-the-books work also took advantage of the welfare-reliant mothers' need to hide their employment by offering them wages below the legal minimum. One woman who found work at a local restaurant told us,

> This new restaurant opened up. But they said since they'd just started, they couldn't pay more than $2 an hour. Then the boss said, "Why don't you just stay on welfare, then I'll pay you under the table."

Many believed they could avoid detection, even using their own social security number, by working only two or three months at a time.[20] In most cases, this strategy worked, apparently because these employers did not list their short-term employees on their quarterly report. One woman told us,

> I worked at a grocery store for a month and a restaurant for a month and I worked at a pizza place for two months, so maybe about four months total I worked last year. That way they can't catch you.

Most mothers felt guilty about not reporting such work. One mother told us,

> I wish I could report my job, I really do. But then I just couldn't make it right now, not until I get a raise or some overtime. I dream about the day when I can go in and tell my caseworker, "I don't need your assistance, I got a job." I dream about the day I can kiss welfare good-bye.

Welfare-reliant mothers who took jobs in the informal economy felt far less guilty about failing to report such work to their caseworkers than those who worked under false identities in formal sector jobs. Since they did not see these as "real" jobs, and since they were virtually undetectable, most mothers found it inconceivable that any mother would report these earnings to the caseworker. The urban economies of all four sites provided various forms of unreported work in the informal economy, such as housecleaning, babysitting, laundry, yard work, house painting, apartment-building maintenance, operating neighborhood taxis, cooking meals for others, and sewing.

These occupations provided crucial supplemental income for welfare recipients, though earnings were very unpredictable. One mother told us,

> I'm pretty resourceful. Where I live we have a pretty big garage, and I collect junk, trash pick—I'm the ultimate trash picker—and I go to garage sales. I have my friends picking up stuff in alleys and at garage sales for me too. They're all like, "Oh, let's grab this for her!" whenever they see some old crap. Then on the weekends, I'll get this friend of mine to help me load his pickup and we get a table at the flea market for about $50. Some weekends I'll make $200 or $300 on old junk I might have paid $20 total for, but that's not all the time.

Another recipient ran her own lottery. She purchased counterfeit bus passes each month and sold $1 chances to win a $60 bus pass. She determined the winner according to the last two digits of the winning state lottery number on the last day of each month. Though she paid roughly $30 each for the passes (legitimate passes cost $60), she still netted a profit of over $200 in a typical month. When the city police began cracking down on users of counterfeit passes, she started purchasing $20 or $30 items from pawn shops to sell chances on and netted roughly the same profit.

Unreported work was not limited to welfare recipients but was an important income-generating strategy for *wage-reliant mothers* as well. In our coding scheme, supplemental unreported work included all earnings that workers did not report to the IRS or to any means-tested program. Those who worked at such jobs earned an average of $207 a month.

Working mothers were motivated to hide side-income to maintain eligibility for food stamps, housing subsidies, Medicaid, and student aid, as well as to avoid paying additional income taxes. Those receiving means-tested benefits had the strongest motivation to hide earned income, because reductions in such benefits constituted an extra "tax" on additional earnings. Not surprisingly, workers receiving these subsidies were far less likely to engage in supplemental reported work and somewhat more likely to take on an unreported job than nonbeneficiaries were.

For those receiving means-tested benefits, hiding work was nearly as risky as it was for welfare-reliant mothers, because if they were caught they had to reimburse the program that had "overpaid" them. One working mother recounted,

I was working a second job and they said that I didn't notify the food stamp program because it was only on the weekends. And they found out through their computer systems that I was working a second job and ugh. . . . They said that they overpaid me in food stamps for $500 and some dollars. So now they're taking that away from me. I thought that was very unfair because regardless I was only working on weekends, I mean, I wasn't really making anything and I'm not on public aid anyway because of my original job that I have. I couldn't argue with them.

Wage-reliant mothers who were no longer eligible for food stamps once their other earnings were known had to reimburse the program in cash. If they did not, their wages could be garnisheed or their EITC seized.

## Underground Work

The fiscal incentives not to report one's work applied even more strongly to the third type of work we have distinguished. We differentiate it from other work because it was inherently illegal and literally unreportable to welfare caseworkers. "Underground" work included selling sex, drugs, and stolen goods. Prostitution was the most highly paid work available in the underground economy, netting women up to $40 an hour. Fencing stolen goods and selling drugs usually yielded hourly wages approximating the minimum wage, because the mothers we interviewed generally found employment at the lowest (and least dangerous) levels of these trades.

Eight percent of our *welfare-reliant* sample told us they had engaged in underground work during the previous year to supplement their welfare checks. For this minority, underground work generated $228 in an average month. These low rates of underground work were not a product of ignorance about underground work or of inadequate opportunities to engage in it. Mothers who grew up in poor households or lived in poor neighborhoods usually knew a relative or friend who engaged in illegal work and could have found such work relatively easily. Like most Americans, however, our mothers believed that criminal activities were not compatible with good mothering. One mother told us,

> My brother, he sells stuff out of the back of his car, you know, like stolen stuff for real cheap prices. I could work for him any time I wanted to, but I don't want my kids to think I'm a criminal.

Another mother with a cocaine-dealing boyfriend told us,

> I don't sell that stuff, because you got to go to the school yard. What kind of a mother would I be if I sold drugs to kids like my own? When he's over here, he has to keep that stuff out of the house.

Because prostitution paid more than other unreported or reported work, welfare-reliant mothers had a strong incentive to engage in it. Other forms of illegal work paid less well, but were nonetheless tempting when other strategies fell through. But most mothers reported that underground work (particularly prostitution) not only lowered their self-respect, it incurred considerable risks.

Since the main goal of almost all welfare-reliant mothers was to keep their families together, losing their children was the last thing they were willing to risk. For this reason, most mothers either refused opportunities in the underground economy or limited their underground work to emergency situations when other income-generating strategies had failed. Yet the desire to keep custody of their children could also pull mothers into underground work, since those who could not afford to feed, clothe, and house their children could lose custody due to neglect. One mother recounted,

> Some of our friends will sell drugs. I know some of my friends who have turned tricks. Usually, some people do it for their family, and some people do it for drugs. At one point I did sell drugs in order to keep my family [together]. When my husband left, and I had to make sure I could pay my bills. That's what I did.
>
> BUT YOU DON'T DO IT ANY LONGER?:
>   No, it's dangerous for my kids. It was not that I was afraid for myself, it was that they were gonna take my kids away. I never got caught with anything, but they knew I was doing it. The police knew and they just couldn't catch me.
>
> HOW DID THEY KNOW?:
>   People tell. People talk. To keep their own self out of jail they would tell. They didn't catch me with anything but they would threaten to take my kids away. That's all I needed to hear to quit.

The risks posed by underground work kept away the vast majority of both wage- and welfare-reliant mothers. Whereas not quite one in ten welfare-reliant mothers generated extra cash in this way, only 1 percent of *wage-reliant* mothers did so. In San Antonio, one wage-reliant mother told our interviewers that she earned $40 from fencing stolen goods in a typical month. A Chicago working mother reported earning $300 a month from prostitution. But these women were a tiny minority (though a somewhat larger group of wage-reliant mothers told us they had engaged in occasional underground work in the past, usually while they were on welfare). Because wage-reliant mothers risked losing their relatively respectable status as workers if the police caught them committing a crime, they felt they had even more to lose than their welfare counterparts.

## AGENCY-BASED STRATEGIES

Many mothers also relied on public or private agencies for cash and in-kind help. Most mothers told us they used agencies when other strategies had failed or were not available to them. Thirty-one percent of *welfare-reliant mothers* had received direct assistance from a private charity in paying their rent or utilities, received cash or vouchers for food or clothing, or squeezed extra cash from student loans and grants. For simplicity, we have termed all of this assistance "agency-based." Agency-based assistance added an average $117 a month to the budgets of welfare-reliant mothers who received it.

Twenty-two percent of *wage-reliant mothers* relied on direct assistance from agencies in paying their bills or on cash from student loans and grants. Though working mothers were somewhat less likely to receive agency-based assistance than their welfare-reliant counterparts, those working mothers who got help received somewhat more ($165 versus $117). Our notes and observations suggest that workers who approached community organizations for help were more successful in securing cash or vouchers than welfare mothers. We think this is because agency personnel often felt that working mothers were a better investment than welfare recipients. The agency personnel with whom we spoke during our fieldwork often expressed frustration at having such limited resources in the face of such tremendous and growing need. Because their resources were insufficient to assuage even a tiny portion of this need, agencies often rationed their services. Some organizations, for example, provided assistance in a single domain, whereas others limited the number of times a given family could receive help in a month or year. Beyond these formal rules, agency personnel often formulated a set of informal rules that guided their decisions. When it came to cash or voucher assistance, for example, agency personnel preferred to target their scarce resources to the mothers whom they perceived to be in short-term need (the workers) rather than chronic need (the welfare recipients). Interestingly, the results in chapter 4, showing that working mothers suffered more material hardship than welfare mothers, suggest that agencies' evaluations of short-term versus chronic need were probably inaccurate—at least for mothers working at low wages.

We also included funds received from student loan and grant programs in agency-based strategies. Wage-reliant mothers had far more difficulty in securing grants; since their income typically made them ineligible, they had to take out loans instead. Though mothers could legitimately use these loans for living expenses, they eventually had to be paid back. As a result, educational debt was common. The working mothers reported that they were carrying an average of $1,000 of debt (welfare mothers had slightly lower levels). About half was due to unpaid medical bills; most of the rest was student loans.

In addition to cash help, over half the welfare-reliant mothers and nearly a third of the workers we interviewed had received in-kind assistance from an agency during the last year. Many agencies gave away used clothing or toys, and while these items had little market value they saved mothers a good deal of money. Other agencies gave away food and cleaning products, but some provided mothers with items they did not need—our favorite examples being caviar, antique furniture polish, and elaborately decorated cakes. Some foods were not ordinarily part of a family's diet (boiled cod pieces, five-pound bags of lima beans, and powdered milk, for example). These items remained at the backs of cupboards and were reserved for when families ran out of other food. In addition, some mothers received bulk food that might have spoiled before they could have used all of it, so they shared it with their relatives or neighbors. For these reasons, the value of in-kind goods was hard to assess.[21]

Both in-kind and cash agency contributions were crucial to many of our single-parent families' survival. Mothers often relied on agencies for food after their food stamps ran out, and for clothing and shoes. One mother who went to churches for help several times a month said,

> If I run out of food stamps and ask for help, my caseworker says, "Oh that's not my problem." I have to go to the churches as Public Aid won't help. The churches give clothing and food.

During the summer months, when children ate their lunch at home, agencies that provided food were particularly important.

As we pointed out earlier, most agencies provided only one or two types of assistance, so that mothers who needed both food and clothing, for example, had to go to at least two different agencies.[22] Most agencies also limited clients to one visit a year or one visit every three months (although sympathetic volunteers sometimes bent these rules). Mothers felt stigmatized if they used any one agency too often. One mother told us,

> I don't like to beg, but I will for the kids. I go to a church where they give you canned goods, tuna, spaghetti, tomato sauce, eggs. . . . I've been twice in two months. They don't like you to show up too often, but if you really need it, they'll give it.

Most mothers who routinely relied on such agencies developed an extensive network of agency contacts. When we conducted our interviews, mothers reported that many of the programs they used were being cut back, and they were having to adjust their strategies accordingly. One Boston mother told us,

> This morning I went to Catholic Charities and got a $20 voucher for the Market Basket [grocery store]. You can only go once a year. They're cutting back a lot of programs: no more emergency assistance, no more back payments in rent, no more rent assistance. These cuts will affect me a lot. I will have to dig deep. I don't know what I am going to do.

## SITE DIFFERENCES IN SURVIVAL STRATEGIES

In a previous analysis of these data, we showed that the four cities we studied differed in many ways: the strength of the local labor market, the size of the city, the character of the underground economy, the practices of local welfare officials, and the number and types of charitable agencies (Edin and Lein forthcoming). All five of these factors affected welfare mothers' survival strategies (see tables 6-4 and 6-5).

We expected the strength of the local labor market to affect welfare-reliant mothers in two ways. First, we believed that cities with tighter labor markets might provide welfare-reliant mothers with more opportunities for both reported and unreported work. In addition, we were curious about how the strength of the for-

TABLE 6-4. **Survival Strategies for Welfare-Reliant Mothers by Site**

| | Charleston | San Antonio | Chicago | Boston | Sig. |
|---|---|---|---|---|---|
| *Number in sample* | *44* | *63* | *62* | *45* | *N/A* |
| Total % work strategies | 36% | 41% | 60% | 44% | * |
| Mean monthly income | $108 | $111 | $180 | $101 | |
| % Reported work[a] | 9 | 6 | 2 | 2 | |
| Mean monthly income | 25 | 29 | 5 | 16 | |
| % Unreported work | 32 | 35 | 52 | 36 | |
| Mean monthly income | 79 | 81 | 133 | 54 | * |
| % Underground work | 2 | 3 | 19 | 7 | *** |
| Mean monthly income | 3 | 1 | 40 | 31 | * |
| | | | | | |
| Total % network strategies | 91 | 71 | 77 | 69 | * |
| Mean monthly income | 253 | 114 | 157 | 126 | *** |
| % Family/friends | 55 | 40 | 40 | 53 | |
| Mean monthly income | 147 | 60 | 104 | 82 | ** |
| % Cash from men | 59 | 57 | 50 | 44 | |
| Mean monthly income | 147 | 60 | 104 | 82 | ** |
| % Boyfriend | 32 | 29 | 24 | 31 | |
| Mean monthly income | 78 | 32 | 60 | 62 | |
| % Absent father | 41 | 32 | 32 | 27 | |
| Mean monthly income | 69 | 27 | 45 | 20 | ** |
| % Covert support | 36 | 16 | 21 | 24 | * |
| Mean monthly income | 60 | 17 | 40 | 18 | ** |
| % Formal support | 18 | 21 | 13 | 4 | |
| Mean monthly income | 9 | 10 | 4 | 2 | ** |
| | | | | | |
| Total % agency strategies | 25 | 30 | 27 | 44 | |
| Mean monthly income | 49 | 15 | 58 | 26 | |

*Source:* Authors' calculations using Edin and Lein survival strategies data.
[a]The very low benefits in southern states heightened the level of desperation of mothers who received welfare. Mothers in Charleston and San Antonio had so much difficulty making ends meet and experienced material hardship so frequently that they were likely to jump at any job that would help sustain them.
*Note:* Two-tailed tests for significance of differences in means between cities given by * > .10; ** > .05; *** > .01.

mal economy might affect opportunities for work in the underground economy (see below). Finally, we thought that the relatives, boyfriends, and fathers who contributed to these mothers' household budgets might be better off in a strong economy and that the money might "trickle down" to the families as a result. We studied one very tight labor market (Charleston), one aver-

**TABLE 6-5. Survival Strategies for Wage-Reliant Mothers by Site**

| | Charles-ton | San Antonio | Chicago | Boston | Sig. |
|---|---|---|---|---|---|
| Number in sample | *47* | *41* | *43* | *34* | *N/A* |
| Total % work strategies | 43% | 29% | 44% | 38% | |
| Mean monthly income | $121 | $35 | $80 | $118 | * |
| % Reported work | 13 | 12 | 7 | 18 | |
| Mean monthly income | 20 | 17 | 13 | 68 | * |
| % Unreported work | 32 | 20 | 37 | 24 | |
| Mean monthly income | 100 | 18 | 60 | 50 | * |
| % Underground work | 0 | 2 | 2 | 0 | |
| Mean monthly income | 0 | 1 | 7 | 0 | |
| | | | | | |
| Total % network strategies | 87 | 63 | 100 | 76 | *** |
| Mean monthly income | 298 | 135 | 293 | 280 | *** |
| % Family/friends[a] | 38 | 32 | 74 | 41 | *** |
| Mean monthly income | 58 | 35 | 103 | 64 | ** |
| % Cash from men | 74 | 51 | 60 | 53 | |
| Mean monthly income | 240 | 101 | 190 | 216 | ** |
| % Boyfriend[b] | 26 | 17 | 40 | 24 | |
| Mean monthly income | 63 | 21 | 112 | 37 | *** |
| % Absent father | 60 | 39 | 33 | 35 | ** |
| Mean monthly income | 177 | 79 | 77 | 179 | ** |
| | | | | | |
| Total % agency strategies | 17 | 34 | 12 | 26 | ** |
| Mean monthly income | 32 | 43 | 4 | 75 | |

*Source:* Authors' calculations using Edin and Lein survival strategies data.
[a]This difference is an artifact of our sampling strategy. Edin conducted the Chicago study prior to our work in the other sites and imposed slightly different sample selection criteria. Thus, although about half of the workers in the other sites received a housing subsidy, only about one-quarter of the Chicago workers did. Since fewer Chicago workers received subsidies, they had higher expenses and needed more help from their families. When we looked at the mean contributions Chicago's privately-housed workers got, they resemble those of privately-housed mothers in other sites.
[b]High Chicago rates were due to the fact that Chicago workers were more likely to live in market-rate apartments and thus had more need for a boyfriend who could "pay and stay."
*Note:* Two-tailed tests for significance of differences in means between cities given by * > .10; ** > .05; *** > .01.

age labor market (Chicago), and two relatively weak labor markets (Boston and San Antonio).

We expected city size to influence a single mother's survival strategies because a mother living in a large city might be able to hide unreported work more easily. Edin began by studying

Chicago, a city with a metropolitan-area population of more than seven million. Because of Chicago's size and density, a welfare mother's chances of encountering someone who knew she was a recipient were quite slim, and many women were able to work under false IDs outside their neighborhoods. (Many women living in poor neighborhoods could remember an instance in which a neighbor had "turned in" another neighbor for alleged abuses of the welfare system.) Chicago mothers were also able to hide illegal work like prostitution more easily from those who might have reported their activities to the welfare authorities or the child protection agency. We thought that such activities would be somewhat harder to hide in the Boston metropolitan area, as its population of 3.2 million residents was less than half that of Chicago. We believed such work would be even harder to hide in San Antonio, where the metropolitan-area population totaled about 1.3 million, and Charleston, where the metro-area population numbered about half a million.[23]

From previous on-site research, we also had quite a bit of anecdotal evidence about the underground economies of the San Antonio and Chicago areas before we began this study. In Chicago, we knew that mothers could get a false ID quite easily, probably because of the large number of illegal migrants who worked there. Charleston had few illegal migrants, so we expected that false documents would be harder to obtain. We also knew that in most poor neighborhoods in San Antonio, families could buy stolen goods at cut-rate prices. Though we had seen people shopping out of the trunks of cars in Chicago, we did not think the practice was nearly as prevalent. Also, as noted above, it seemed reasonable to look at the links between the formal economy and the underground one: on one hand, we might assume that a strong formal economy would produce a strong underground economy (because consumers would have more to spend on illegal goods); on the other hand, we also thought that a slack formal economy might force more people into underground work, even though the average "take" per worker might be lower.

We also knew that the practices of local welfare officials varied. Lein and her family had lived across the street from a federal housing project in San Antonio for a summer and found few project households where a mother let her boyfriend live with the family. When she asked people there why, they told her that the housing authority "visited" apartments in search of anyone whose name was not on the lease.[24] A boyfriend's or father's presence gave the housing authority cause to evict the mother and her children. Though such practices were not unknown in Chicago, they were less frequent and residents were nearly always forewarned. Thus, Chicago mothers who lived in the projects were more likely to have a boyfriend or a child's father living with them. We expected that this might enable Chicago mothers to make more successful claims on men's income.

Child support enforcement practices also varied from state to state. We thought that states with strict enforcement might help mothers to get more support through the formal system (we did not know much about the informal system when we started our work). We also thought that strict enforcement might motivate fathers to leave formal sector jobs, where their wages could be garnisheed, for informal jobs, leaving mothers with no support at all.

Finally, we knew that some locales offered a richer mix of services than others, which would affect a mother's survival strategies. In her previous fieldwork in San Antonio, for instance, Lein had documented that families in one large housing project utilized between twenty and thirty different agencies in a given year. These agencies provided food, clothing, over-the-counter medicines, and summer recreation programs for children. Sometimes mothers could also get cash help or vouchers for overdue bills in an emergency. In other sites, a different mix of services was possible.

### Strength of Local Labor Market

As we have shown elsewhere (Edin and Lein forthcoming), tight labor markets affected *welfare-reliant mothers'* survival routines in two ways. First, tight labor markets provided welfare recipients with more opportunities for side-work. In Chicago, where the labor market was quite tight, recipients were the most likely to report that they worked on the side. Charleston also had a very tight labor market, but as we demonstrate below, the city's relative size and the distinctive features of the informal economy made it difficult for Charleston recipients to take side-jobs.

Second, tight labor markets benefited welfare-reliant mothers' budgets because they increased the earnings of network members. In Charleston and Chicago, men provided more help, on average, than in Boston and San Antonio. Charleston's thriving tourist economy provided seasonal service-sector work for men. During the spring and fall, when tourists flood the city, men could find work in the various hotels, resorts, and restaurants that catered to tourists. In addition, the hurricane that hit Charleston in 1989 had created a vigorous demand for construction workers.

The patterns for *wage-reliant mothers* were similar to those of the welfare recipients. In our slackest labor market, San Antonio, the total amount gleaned from side-work was lower than the amount in the other sites. In our strongest labor market, Charleston, mothers earned more from second jobs than mothers in the other sites. Boston-area mothers earned more from side-work than we would have expected given the relatively slack labor market there.

The strength of the local labor market also affected wage-reliant mothers' network contributions. Workers were much more likely to get cash help from a relative or friend in Charleston and Chicago than in San Antonio or the Boston area. San Antonio workers, who faced the slackest labor market, were the least likely to get any substantial network help.

Finally, for the workers, weak labor markets meant that mothers relied more frequently on agencies.

## City Size

As we had expected, city size affected *welfare recipients'* survival strategies in two ways. First, in large metropolitan areas like Chicago, welfare-reliant mothers who worked at unreported formal sector jobs had little chance of being detected. In the smaller cities, less visible work in the informal sector presented the best opportunity for welfare-reliant mothers to combine welfare with covert work. Conversely, the anonymity available to mothers in our largest city (Chicago) made it easier to work in the underground economy.

City size did not affect *wage-reliant mothers'* ability to take side-work, probably because getting caught was of less concern for workers than for welfare recipients.

## Character of the Informal and
## Underground Economy

The character of each city's informal and underground economy also served to constrain or enhance *welfare-reliant mothers'* range of possible survival routines. First, only in Chicago and San Antonio did welfare recipients tell us they knew how to obtain a false ID, probably because the larger numbers of illegal migrants in these cities had created a market for false social security cards and other proofs of citizenship. Boston had fewer illegal migrants, and Charleston had virtually none. Welfare-reliant mothers in these sites had generally not even considered the possibility of working a formal sector job using a false social security card. Though our mothers told us that false IDs were also easy to come by in San Antonio, not many reported using them. (This could have been because the slack economy in San Antonio allowed employers to choose more highly skilled workers for menial jobs).

Second, we observed a sharp racial division of labor in Charleston's informal economy. In a city where jobs were highly segregated by race, whites seldom worked in most menial occupations no matter how desperate their circumstances. Many jobs in this informal economy—heading shrimp at the commercial fishing docks, selling one's own seafood catch along the roadside, and cleaning houses—were fairly race-specific. Thus, we found that white welfare recipients were not as likely to pursue work-based strategies in Charleston but relied more heavily on their relatives.[25] This is another reason why fewer Charleston recipients worked at side-jobs than Charleston's tight labor market led us to expect.

We did not see sharp distinctions by site among wage-reliant mothers in any of these areas, probably because side-jobs did not threaten AFDC receipt for this group.

### Practices of Local Welfare Officials

The practices of local welfare officials played a role in enhancing or limiting *welfare recipients'* claims on men's income. In San

Antonio, the housing authority's de facto "man in the house" rule limited the amount of money recipients could get from men in a typical month. San Antonio mothers were less willing to risk their housing subsidy in order to let a man live with them. Since men who stayed with mothers typically contributed twice as much as men who did not, this informal rule diminished men's contributions (San Antonio mothers in private housing looked like mothers elsewhere in this regard). In other sites, housing authorities were less vigilant. The same pattern was evident among those workers who lived in private housing.

Child Support Enforcement system practices also varied a lot from place to place. In Charleston, where enforcement was much stricter than in the other sites, county judges routinely put absent fathers in the county jail for failing to comply. Welfare recipients here were more successful in getting covert contributions from absent fathers than mothers in other sites. Charleston's strict enforcement rules made welfare-reliant mothers' threats of turning fathers over to the authorities more credible.[26] These rules also meant that recipients who chose to use the formal system received more substantial formal child support. However, the Charleston welfare-reliant mothers were far more likely to say that they feared their child's father would "go underground" cease to work in the formal economy, where wages could be garnisheed, and work in the informal or underground economy to evade child support than mothers in the other sites. Charleston's enforcement procedures had probably not been in place long enough for our data to show whether mothers' fears were justified (in which case we would have found that more mothers here were left with nothing than mothers in the other sites). Charleston's procedures helped *wage-reliant mothers* as well as welfare recipients, since both groups had access to free services from the Child Support Enforcement system.

## Presence and Practices of Agencies

*Welfare-reliant mothers'* success in generating cash assistance from agencies did not vary substantially according to where they lived, but *wage-reliant mothers'* success did, and the general pattern is the same for both groups. The Boston and San Antonio service environments were more highly developed than those in Charleston and Chicago. Private charities in both cities gave mothers a lot of in-kind assistance. Cash or voucher assistance was more common in Boston, mostly because of a single Boston-area charity that provided poor mothers with vouchers to purchase their children's school clothing. Boston-area mothers also told us that they used a community program that sometimes paid mothers' utility bills when they presented a shutoff notice from the light or gas company.

In San Antonio, there was no cash or voucher program for school clothing or utilities, but mothers could persuade a local charity or church to help with a specific need. San Antonio mothers could also get in-kind donations of food and used clothing from agencies (these results are not shown), and these mothers often developed an elaborate network of agency contacts so they could routinely utilize in-kind assistance to reduce their monthly expenses.

Because Chicago and Charleston had less-developed service environments, many private charities had chosen to limit their cash assistance to victims of emergencies. The Charleston mothers who got large amounts of agency assistance had usually become homeless during Hurricane Hugo. They had often received security deposits for market-rate apartments, plus vouchers for clothing and furniture from community groups set up specifically to meet posthurricane needs. In Chicago, most of those who got help from agencies had been burned out of their apartments or were precariously doubled up in an overcrowded apartment. They usually received large lump sums for a place of their own.

## CONCLUSIONS

Poor mothers, whether working or on welfare, constantly faced a yawning gap between their income and expenditures. Each month they pursued a wide range of strategies aimed at filling the gap and providing for their families. In this chapter we have focused on how mothers used different strategies and how they chose between them. Most mothers preferred network-based strategies over side-jobs or help from agencies, particularly when mothers felt their benefactor had an obligation to contribute. But not all mothers chose to rely on members of their networks. Some did not do so because they had no generous friends or relatives. Others had friends and relatives who might have contributed but who demanded too high a price for that help, such as tolerating domestic abuse.

We first learned about the role of networks in poor women's lives from Carol Stack's *All Our Kin* (1974). Stack collected data nearly three decades ago during a period when both welfare benefits and the minimum wage were substantially higher in real terms than they were in the late 1980s and early 1990s. Not surprisingly, the data presented here show that network-based survival strategies are still alive and well among unskilled and semi-skilled single mothers. Networks serve two functions: smoothing income flows over time (a type of mutual exchange within the network, which Stack observed) and equalizing distributions across individuals in the network (where those at the bottom never repay). Because we observed mothers' behaviors at a point in time, we found little mutual exchange and a lot of support for poor mothers from their better-off kin. Had we been able to follow mothers over time, we might have seen some of our mothers move into a position to help others in their network.

This study also allows us to make some comparisons that Stack could not, because her data were limited to welfare-reliant mothers. Although half of both our wage- and welfare-reliant mothers received cash assistance from their families, far more working mothers received cash from boyfriends and absent fathers. In fact, help from a male wage earner was crucial in allowing poor single mothers to work rather than receive welfare.

Further, fathers who knew that the state would keep all but $50 of what they paid in child support often felt that any participation in the formal system was foolish. They may have also felt that any covert contribution over $50 was generous. When mothers left welfare for work, these disincentives no longer applied, and the absent fathers may have felt that their contributions counted for more. Many absent fathers, however, had little ability to pay, and some women turned to welfare precisely because the fathers were not sufficiently employable or hardworking.

For these reasons, we argued that a primary difference between those women who chose to work and those who chose welfare was not their willingness to hold a job but their ability to do so, an ability that hinged on special circumstances and steady help from others. Eliminating welfare would force more women into situations where they would have to depend on men's wages to survive, and sometimes the cost of those relationships could be quite high, as we have shown.

When mothers could not get enough help from their networks, or felt that the price of the help was too high, they generally took a side-job to pay their bills. Nearly half the welfare-reliant mothers we interviewed had engaged in work during the previous twelve months to supplement their incomes. These findings suggest that images of welfare-reliant mothers as completely detached from the formal labor market are wrong. Most mothers preferred informal work or cash work to that which required the use of a false ID or work in the underground economy. These preferences reflected widely shared norms against mothers resorting to fraud or crime.

While there may be a "culture of dependency," which is at odds with the "culture of work," we did not find much evidence for it among the mothers we interviewed. Not many welfare mothers were predisposed against work, and few were ignorant about the world of work. Almost all were aware that employees must get to work on time, respect the boss, and exhibit a professional demeanor. After all, roughly four-fifths had held formal sector jobs at one time or another.

The main exceptions were teenage mothers, whom we interviewed but did not include in our analysis. Poor teenage mothers were still learning adult roles, just as other teenagers do. Because they had the added responsibility of caring for a child, many had learned to act like adults much sooner than more privileged teens. Most teen mothers recognized their obligation to provide for, as well as to parent, their children. Sadly, labor market opportunities and wages for unskilled or semiskilled mothers did not support the labor-market aspirations of either teenagers or adults.

When other strategies failed or were not available, mothers turned to agencies to get what they needed, even though they found the "begging" humiliating. Most often, welfare-reliant mothers received in-kind assistance from private charities, but some got cash. Working mothers were less likely to receive agency assistance, but when they did, they typically got more than welfare mothers received. Working mothers also depended on welfare-based sources of assistance—especially food stamps and housing subsidies. Because their wages were insufficient, these benefits were often crucial to their family's survival.

If future policies limit welfare, mothers will still need welfare-like benefits to keep their families together, and they will have to come either from government agencies or from private charities. During the course of this study, we spent hundreds of hours in local food pantries, community centers, and other grassroots organizations. In our experience, mothers who need regular help and present themselves time and again at a local food shelf are likely to be turned away, no matter how convincing their story. Local charities are willing to help in emergencies, but they simply do not have the resources to provide the regular assistance that these families need.

Finally, a mother's place of residence, as well as her personal situation, constrained the range of survival strategies open to her. Larger cities permitted more mothers to work under false identities and in the underground economy. Tight labor markets made it easier for mothers to earn more from off-the-books work and also improved the ability of network members to contribute to mothers' budgets. The nature of the underground and informal economies shaped the type of side-work mothers could get, as did the local service environment and the practices of local welfare officials. Despite these constraints, mothers in each city engaged in the whole range of income-generating strategies we have outlined in order to fill the gap between their incomes and expenses.

# Chapter 7

# Differences Among Mothers

THE READER MAY wonder whether the spending patterns, hard-ships, and survival strategies we have observed are similar across different groups of low-income mothers, or whether these behaviors vary significantly by race and ethnicity, neighborhood, family background, or other factors. Public discourse about welfare often refers to the supposedly distinctive value systems shared by minorities, residents of inner-city ghettos, never-married mothers, or second-generation welfare mothers. According to these arguments, destructive subcultural norms, which destigmatize welfare use, criminal activity, and out-of-wedlock childbirth, are supposed to explain why such groups ignore mainstream mores about work and obeying the law.

Because our sample consists of only low-income single mothers, we cannot say much about how group differences affect a young woman's chances of ending up in this category. Our sampling strategy also rules out rigorous tests of whether group differences can explain which mothers use welfare and which do not. Other researchers have studied these issues extensively with more appropriate data. Using large representative samples, several studies suggest that girls who grow up in families receiving welfare are more likely to use welfare as adults and to use it long term (Duncan, Hill, and Hoffman 1988; Furstenberg, Brooks-Gunn, and Morgan 1987; Hill and Ponza 1984; Testa et al. 1989), though the rate of intergenerational transmission is rather low. Sara McLanahan and Gary Sandefur (1994) document that the marital status of a girl's parents also is related to her own chances of being poor, becoming a single parent, and using welfare as an adult (girls from single-parent homes are more likely to experience all these problems than girls from two-parent homes). Mary Jo Bane and David Ellwood (1994) have found that a mother's own marital status is a strong predictor of whether she will become a long-term welfare recipient (never-married mothers use welfare for longer periods). Other studies suggest that race is related to welfare use (U.S. House of Representatives 1995, tables 10-45–10-47). We could find no study that looked at whether living in a ghetto neighborhood affected welfare use, but several studies have found that growing up in a ghetto neighborhood makes it more likely that a young woman will bear a child in her teenage years (see Jencks and Mayer 1990 for a review of this literature), and others have shown that early childbearing is a correlate of welfare use (Bane and Ellwood 1994).

All these studies must be interpreted with caution, however, because it is difficult to control for certain aspects of a mother's family background and current situation, factors that may affect the likelihood of receiving welfare. For example, human and social capital probably have a powerful independent effect on a given mother's probability of receiving welfare. For example, Mark Rank (1988) has found that after controlling for variation in such measures, the relationship between race and welfare use disappears.

Our data do, however, offer a unique chance to explore whether unskilled and semiskilled mothers in various groups get and spend their money differently. If patterns do not vary much, we can infer that the expenditure patterns, survival strategies, and hardship rates are mainly the result of the common constraints imposed by having children, not having valuable job skills, and not having another parent with whom to share the load.[1] If patterns do vary, subcultural differences may play a role.

In this chapter, we show that the mothers in our sample varied little by subgroup in what they spent, how they bridged the monthly gap between spending and income, and the extent to which they suffered material hardship. Rather, the weight of evidence supports the notion that unskilled and semiskilled mothers made economic choices based primarily on a shared set of constraints. Since the women were all the primary caretakers of children, their foremost consideration was the need to balance their families' income needs with their children's needs for nurturance and supervision. This balancing act was one that all mothers faced and accounts for much of the similarity we find across different groups of mothers.

There were some group differences, however, mainly arising from variations in structural opportunities and constraints. For example, mothers from the more-advantaged, or "mainstream," groups generally had the best access to those survival strategies that facilitated the transition from welfare to work. Mothers from the less-advantaged groups, on the other hand, sometimes had more access to the money-saving strategies that enabled them to live on a very tight budget and still escape material hardship.

## CULTURAL THEORIES OF POVERTY

We looked at five cultural "fault lines" on which both popular discourse and academic literature suggest our respondents might differ. The first two are those that loom largest in public discussions of this population and reflect widespread perceptions about the "underclass": namely, disproportionate welfare use and out-of-wedlock childbearing. The third is a mother's own family history, for which we draw on the work of Oscar Lewis (1959, 1965, 1968). The fourth, suggested by William Julius Wilson (1987), is the neighborhood in which a mother lives. The fifth fault line is race or ethnicity, as indicated in work by Douglas Massey and Nancy Denton (1993).

The notion that welfare is deleterious to values and promotes "behavioral dependency" predates the American welfare state and has its roots in the English Poor Laws (Handler 1995). According to this view, the problem of welfare dependency arises from the values of the individual recipient, not from the larger social and economic system. It is assumed, therefore, that even among unskilled and semiskilled single parents, those who choose welfare do so primarily because they lack the correct values. We dub this argument the "culture of welfare" hypothesis. In 1982, Ken Auletta (1982) argued along these lines that welfare-reliant mothers transmit a set of values to their children that devalue work and self-sufficiency (Auletta 1982). Ten years later, Lawrence Mead (1992) claimed that the poor differ from the nonpoor because they do not work as much, and Mead's theory has broad public support. In 1994, 65 percent of respondents to a national public opinion poll named the lack of willingness to work as a major reason why people use welfare (Blendon et al. 1995).

Another aspect of the "culture of welfare" argument is that the poor are much more accepting of out-of-wedlock childbirth. The phenomenon of nonmarital childbearing is often tied to the same set of deviant values that are allegedly at the root of welfare use. Public resentment of single women who choose to have children and then support their children by relying on government largesse infuses public debates over welfare reform. In the same opinion poll cited above, 56 percent of respondents agreed with this view (Blendon et al. 1995).[2] Bill Moyers and other journalists have created powerful documentaries that portray whole communities of women and men who have abandoned the marriage ethic and have babies they cannot support because they know the mother can rely on state handouts. In his 1985 documentary *The Vanishing Family*, Moyers interviewed several unmarried African American fathers of welfare-dependent children in Newark, New Jersey. When Moyers asked one father of three how his children survived, he responded, "What I don't do, the government does." Later, this same father quipped, "You know what they say, 'Mama, baby. Papa maybe'."[3]

In response to the pervasive sense that welfare has contributed to dramatic changes in American family structure, many states have taken measures to limit nonmarital births among welfare recipients. In the early 1990s some states denied additional benefits to women who had more children while on the rolls. Other states requested federal waivers that allowed them to require mothers who wanted to continue receiving welfare to use contraceptives (see Handler 1995).

The "culture of welfare" arguments discussed above are similar, though not identical, to Oscar Lewis's notion of the "culture of poverty." Between 1959 and 1968, Lewis published a series of books based on observation of and life history interviews with

Latin Americans living in poverty. On the basis of his fieldwork, Lewis argued that the poor, who are driven into economic marginality by a capitalist society, tend to form a "culture of poverty":

> The culture of poverty, however, is not only an adaptation to a set of objective conditions of the larger society. Once it comes into existence it tends to perpetuate itself from generation to generation because of its effect on the children. By the time slum children are age six or seven they have usually absorbed the basic values and attitudes of their subculture and are not psychologically geared to take full advantage of changing conditions or increased opportunities which may occur in their life-time. (Lewis 1968, 188)

William Julius Wilson believes that "social isolation" rather than childhood socialization is primarily responsible for the deviant behavior of the poor. In attempting to explain the rise of deviant behavior among the poor, Wilson points to a host of structural forces that have taken manufacturing jobs and middle-class residents from central-city neighborhoods. Consequently, poor persons are much more likely to live in ghetto neighborhoods now than in previous generations. Bereft of job opportunities and middle-class role models and institutions, the residents of these neighborhoods have less contact with mainstream norms than in previous decades and are more likely to adhere to subcultural value systems:

> Today's ghetto neighborhoods are populated almost exclusively by the most disadvantaged segments of the black urban community, that heterogeneous grouping of families and individuals who are outside the mainstream of the American occupational system. Included in this group are individuals who lack training and skills and either experience long-term unemployment or are not members of the labor force, individuals who are engaged in street crime and other forms of aberrant behavior, and families that experience long-term spells of poverty and/or welfare dependency. These are the populations to which I refer when I speak of the underclass. I use this term to depict a reality not captured in the more standard designation lower class.
>
> In our conception, the term underclass suggests that changes have taken place in ghetto neighborhoods, and the groups that have been left behind are collectively different from those that lived in these neighborhoods in earlier years. It is true that long-term welfare families and street criminals are distinct groups, but they live and interact in the same depressed community and they are part of the population that has, with

the exodus of the more stable working and middle class segments, become increasingly isolated socially from mainstream patterns and norms of behavior. (Wilson 1987, 8)

Finally, in their book *American Apartheid*, Massey and Denton claim that the changing conditions of American ghettos do not tell the whole story. In their view, the increase in deviant behaviors like crime and welfare use can be tied to what they call the "culture of segregation," which has resulted from the fact that African Americans and other minority groups are likely to live in neighborhoods that are segregated by race as well as class.

In concentrating poverty . . . [residential] segregation . . . also concentrates conditions such as drug use, joblessness, welfare dependency, teenage childbearing, and unwed parenthood, producing a social context where these conditions are not only common but the norm. . . . In adapting to this social environment, ghetto dwellers evolve a set of behaviors, attitudes, and expectations that are sharply at variance with those common in the rest of American society. (Massey and Denton 1993, 12–13)

## TESTING THE
## CULTURAL THEORIES OF POVERTY

We evaluate these competing theories by examining subgroup differences within our sample. Specifically, we compare our 214 welfare-reliant mothers with our 165 wage-reliant mothers, our 210 ever married mothers with our 169 never married ones, our 102 respondents whose own mother had received welfare with our 277 respondents who never received welfare as children, our 89 respondents who lived in very poor neighborhoods (census tracts with a poverty rate of at least 40 percent in 1989) with our 290 who did not, and our African and Mexican American mothers with our white mothers. Our sample is 46 percent African American, 45 percent non-Hispanic white, and 9 percent Mexican American; these proportions roughly reflect the racial and ethnic distribution of the welfare population as a whole in the early 1990s (U.S. House of Representatives 1993, 697). Our Mexican American sample is not representative, however, of Latina welfare recipients nationwide, since it was drawn from a single site in Texas with a distinctive border culture. San Antonio's second-generation Mexican Americans can be distinguished from other U.S. groups of Latin heritage by their very close ties to Mexico, low educational attainment, and some distinctive health problems (Frisbie and Cruz 1992; Frisbie et al. 1992; Pendry 1995).[4]

Our research focuses on expenditure patterns, survival routines, and hardship among poor single mothers. By comparing these variables across subgroups, we can examine whether the behaviors we studied are best understood as widely shared responses to structural constraints, or whether they vary across different groups of mothers, as both the popular discourse and some of the academic literature suggest. Also, before assuming that any observed difference is attributable to a distinctive subculture within a group, we carefully examine whether it can be more readily explained by other factors.

## Expectations Regarding Expenditure Patterns

If welfare use itself represents adherence to a set of deviant values, we might expect to find that mothers who rely on welfare waste more money on nonessentials and budget less efficiently than wage-reliant mothers. If a mother's marital status is a proxy for her value system, we might see similar differences between ever-married mothers and never-married ones. If single mothers raised on welfare have been socialized into the "culture of poverty," we should see differences between mothers raised on welfare and mothers who grew up in nonwelfare households. Wilson's "social isolation" theory suggests that we should find differences between single mothers living in the poorest neighborhoods versus those living in better ones. Finally, Massey and Denton's "culture of segregation" argument would lead us to expect differences among racial and ethnic groups (see table 7-1).

## Expectations Regarding
## Work-Based Survival Strategies

If either welfare use or lack of a marital tie indicates adherence to a deviant set of values, those raised on welfare and those who have never married might pursue work-based survival routines that are distinctively different from those of mothers from more "mainstream" backgrounds.[5] Specifically, mothers who use welfare or never-married mothers might avoid formal-sector work and gravitate toward illegal activities. A "culture of poverty" perspective would suggest a similar finding for mothers who grew up on welfare compared with mothers who did not. A "social isolation" approach would predict the same differences along neighborhood lines, while a "culture of segregation" approach predicts that the differences in work choices should follow racial or ethnic lines.

## Expectations Regarding Network-Based Strategies

Mothers' willingness to employ the covert child support strategy might vary by subgroup because mothers in more disadvantaged groups might be more willing to break the rules in order to garner under-the-table payments from absent fathers. Alternatively, the subcultural technology necessary to employ this strategy might be differentially available depending on whom a mother associates with and where she lives. We did not make any other specific predictions in the area of social networks, but we did look at whether variation in social networks could produce the differences in resources and opportunities that explained other differences among groups.

## Expectations Regarding Agency-Based Strategies

The cultural theories we have discussed throughout this chapter might also predict that mothers in the disadvantaged groups would be more willing to ask churches and neighborhood organizations for financial help because they felt less stigma in doing so.

## ACTUAL PATTERNS OF BEHAVIOR

In other chapters, we have taken a very simple approach to describing similarities and differences in expenditures, survival

## TABLE 7-1. Predicted Patterns in Expenditures and Survival Strategies

| | Welfare Status | Marital Status | Family Background | Neighborhood | Race/Ethnicity |
|---|---|---|---|---|---|
| Expenditure and hardship | Mothers receiving welfare would (a) spend more money, especially on non-essentials, and (b) experience more material hardship due to their inability to budget their incomes effectively. | Mothers who had never been married would . . . | Mothers with welfare backgrounds would . . . | Mothers living in ghetto neighbor-hoods would . . . | African and Mexican American mothers would . . . |
| Work-based strategies | Mothers receiving welfare would (a) earn less from reported work, (b) earn less from un-reported work, and (c) earn more from underground work. | Mothers who had never been married would . . . | Mothers with welfare backgrounds would . . . | Mothers living in ghetto neighbor-hoods would . . . | African and Mexican American mothers would . . . |
| Network-based strategies | Mothers receiving welfare would (a) receive more from covert child support. (b–c) No prediction for other network-based contributions. | Mothers who had never been married would . . . | Mothers with welfare backgrounds would . . . | Mothers living in ghetto neighbor-hoods would . . . | African and Mexican American mothers would . . . |
| Agency-based strategies | Mothers receiving welfare would (a) receive more from agencies | Mothers who had never been married would . . . | Mothers with welfare backgrounds would . . . | Mothers living in ghetto neighbor-hoods would . . . | African and Mexican American mothers would . . . |

*Source:* Authors' summary of predicted patterns.

strategies, and hardships among welfare and working mothers. This approach is somewhat problematic for understanding subgroup differences because, as the reader might suspect, the groups overlap. For example, mothers whose own mothers received welfare were also more likely to live in ghettos, and fewer of them were white.

In addition, subgroups differ in ways that might explain the patterns we want to understand. A difference in spending patterns between Mexican American and white mothers, for example, might reflect our sampling design (the Mexican American mothers lived in San Antonio, where mothers of *all* racial and ethnic backgrounds spent less than those in the other sites). Alternatively, it might reflect the higher marriage rate among this group, which provides easier access to formal child support.

To understand subgroup differences in expenditures, we pooled welfare- and wage-reliant mothers and controlled for the variables that we used to select our sample as well as other sociodemographic variables. In the first step, we controlled for exogenous variables (family background, race, and site). In subsequent steps, we added other variables that might be said to reflect a mother's choices and values—marital status, family size, welfare status, rent subsidy status, and neighborhood residence. We looked at how these variables were related to total expenditures, total nonhousing expenditures (because housing costs varied so much by site), expenditures on "necessities" other than housing, and expenditures on nonessentials.

We developed a somewhat more complex approach to look at material hardship by controlling for all of the variables listed above plus mothers' total expenditures, the quality of their networks (measured in dollars received from these networks), and whether they had a live-in boyfriend—variables that our previous analysis (chapters 4 and 5) suggested might be important predictors of a mother's overall well-being.

To sort out subgroup effects on survival strategies, we looked at the amount of money mothers generated from a particular strategy. Here, we employed the same method used for measuring differences in expenditure, but added an additional step controlling for the amount of money generated from alternative survival strategies.[6] We added this last step because we reasoned that some subgroups might be more likely to employ a certain strategy if they had less access to others. For example, mothers raised on welfare might work in the underground economy more than other mothers because they had less access to network-based survival strategies.

The results of these analyses are summarized in table 7-2 (the regression results are shown in appendix B). We draw three main conclusions from the findings. First, only a few results support the notion that cultural values play a large role in mothers' spending, survival strategies, or hardships (these results are printed in bold type). Moreover, for some of these results, we cannot rule out the possibility that observed differences may not reflect differences in resources and opportunities. Second, many of our findings directly refute these culture-based arguments (these results are italicized). Third, the most interesting and analytically important differences we found suggest strongly that mothers in the disadvantaged subgroups suffer from reduced access to opportunity structures. All the results are discussed more specifically below.

## Welfare Status

### Expenditure and Hardship

There were significant differences in spending among subgroups of mothers. When all else was equal, welfare-reliant mothers spent roughly one-third *less* than wage-reliant mothers. With the exception of spending on non-necessities, this difference was primarily due to additional work-related expenses for working mothers, though a small but significant difference remained even when controlling for work-related expenses; the increased costs of working could not account for the fact that working mothers spent more for nonessentials. Finally, the welfare-reliant mothers with whom we spoke reported fewer material hardships over the twelve months preceding the interview, even when controlling for their lower expenditures. Thus, the welfare-reliant mothers appeared to use their scarce resources to better effect than the wage-reliant mothers, a finding in sharp contrast to what current rhetoric might suggest.

## Work-Based Strategies

The amount of income from reported supplementary work did not vary significantly by welfare status. Welfare status was positively related to earnings in the informal economy, however, with welfare-reliant mothers earning nearly seven times more from unreported supplemental work than wage-reliant mothers. Differences in earnings from this type of work persisted when we took earnings from other strategies into account but were not nearly as large.

Finally, welfare status did not significantly affect earnings from illegal work, suggesting that welfare mothers are not disproportionately drawn to criminal activity.

## Network-Based Strategies

Welfare status did not significantly affect the amount of cash mothers received from their family members and friends. The same held true for boyfriends. Welfare status did have a powerful effect, however, on the amount of cash absent fathers contributed: mothers who did not receive welfare generated about three-fifths more from absent fathers than mothers who did. We discussed possible reasons for this disparity in chapters 5 and 6. Both the significance and strength of this result persisted when controlling for income from other strategies.[7]

## Agency-Based Strategies

Welfare status was not related to the amount of cash assistance mothers received from agencies.

## Marital Status

### Expenditure and Hardship

Overall, expenditures and material hardship varied little according to whether a mother had ever been married, the exception being spending on nonessentials. Mothers who had been married spent *more* in this category than never-married mothers, though

## TABLE 7-2. Actual Patterns in Expenditures and Survival Routines

| | Welfare Status | Marital Status | Family Background | Neighborhood | Race/Ethnicity |
|---|---|---|---|---|---|
| Expenditure and hardship[a] | (a) *Mothers who received welfare spent less in all four categories than those who did not.* (b) *Mothers who received welfare reported fewer hardships than those who did not.* | (a) No difference overall, though mothers who had married in the past spent somewhat more for nonessentials. (b) No difference. | (a) No difference. (b) **Mothers who were raised on welfare reported more material hardship than mothers from nonwelfare backgrounds.** | (a) *Mothers living in very poor neighborhoods spent less overall and* (b) *experienced fewer hardships than mothers living in better neighborhoods.* | (a) *African and Mexican Americans spent significantly less than whites.* (b) No significant difference. |
| Work-based strategies | (a) No difference in income from reported side-jobs. (b) *Mothers who received welfare earned far more from unreported supplemental work.* (c) No difference in earnings from illegal work. | (a–c) No difference. | (a–b) No difference. (c) **Mothers who were raised on welfare earned more from underground work, even when access to other survival strategies was taken into account.** | (a) No difference. (b) **Mothers living in very poor neighborhoods earned less from informal work.** (c) No difference. | (a) No difference between African Americans and whites, but *Mexican Americans were less likely to engage in reported work than whites.* (b–c) No difference. |

204

| | Welfare Status | Marital Status | Family Background | Neighborhood | Race/Ethnicity |
|---|---|---|---|---|---|
| Network-based strategies | (a–b) No difference in what mothers received from family, friends, and boyfriends. (c) Mothers who received welfare received far less from absent fathers. | (a) Mothers who had married in the past received more from family, friends, and (b) received less from boyfriends and (c) more from absent fathers overall (no significant differences in the amount of covert support received). | (a–b) No significant difference. (c) No difference in overall level of support from absent fathers, though **mothers who were raised on welfare received more from covert child support than mothers who were not.** | (a) Mothers living in very poor neighborhoods received less from family members than residents of better neighborhoods. (b–c) No significant difference. | (a) No significant differences between African Americans and whites, though Mexican Americans received less cash from family and friends than whites. (b) No significant difference. (c) African Americans received less from absent fathers than whites overall (no significant differences in the amount of covert support received). |
| Agency-based strategies | (a) No difference. | (a) No difference. | (a) No difference. | (a) *Residents of very poor neighborhoods received less.* | (a) No difference. |

*Source:* Based on authors' calculations using Edin and Lein survival strategies data. (See appendix B).

[a] Expenditures were broken down into four categories: total, total nonhousing, nonhousing necessities, and nonhousing nonnecessities.

the effect was modest. This finding suggests mothers who had never married were a bit more frugal than those who had.

### Work-Based Strategies

Marital status did not significantly affect mothers' earnings from any work-based strategy, suggesting that mothers who had never been married were about as ambitious (in the case of reported and informal work) and as willing to break the law (in the case of underground work) as mothers who had married.

### Network-Based Strategies

Mothers who had been married received a lot more cash help from family members and friends (roughly a third more). This result persisted when controlling for income from other strategies. They also received far more from absent fathers, almost entirely because they were far more likely to receive child support through the formal system (income from covert support did not vary significantly by marital status). The opposite was true for boyfriends, who contributed more to never-married mothers, and partly offset the lack of help from absent fathers.

### Agency-Based Strategies

A mother's marital status had no significant effect on her cash income from agencies.

## Family Background

Our data lend mixed support to the notion that family background may affect mothers' spending, survival strategies, or hardships.

### Expenditure and Hardship

We found no significant differences in total expenditures along family background lines. Though it appeared that mothers whose own mothers raised them on welfare spent somewhat less for both total nonhousing and nonhousing necessities, the results disappeared when we controlled for a mother's welfare status (in our sample, mothers from disadvantaged backgrounds were more likely to receive AFDC). Differences in family background did not affect spending on nonessentials.

Mothers who grew up in welfare-reliant households did experience more material hardship than mothers who had not. Though this could indicate a lack of budgeting ability among second-generation welfare recipients, it could also have resulted from unmeasured differences in the in-kind assistance from family and friends.

## Work-Based Strategies

Family background did not have a significant effect on the amount earned from either reported or unreported supplemental work. However, mothers who were raised on welfare earned nearly two-and-one-half times more from underground work than mothers from nonwelfare backgrounds. This difference persisted when controlling for earnings from other strategies and suggests that a small minority of persons from intergenerational welfare families might be more willing to engage in criminal activity. This increased likelihood may result from deviant socialization during childhood, which influenced a mother's willingness to engage in crime as an adult. However, our observations also indicated that underground workers were typically recruited into illegal trades by family members (especially brothers and male cousins). If other mothers had comparable access to such strategies, they might have been equally tempted to use them. Regardless of whether this was due to willingness or access, it can still be viewed as a cultural difference. However, the reader should remember that only a small minority of any group used underground work as a survival strategy.

## Network-Based Strategies

Growing up in a welfare household did not affect the level of a mother's family-based support nor did it significantly affect the contributions of boyfriends. In addition, family background had virtually no impact on what an absent father contributed. However, welfare-reliant mothers who grew up on welfare generated more covert support than those welfare-reliant mothers who did not receive welfare as children. When we added controls for income generated through the formal child support system and other survival strategies, this difference persisted, although the effects on income from covert support were not as strong. This finding suggests that mothers who grew up in a welfare-reliant family might be more able or more willing to circumvent the welfare rules and receive child support covertly. It also might indicate unmeasured differences in the employment prospects of the fathers of these mothers' children (which would make them less willing to use the formal system, for reasons outlined in chapter 6).

*Agency-Based Strategies*

Family background was not closely related to the amount of cash a mother received from agencies.

In sum, our findings lend a modicum of support to the notion that a mother's background may influence her willingness to break the law (by selling sex, drugs, or stolen goods) and to violate the welfare rules in regard to child support. Even among mothers who were raised on welfare, however, only a tiny portion reported working in the underground economy. These findings clearly did not offer strong support to the idea that within our very select group of mothers, those from disadvantaged backgrounds had inherited less impulse control than the other mothers, at least as reflected in their ability to budget their money, or were more averse to reported work. Nor did their backgrounds seem to make them less sensitive to the stigma they felt when asking agencies for cash handouts.

## Neighborhood Residence

When all else is equal, the neighborhood in which a family lived does appear to have had some influence over expenditures, hardship rates, and survival strategies. Many of these relationships, however, are the opposite of those outlined in table 7-1.

## Expenditure and Hardship

Living in a very poor neighborhood substantially lessened a mother's overall spending (though differences within subcategories were not significant). In addition, mothers from very poor neighborhoods experienced fewer hardships than other mothers, even when controlling for differences in total expenditures. (Mothers in poor neighborhoods often lived in housing projects, which cost less than a private apartment.) One possible explanation for this finding is that mothers in poor neighborhoods were better able to manage their money somehow, a point we discuss below.

## Work-Based Strategies

Neighborhood residence did not affect a mother's earnings from supplemental reported work or from underground work. It did, however, lower mothers' earnings from unreported work, and the effect was substantial. These findings offer some support to the theory that residents of very poor neighborhoods are isolated from the social networks that would help them find jobs or are physically so remote from such jobs as to make work inaccessible. In our experience, unreported work requires the proximity of friends and neighbors with enough excess cash to hire out their cleaning, lawn work, and other chores. It also requires the presence of small businesses that need part-time and casual laborers and that pay cash. In many very poor neighborhoods, both are in short supply.

## Network-Based Strategies

Though the amount of cash that mothers received from boyfriends or their children's fathers (either through the formal system or covertly) did not vary significantly by neighborhood residence, mothers living in very poor neighborhoods did receive less cash from family and friends. Presumably, mothers living in very poor neighborhoods had fewer relatives with surplus resources than other mothers living elsewhere.

*Agency-Based Strategies*

Residents of very poor neighborhoods also received significantly less cash from agencies than residents of other neighborhoods. This difference persisted when we controlled for a mother's ability to garner supplemental income from other sources. Our records suggest that most of this difference arose because mothers living in better neighborhoods had stronger ties to churches and other community groups, had the know-how to get student loans and grants, and were better able to convince agency personnel that cash help would help them get back on their feet.

These findings imply that a mother's contacts with other mothers in poor neighborhoods may influence their spending and survival patterns. The spending differences suggest that mothers who live in very poor neighborhoods learn how to manage their budgets more efficiently by exchanging money-saving techniques with neighbors. We routinely saw mothers engage in such talk on front stoops, in laundromats, at bus stops, on the job, and in their local welfare office.[8] In our experience, mothers who lived in better neighborhoods did not have as much access to the money-saving techniques they needed to survive poverty.

The data also indicate, however, that mothers who live in very poor neighborhoods may lack access to informal work opportunities because of their lack of physical proximity to prospective casual employers. Finally, our data suggest that agencies might be hesitant to expend their limited resources on mothers from ghetto neighborhoods, since agency personnel sometimes perceive ghetto residents as less likely to better themselves than residents of better neighborhoods. In our experience, some agency personnel felt that offering cash assistance to mothers living in notorious ghettos, such as Charleston's Eastside or Union Heights neighborhoods, or Chicago's North Lawndale or Cabrini Green, was not the optimal way to invest limited agency resources.

Family members might have made similar assessments, which would explain why mothers living in very poor neighborhoods received less from family members. On the other hand, differences in family-based contributions might really be the result of unmeasured variance in the quality of a mother's family-based network (we only controlled for whether a mother's own mother had received welfare).[9] Because we do not have more precise measures of a mother's class background, we cannot be sure.

## Race and Ethnicity

When looking at differences in mothers' behaviors and attitudes by race and ethnicity, we observed strong effects, but none in the direction outlined in table 7-1.

### Expenditure and Hardship

Minority mothers spent less overall than white mothers. African American mothers spent about 10 percent less each month than whites, while Mexican American mothers spent almost 20 percent less. This difference runs opposite to what a "culture of segregation" approach would predict. When we subtract housing costs from total expenditures (minority mothers spent less, on average, for housing), minority mothers still spent less than whites. Mexican American mothers also spent less than whites on nonhousing necessities and on nonessentials.

We can view this frugality as cultural, since the techniques needed to live on very little are almost certainly learned from others in the same environment. In addition, since low-income African Americans and Mexican Americans are typically segregated into neighborhoods where there are a lot of other poor people (even if they do not meet our criteria of a very poor neighborhood), the social interactions with other poor people are almost certainly more frequent for them. Thus, our observations suggest that, contrary to the "culture of segregation" argument, racial isolation does not necessarily lead to a breakdown of frugality and sound financial management.[10] Instead, people learn from each other how best to manage poverty.

Though both African American and Mexican American mothers spent significantly less than white mothers in the early 1990s, Mexican Americans' expenditures were far below those of African Americans. We believe these differences were more apparent than real, however. Most Mexican American mothers used between twenty and thirty agencies on a regular basis for in-kind assistance, so they did not need as much cash as other mothers.

African American mothers also experienced less hardship than white mothers, even when controlling for expenditure. This suggests that African American mothers may have been better at managing their money. Mexican American mothers did not experience significantly less hardship than whites. In fact, we believe that had we used more precise measures of hardship, the figures for the Mexican American group would have been far worse off than those for either the African American or white groups, even when controlling for their reduced expenditures. These mothers faced more frequent and more serious hardship (including monthly shortages of food, no indoor plumbing, raw sewage in the homes, and so on) than our scale reflected.[11]

## Work-Based Strategies

Though there were no reliable differences between African American and white mothers, Mexican American mothers were much less likely to engage in reported work than whites. We doubt this reflects cultural differences in this group's willingness to work, but these mothers also faced unique constraints on their employment, including a language barrier and some unique health problems. Race and ethnicity made little difference in either unreported or underground work.[12]

## Network-Based Strategies

African American and Mexican American mothers were less likely than white mothers to receive cash assistance from their family members and friends. For African Americans, the difference became insignificant when we controlled for neighborhood residence. For Mexican Americans, the differences remained when we controlled for neighborhood.

African American mothers received fewer dollars from fathers each month than white mothers did. This pattern is not surprising, since African American men are poorer than white men. Though it appeared that African American mothers partly compensated for the lack of help from fathers by enlisting the aid of boyfriends, differences between African Americans and whites in the level of boyfriends' help were no longer significant once we controlled for marital status.

Race and ethnicity played no significant role in welfare-reliant mothers' receipt of covert support.

## Agency-Based Strategies

A mother's success in garnering cash or direct assistance from agencies was not significantly affected by her race or ethnicity.

## Summary of Findings

Our data do not tell a strong story of cultural forces shaping mothers' spending, survival strategies, or hardship, though they do suggest some unexpected differences among groups. Foremost, mothers who received welfare, mothers who had never married, mothers who lived in very poor neighborhoods, and mothers who were from a minority group exhibited *more* frugal spending behavior than their more advantaged counterparts. These mothers seem to have acquired what some sociologists term "cultural tools," techniques that equip them to make do with less and avoid serious material hardship (Swidler 1986).[13]

The exceptions to this pattern were mothers who had been raised on welfare. Though their spending patterns were not significantly different from those of mothers from nonwelfare backgrounds, they did report higher rates of material hardship. It is possible that this difference reflected a lack of budgeting ability. It is also possible that it reflected unmeasured variation in mothers' receipt of in-kind assistance from kin.

Overall, the variables in our model predicted about half of the variance in total expenditures, roughly a third of the variation in expenditures for nonhousing necessities, and about 10 percent of the variance in spending for nonessentials. In the total expenditures category, a mother's age and family size were positively related to spending, while mothers with a rent subsidy spent less.

Our model explained only 17 percent of the variance in hardship rates among poor mothers. We found that higher expenditures, receipt of welfare, residence in a poor neighborhood, minority status, and the cash-generating strength of a mother's social network all reduced hardship. Growing up on welfare and having a large family tended to increase a mother's material hardship. Older mothers reported more hardship than younger mothers, probably because older mothers tended to have older children, who were more expensive to feed and clothe. Chicagoans were less likely to experience hardship than mothers in other sites, entirely because of differences in housing quality.

In terms of work-based strategies, all groups of mothers were equally likely to work at a supplemental reported job (with the exception of the Mexican American mothers), and mothers who received welfare actually earned more from supplemental unreported work. Mothers living in very poor neighborhoods earned less from unreported work, probably because the physical isolation of their neighborhoods separated them from casual employers. In addition, mothers receiving welfare, mothers who had never been married, mothers from very poor neighborhoods, and minority mothers were no more likely than other mothers to work in the underground economy, though mothers who were raised on welfare were more likely to do so. All in all, subgroup differences explained none of the variance in earnings from reported jobs, only about 7 percent of the variance in earnings from unreported work, and only about 3 percent of the variance in earnings from underground work.

Turning to differences in network-based strategies, our subgroups differed little in the amount of covert support they received, with the exception of those mothers who had grown up on welfare, who received more. We did not predict differences in other network-based strategies but did observe that a marital tie enhanced contributions from family members, while living in a very poor neighborhood and having a Mexican American heritage were negatively related to cash contributions from relatives. We believe these differences resulted from unmeasured differences in mothers' class backgrounds, though we cannot be sure. A past marital tie lowered cash contributions from boyfriends, presumably because mothers who had been or were married were less likely to have a boyfriend (though we did not measure this). Help from boyfriends was not, however, significantly affected by welfare status, family background, neighborhood residence, or race and ethnicity.

There were no significant differences among subgroups in contributions from absent fathers, except by welfare status. This is partly an artifact of the federal welfare rules, which deemed that mothers receiving substantial payments through the formal Child Support Enforcement system were ineligible for welfare and limited the pass-through payment to mothers receiving formal system support to $50. Other possible explanations for why fathers of children with wage-reliant mothers might have been more able or willing to contribute were discussed in chapters 5 and 6.

Overall, group differences explained only a little of the variation in network-based contributions. We predicted about 10 percent of the variance in cash contributions from family and friends, about 6 percent of the variation in cash from boyfriends, about 15 percent of the variation in overall contributions from absent fathers, and, for welfare-reliant mothers, about 10 percent of the variance in covert contributions from absent fathers.

In terms of agency-based strategies, mothers with more-advantaged characteristics seemed no less willing to seek cash assistance from agencies than those with less-advantaged characteristics. In fact, mothers from very poor neighborhoods received less cash from agencies than mothers living in better neighborhoods. We suggested earlier in this chapter that this is probably because of formal and informal criteria utilized by agency personnel.

Group differences predicted only about 5 percent of the variance in cash contributions from agencies. Beyond the variables already discussed, age was also positively related to getting cash help from an agency, as was having a rental subsidy. Presumably, older mothers were more successful at getting help because they were more experienced. Similarly, mothers who were clever enough to get Section 8 housing might also be quite good at getting cash help from an agency.

## A FINAL WORD ABOUT
## CULTURAL THEORIES OF POVERTY

In *All Our Kin,* Carol Stack vividly described how poor African American mother-only families participated in kin-based networks to ensure their economic survival. In Stack's account, kin shared meals, loaned each other small sums in emergencies, and assisted each other with childrearing and other household chores. We uncovered similar evidence of survival networks, particularly among women who lived in very poor neighborhoods. Indeed, their reliance on these networks was one of the reasons mothers gave for not moving to the suburbs or to other cities with somewhat better employment prospects.

However, our primary interest was in cash survival strategies, which Stack did not emphasize. Mothers belonging to more advantaged subgroups were able to get both in-kind and cash assistance from their kin-based networks. Cash contributions tended to free these mothers from having to engage in more time-consuming strategies. Therefore, mothers from more-advantaged subgroups generally had more time to study for their GED, participate in a training program, or attend college.

This difference in the cash resources of one's network was important, because it provided the most-advantaged mothers with more tools to substantially improve their human capital. Women who received high-quality training or a college degree were better able to enter the primary sector of the labor market and earn a living wage. These women are also more likely to marry or remarry and become even better off. Daniel Lichter, Diane McLaughlin, George Kephart, and David Landry's (1992) analysis of National Longitudinal Survey of Youth (NLSY) data showed that while welfare receipt was unrelated to women's entry into marriage, women's education, earnings, and current employment were all positively related to marriage.

These differences in mothers' ability to get network-based support as well as the role that network-based support played in decreasing material hardship suggest that the composition of these mothers' social networks enhanced their ability to make the transition from welfare to work and to survive the ups and downs of income flow associated with leaving welfare for a low-wage job with uncertain stability and few fringe benefits. Though this issue merits further study, these findings also hint at possible reasons why national data show that these mothers are more likely to choose work over welfare and to experience much shorter welfare spells (Edin and Harris forthcoming; Harris 1996).

Though various experts have argued that the reasons behind these differences lie in cultural variation, skill differences, or even differences in intelligence, too little research has looked at differential network composition and how it affects material well-being.[14]

While we find evidence that family background can have an insidious effect on *some* mothers' survival strategies, the majority of mothers from disadvantaged backgrounds seem firmly committed to mainstream norms and work attitudes. Those that did not may constitute a very small hard-core group who, as Oscar Lewis predicted, might not respond to any intervention policymakers devise. If subjected to harsh sanctions, these mothers might respond by raising their children on the streets or in shelters. In that case, the state might take custody of some of the children. Americans first learned how expensive it was to break families apart during the "poorhouse" era, when poor single parents often lost their children to orphanages. Local officials soon learned that it was cheaper to allow these parents to receive relief and keep their children at home (Katz 1986). We know of no study that measures the long-range effects of persistent welfare use on children's outcomes. We do know, however, that the long-term prospects for children raised in institutions and foster homes are extremely poor (see Penzerro and Lein 1995 for a review of the literature).

# Chapter 8

# The Choice Between Welfare and Work

Τ HIS BOOK TELLS the story of single mothers all over America who face a desperate situation recognized by neither politicians nor the media: neither welfare nor low-wage work provides enough income to cover basic needs.

The federal welfare rules present welfare-reliant mothers with a stark choice: follow the rules—which disallow supplemental income—and subject their families to severe hardship, or break the rules. Virtually all welfare-reliant mothers with whom we spoke during the course of our research chose their family's welfare. In Chicago and Boston, many welfare-reliant mothers coped by taking off-the-books work. Many San Antonio mothers subsisted by purchasing stolen bread, meat, and tennis shoes out of the backs of cars and spent the early morning hours of many weekdays waiting in long lines for government surplus food, used clothing, or assistance in paying an overdue bill. In Charleston, descendants of antebellum Sea Islanders of African heritage did what they had always done to subsist: made and sold handicrafts, worked for cash at fishing docks heading shrimp, and cleaned the houses of rich northern retirees; poor white mothers lived off under-the-table handouts from better-off relatives and friends.

When they could, the welfare-reliant mothers in all these cities persuaded the fathers of their children to circumvent the Child Support Enforcement system, which would have passed through only $50 of the money the father contributed legally, keeping the rest as partial repayment of the family's welfare benefits. Instead, mothers urged fathers to contribute to their children's well-being

218

covertly, enforcing their claims with threats to "turn them in" to child support officials, who could dock their pay, seize their tax returns, revoke their driver's licenses, or, in some cases, throw them in jail if their identities were known.

Some mothers had lost contact with their children's fathers. Other fathers were abusive, violent, addicted, incarcerated, or dead. These fathers rarely contributed in any way, so some mothers turned to other men—boyfriends—whose intermittent earnings could help keep the household afloat. Because of the dire economic needs of their families, some women allowed these men into their homes on a "pay and stay" basis. Sometimes these men became the father of the next child in the family, and sometimes they did not. In either case, when men lost their jobs or stopped bringing home a portion of their paycheck, they were forced back into the households of their own mothers, grandmothers, or sisters or onto the streets. The mercenary tone of these male/female relationships eroded much of whatever trust existed between women and men in poor communities.

For those mothers who did not receive welfare and relied instead on earnings from low-wage work, every dollar they earned meant a decrease in their food stamps and housing subsidies; wage income also threatened their Medicaid eligibility. In addition, working entailed increased costs for child care, transportation, and clothing. Thus, wage-reliant mothers had to generate even more outside income from various survival strategies in order to balance their budgets.

The reality of economic life among unskilled and semiskilled mothers is sharply at odds with the perceptions held by most citizens. Average Americans depend on newspapers, magazines, television, and radio for their information about public policy issues. Journalists and their editors, in turn, publicize those stories that they think will attract the most interest or outrage. Thus, the public has been influenced by stories of welfare queens who used their ill-gotten gain to buy fancy cars and vacation homes or of mothers who exchanged AFDC and food stamps for crack or heroin while their children huddled in filthy unheated hovels.

A lot of Americans also depend on the reports of friends and relatives who have more direct contact with the poor—those whom Michael Lipsky (1980) terms "street level bureaucrats":

police officers, social workers, and others whose professional lives place them in close contact with those mothers who are having the most difficulty surviving the harsh world of subsistence living. Finally, ordinary citizens often form opinions based on their own observations in the grocery store, where they inspect the carts of those mothers who pay with food stamps, or when they drive by street corners of poor neighborhoods and see working-aged adults loitering.

Some of the single mothers we interviewed fit these stereotypes in one way or another; some did exchange their food stamps for drugs, and some bought junk food for their kids in the grocery store (though food stamps cannot be used to pay for soda pop, candy bars, frozen dinners, or other nonstaples). The vast majority, however, were managing as well as they could given their resources. Typically, mothers traded food stamps for cash only when they were short on the rent—a common occurrence in cities where rent alone often cost as much as the family received from welfare.

The primary lesson we have taken from their stories is not that the welfare system of the early 1990s engendered psychological dependency or encouraged the formation of a set of deviant behaviors. The real problem with the federal welfare system during these years was a labor-market problem. The mothers we interviewed had made repeated efforts to attain self-sufficiency through work, but the kind of jobs they could get paid too little, offered little security in the short term, and provided few opportunities over time. Meanwhile, mothers who chose to work were even worse off in material terms than their welfare counterparts. To "make it" while working, unskilled single mothers had to be extraordinarily lucky: they had to have a set of special circumstances that artificially lowered the cost of working and they had to be able to employ a set of survival strategies that were consistent with work.

The public tends to see welfare-reliant and wage-reliant single mothers as if they were two distinct populations. In reality, however, a very large proportion of unskilled and semiskilled mothers cycle between the low-wage sector of the economy and the welfare rolls. Welfare- and work-reliant mothers should be seen as two overlapping populations on a single continuum.

Roberta Spalter-Roth and her colleagues' (1995) analysis of the Census Bureau's Survey of Income and Program Participation, for example, shows that welfare-reliant mothers have substantial work histories—4.2 years on average. Recall that, in our sample, 65 percent of the welfare-reliant mothers had worked in a formal sector job during the previous two years, and 84 percent had held such a job during the past five years. We also have shown that about half of all welfare recipients had done some kind of paid work in the past year. We do not know how many low-wage single mothers nationwide have welfare histories, but 60 percent of the work-reliant women in our sample had used welfare recently. In addition, a large fraction of our wage-reliant mothers used federal, state, or community-based assistance while they were working.

Throughout this book, we have argued that the behaviors we observed were shaped partly by the particularities of our sites and certain group characteristics, but our data even more strongly suggest that most women usually behaved in ways that reflected reasoned calculations of which alternatives would be likely to expose their children to the least harm. If we want more single mothers to work without endangering the well-being of their children, we will need to be more realistic about the cost of subsistence and dramatically increase the earnings of both unskilled mothers and the fathers who contribute to their households.

## WHAT POOR SINGLE MOTHERS SPEND

On average, the 214 *welfare-reliant* mothers we interviewed spent $876 in cash and food stamps each month (in 1991 dollars). They spent 24 percent of their cash on housing, even though half of the sample received housing subsidies and some of the rest were doubled up with relatives. They spent another 30 percent on food, and 39 percent on clothing, transportation, laundry and cleaning supplies, diapers, school supplies, and other necessities. The remaining 7 percent went for nonessentials: a few video rentals or a basic cable subscription, an occasional trip to see relatives or go to an amusement park, a carton of cigarettes or a six-pack of beer, a bingo card or lottery ticket, or an occasional meal at a fast food restaurant. These small expenditures helped mothers survive psychologically and helped them to keep their children in school, off the streets, and out of trouble.

The expenditures of our *wage-reliant* mothers closely matched those of our welfare-reliant mothers with six notable exceptions. First, wage-reliant mothers earned more, so those who lived in a subsidized apartment had to pay more rent. While roughly half of the wage-reliant mothers in our sample received housing subsidies and many more doubled up, the wage-reliant sample as a whole paid about $100 a month more for housing than the welfare-reliant group. This was true even though we recruited our wage-reliant and welfare-reliant mothers from roughly the same neighborhoods.

Wage-reliant mothers also spent more on medical care, child care, transportation, clothing, and nonessentials. Mothers in the wage-reliant group often made substantial copayments for health care or went uninsured. Even though the working mothers and their children were in better health than members of welfare-reliant families, workers still paid three times as much for medical care as the welfare-reliant group. Wage-reliant mothers also spent about a quarter more for clothing, twice as much for transportation, and nearly ten times more on child care than the welfare-reliant mothers. The large difference in child care costs existed even though hardly any of the working mothers paid market rates for child care. Most wage-reliant mothers told us that they could not work if they had to pay market rates. Finally, wage-reliant mothers spent an average of $20 more each month on nonessentials—a rather paltry reward for choosing work over welfare. In other areas, workers' budgets were as bleak as those of the welfare-reliant group.

All told, our wage-reliant group spent $1,243 a month (in 1991 dollars), or roughly $15,000 a year. If these mothers had paid all of their own bills instead of getting housing subsidies, Medicaid, and the like, they would have had to earn at least $16,500 a year before taxes. This figure is a lower-bound estimate of a family's subsistence needs, because the wage-reliant group had fewer and older children, better health, more access to relatives who could watch their children, and received more in-kind help from friends than our welfare-reliant group.

We compared our mothers' expenditures with those of single mothers in the national Consumer Expenditure Survey. Our mothers spent less in almost every category than mothers in the national sample. We concluded that our mothers' expenditures were at the very low end of what constitutes a minimally acceptable living standard in the United States.

City-to-city differences in expenses were largely confined to housing and transportation. Rents were the lowest in San Antonio, which resembled rents in other southern cities including Little Rock, Louisville, Memphis, and New Orleans. Rents in Charleston were higher and typical of rents in other fast-growing cities in the New South. Rents in Chicago were still higher, but typical of rents in other large Midwestern cities. Rents in the Boston area were the highest and representative of many Northeastern and West Coast cities. Our Boston-area mothers spent less on housing than one would expect, however, because most non-subsidized families doubled up with family members or friends.

Transportation expenditures also varied by site. Chicago and Boston had reasonably good public transportation, so central-city residents could ride the bus or subway and seldom needed a car. Suburban mothers in these cities often had to maintain a car, so they paid more for transportation. Charleston provided minimal public transportation in poor neighborhoods, so mothers had to buy automobiles or use neighborhood taxis. In San Antonio, welfare-reliant mothers spent very little on transportation because they pursued survival strategies that did not require them to leave their immediate neighborhood.

Why have so many Americans come to see welfare as "dependency" and work as "self-sufficiency"? This rhetoric persists partly because most discussions of single parents take place without consideration for what welfare provides and what it actually takes to support a family. The official poverty line is of little help since it does not attempt to measure how much mothers need to spend on goods and services.[1] John Schwarz (Schwarz and Volgy 1992, 67–93) has attempted to estimate what the most basic necessities would cost. His budget includes no money for extras or child care. Even so, he determined that a family of four would have needed $20,660 in 1991, or 155 percent of the poverty threshold, to meet its basic needs. Schwarz's budget closely matches our estimates of roughly 150 percent of the poverty line for a working family of three.

Interestingly, both Schwarz's and our estimates closely match public opinion. Since the 1950s, the Gallup poll has asked Americans what they consider to be the minimum amount of income necessary for a family of four to live in their community. During the 1980s, responses ranged from 140 to 160 percent of the poverty line, suggesting that even the American public considers the official poverty measure too low. In 1987, the last time Gallup asked this question, Americans told the pollsters that a family of four would need to spend an amount equaling 160 percent of the poverty line to subsist.

Without an adjustment of the official measure of poverty, policymakers and social scientists will have trouble understanding the true extent and nature of poverty. Currently, both social scientists and policymakers tend to divide the population into two categories—poor and nonpoor—and sometimes use the term "near-poor" to describe those living just above the threshold. It makes little sense, however, to define a group whose income is too low to pay its bills as "near-poor" or to use such unrealistic measures as eligibility criteria for public programs.

## SURVIVAL STRATEGIES

While making ends meet is far more expensive than previous social science research has indicated, most families are also more resourceful than has been understood. Conventional measures of income miss a lot of the ways in which single mothers make ends meet. In our sample, for instance, welfare-reliant mothers were able to cover only three-fifths of their budgets with welfare, food stamps, and benefits from other means-tested programs in the early 1990s. Wage-reliant mothers could cover about two-thirds of their monthly budgets with wages from their main jobs. Because both welfare- and wage-reliant mothers faced the same fundamental dilemma each month, they relied on similar kinds of survival strategies to generate the additional money they needed to bridge the gap between their income and expenditures.

These survival strategies were dynamic rather than static. They resembled a continuously unraveling patchwork quilt, constructed from a wide variety of welfare- and work-based income; cash and in-kind assistance from family, friends, absent fathers, and boyfriends; and cash and in-kind assistance from agencies. Though welfare- and wage-reliant mothers drew from the same repertoire of strategies, wage-reliant mothers were less likely to rely on supplemental work because they had so little extra time. They were also less likely to get cash help from agencies. For the same reason, they relied much more heavily on their personal networks to meet household expenses. Although maintaining this web of social relations took time, this "work" fit more flexibly into working mothers' schedules. Thus, network-based strategies were much more compatible with full-time work than other strategies.

Mothers living in different cities faced somewhat different constraints and opportunities. For *welfare-reliant* mothers, the feasibility of working an off-the-books job varied by city size and the availability of false IDs. Their ability to get money from family and friends also varied with the strength of local labor markets and that of the local child support system. Robust local labor markets allowed boyfriends, absent fathers, and other network members to contribute more to welfare-reliant mothers' budgets, while a strong child support system helped mothers enforce their claims on fathers. Agency-based differences for welfare-reliant mothers were largely due to the kind of service environment that each site provided.

*Wage-reliant* mothers' strategies varied by site for much the same reasons that welfare-reliant mothers' strategies did. Supplemental work and network-based opportunities were determined largely by the local labor market. Agency-based strategies differed according to the generosity of local service providers.

Although our data are not longitudinal, we can use them to suggest why so many single mothers in the 1980s and 1990s repeatedly cycled between welfare and work. We have argued that the particular strategies a welfare-reliant mother used to make ends meet either constrained or enhanced her ability to make a permanent transition to work. Ironically, our data suggest that for welfare recipients, work-based strategies did not facilitate permanent departure from the welfare rolls unless they resulted in unusually high and stable earnings. Network-based strategies, however, did facilitate such transitions.

Network-based strategies came in three varieties: contributions from family and friends, contributions from boyfriends, and contributions from absent fathers. Workers and welfare recipients received about the same amount of assistance from their family members, but whites received more than African Americans. Whites received more, but they were more likely to have been married when their child was born and because marriage was associated with a larger network. This may also help explain why disproportionate numbers of African American women were on the federal welfare rolls (Bane and Ellwood 1994). If mothers required strong and generous networks to sustain work without endangering their children, and if minority women had less access to such networks, they would have worked less.

The role of family-based networks was also somewhat paradoxical. On the one hand, the cash-generating strength of mothers' networks enabled mothers to work and cushioned some of the worst economic shocks of working at a subsistence level. On the other hand, even strong networks could not fully protect working mothers from the vagaries of the labor market.

In addition, network support was not free. Because mothers often depended on others only marginally better off than themselves, others in their network expected to receive help if the mothers managed to better their situations. So while our mothers seldom contributed cash to the budgets of other network members, we suspect that better-off mothers (not in our sample) devoted a part of their monthly budgets to assisting others in their network. If obligations are reciprocal in this way, even mothers who manage to escape welfare and the $5-an-hour ghetto might have difficulty getting ahead, and so remain vulnerable to economic shocks even as they move up the income ladder. Furthermore, the mothers we interviewed were expected to invest a good deal of time and energy maintaining relationships with their benefactors—time and energy they could not spend going to school or attending training. These encumbrances also could limit a mother's ability to get ahead.

The second source of network assistance was from boyfriends. Interestingly, the amount of support from this source was not greater for welfare-reliant mothers than for workers. Nor were minority mothers more likely than white women to generate cash from boyfriends. Mothers who had never been married did get a bit more from boyfriends, but part of this difference can be explained by the lack of contributions these mothers received from absent fathers.

Absent fathers also helped mothers cover their expenses. For the welfare-reliant group, we distinguished between contributions received through the formal child support system and those received covertly. In both cases, the existence of strong child support enforcement aided mothers who wanted help from fathers. If mothers and children had few ties to the father, a strong enforcement environment helped them to get more money from the father through formal channels. For mothers who wanted to maintain their children's tie with the father, a strong enforcement environment could still be easily circumvented, and mothers were able to better enforce their claims on covert support because they could threaten to turn the fathers in if they failed to pay. This enabled mothers to keep more of the money and yet preserve the father's relationship with the child. We did not make the formal/covert distinction for working mothers, since participation in the formal system was not a legal requirement for this group. On balance, though, strong child support enforcement did help these mothers get more cash from fathers.[2]

We also found that mothers whose boyfriends lived with them were able to make substantial claims on these men's income. Men who stayed were expected to pay. This finding is sharply at odds with many media stories about inner-city men, which portray them as living off of their girlfriends' welfare checks. There is more economic activity among poor men, both in the formal and informal sectors of the economy, than most assume. Understanding the contribution patterns of unskilled and semiskilled single men as they move between formal, informal, and illegal jobs is crucial. Only then can we understand the other side of the story that this book tells.

## MATERIAL HARDSHIP

Despite the broad range of survival strategies that single mothers employ, most told us they had experienced serious material hardship during the prior twelve months. Not surprisingly, welfare-reliant mothers in high-benefit states experienced less hardship than those in low-benefit states; for workers, mothers with higher wages were better off than those with lower wages. It is more surprising that welfare recipients experienced fewer hardships than workers. In fact, if wage-reliant mothers were to bring their hardship levels down to those of our welfare-reliant mothers, they would have to spend roughly twice as much as the welfare mothers do.

The hardships that single mothers face when they move from welfare to work help to explain why so many unskilled and semiskilled mothers in the last three decades have relied on the federal welfare system, and why so many of those who left welfare for work during that time eventually returned to the government rolls. For these women, while welfare did not work very well, it made more sense than low-wage work, largely because it was so stable.

It is striking that welfare-reliant mothers still experienced substantial material hardship despite the assistance they received from the government. This indicates that even under the old welfare system the safety net was weak and that America's most vulnerable citizens, single mothers and their children, were constantly falling through the loose netting.

There is virtually no social safety net for single mothers who work, even when their wages don't pay enough to make ends meet. Transitional benefits for women who leave state welfare programs for work are undoubtedly necessary, but health benefits and child care assistance end after one or two years of work and the wages of those who have left welfare will seldom rise enough to make up the difference.

## CHOOSING BETWEEN WELFARE AND WORK

Unskilled and semiskilled mothers learn vital lessons from their experiences in the low-wage labor market. First, the kinds of jobs these women held in the past (and would get in the future without better skills) did not make them any better off—either financially or emotionally—than they were on welfare. Second, given the unstable nature of the low-wage job market, mothers with whom we spoke believed the transition from welfare to low-wage work might make them worse off and place them and their children at serious risk. Third, no matter how long they stayed at a job and no matter how diligently they worked, few jobs led to advancement. Fourth, past experience made mothers skeptical of the value of job clubs and other work-readiness components of the federal JOBS program, most of which attempted to place mothers in precisely the same types of jobs they held in the past.

Having learned these lessons, many single mothers who had burned out in the low-wage labor market returned to welfare. They did not plan to remain there, however. For these mothers, welfare was often part of a long-term strategy to reenter the labor market more successfully in the future. These plans took two forms. Some planned to stay out of the labor force until the costs of working were lower. This usually meant waiting until their children were in school or they could get a rent or child care subsidy. Others stayed on welfare to get more education and reenter the labor market in a more competitive position.

Most mothers firmly believed that education represented their best hope of breaking out of the $5-an-hour job ghetto. As we have seen, most were cynical about the local JOBS programs. Instead, mothers favored high-quality two- or four-year programs that prepared them for occupations paying a living wage. Pursuing high-quality training required a lot of time—a commodity in very short supply among the single mothers with whom we spoke. Finding time to go to school was even harder for wage earners than for welfare recipients. Furthermore, since they were less likely to qualify for Pell grants or other need-based forms of tuition assistance, going to school was more expensive for workers than for welfare recipients.

Because mothers who relied on wages struggled even harder to make ends meet than those who relied primarily on welfare, most felt that welfare made better economic sense than work did. In a social and psychological sense, however, mothers felt that work held clear merit. They were ambivalent about the toll that work would take on their parenting. On the one hand, mothers feared subjecting their children to the economic and social risks that came with work. On the other hand, they wanted their children to be proud of them and to take them as role models.

Welfare-reliant mothers' estimates of what they would need to leave welfare in the early 1990s reflected the experience of our wage-reliant mothers: they knew they would incur added costs for child care, medical care, transportation, work apparel, and housing. Our welfare-reliant mothers thought they would need $8 to $10 an hour to break even, a rate that closely resembled our estimates based on our wage-reliant mothers' budgets. They also knew they might be able to work for less if they enjoyed a special circumstance that lowered the cost of working or their other expenses.

All else equal, almost all mothers said they would rather work than rely on welfare. They believed work had important psychological benefits and welfare imposed stigma costs. However, mothers who worked knew they must risk their own and their children's well-being to do so. Nevertheless, because most single mothers want to work and most of the public wants them to do so, we advocate work-based solutions to the welfare and poverty problems we describe here. Very simply, then, if we want to make work less costly for unskilled and semiskilled mothers, their earning power must be enhanced. We can raise their wages by making substantial investments in their skill levels, by helping them to get better jobs, or by supplementing the wages and benefits they receive at their current jobs. To make any of these solutions viable, mothers with two children who worked full time and year-round would need to earn at least $16,000 a year—$8 to $10 an hour—in 1991 dollars. This figure assumes very modest child care or health care costs, which, of course, is not necessarily a reasonable assumption to make. Thus, unless affordable, high-quality child care and health care become available, those with expensive health problems or child care needs would have to earn more than we have estimated here or put their children at serious risk. As for the training option, the kind of training necessary to bring unskilled single mothers' earning power up to $8 an hour (1991 dollars) isn't currently available to welfare mothers in most states. However, solutions of this kind can work. We found a model of such a system in a small, rural county in Minnesota, which we will describe at the conclusion of the chapter.

## BEHAVIOR AND
## PERSONAL CHARACTERISTICS

To get at some of the most controversial aspects of the welfare debate, we wanted to know whether a mother's personal or social characteristics influenced how much she spent each month, how much hardship her family experienced, and how she bridged the gap between her main income (either welfare or low-wage work) and her expenditures. We looked at whether the receipt of welfare, marital status, family welfare history, neighborhood residence, and race or ethnicity affected the economic behaviors of mothers in our sample. Although our data do not indicate important distinctions between these groups, some effects were surprising and ran counter to conventional theories about the relationship between culture and poverty.

First, mothers who received welfare, mothers who had never married, mothers living in very poor neighborhoods, and minority mothers budgeted as effectively as their more "mainstream" counterparts. In fact, these mothers were more frugal and spent less on nonessentials. We argued that this was because the mothers had more access to the cultural tools necessary to make do with very little. Mothers who had been raised on welfare, however, did not fit this pattern, possibly because they spent some of their money foolishly but more likely because of unmeasured differences in the level of in-kind assistance from kin.

Mothers from the more disadvantaged groups earned as much from both supplemental reported and unreported work as their more advantaged counterparts. There were three exceptions to this rule: Mexican American mothers earned less than whites from reported work; mothers living in very poor neighborhoods earned less from informal work; and mothers who grew up on welfare earned more from underground work. We argued that the first two exceptions were due to local market conditions in San Antonio and the physical isolation of poor neighborhoods, respectively. The last may have resulted from either a greater willingness to engage in crime or a greater access to family members who engaged in criminal trades.

There was only one important group difference in the amount of covert cash help that welfare recipients received from their social networks: Mothers who had grown up on welfare received more. In addition, mothers from more disadvantaged groups had less access to the social resources that might have enabled them to make the transition from welfare to work. This difference might explain why national data show that throughout the 1980s mothers from these groups spent more time on welfare and had more difficulty permanently leaving welfare for work (Edin and Harris forthcoming).

With regard to generating cash help from agencies, mothers from different backgrounds differed little. In fact, mothers from better neighborhoods received more cash from agencies than mothers living in very poor neighborhoods, possibly because agencies use people's address as a proxy for other socially desirable characteristics, like the perceived desire to better oneself.

These findings suggest that mothers' personal and social characteristics cannot explain most of the economic behaviors of the women in our sample. By and large, once mothers from different walks of life found themselves in the same miserable situation, they responded in similar ways. Though some mothers who grew up on welfare did seem to be somewhat more willing to engage in vice to meet their expenses, a majority did not.

## A PROGRAM THAT WORKS

The bulk of this book has been devoted to describing the mothers' experience in urban welfare systems of four cities between 1988 and 1992 systems that did not work well for those who relied on them. We also interviewed a small group of single mothers living in a rural county in Minnesota in 1991 because it was one of the few places in the nation where mothers could live on their welfare benefits. This was because Minnesota's benefits were among the highest in the nation at that time (identical to those received by Boston-area mothers in 1991) and its rural counties had very low rents. In this rural county, all the respondents we interviewed (nineteen welfare- and seventeen wage-reliant mothers) were white, as the county had virtually no minority residents.

To find a rural county in which both whites and African Americans lived, we would have had to go to a southern state, none of which paid nearly as much as Minnesota did in 1991.

In this county, the welfare-reliant mothers generally managed on their welfare checks and food stamps; they also received a lot of in-kind help from local food pantries and churches when their food stamps ran out (generally three weeks into the month) or their children needed clothing or holiday gifts. Mothers generally supplemented their welfare checks with cash-generating strategies on special occasions only—the holidays, the coldest winter months when heating bills were high, or when their children needed new coats, boots, or something for school. When these needs arose, mothers worked informally, relied on members of their personal networks, or went to agencies for help.

In this rural county, side work included scrounging the local forests for firewood and selling it door to door, working the holiday rush at a local turkey farm, doing household chores or running errands for neighbors, shoplifting items from the local hardware store and then pawning them, and occasionally turning tricks. Network contributions came primarily from family members, because in a rural county it was nearly impossible for a father or boyfriend to live with the family without the authorities finding out. The county also had three food pantries and many churches that routinely assisted poor members (and nonmembers) with overdue bills and other special needs. What made this site different from the urban sites we studied was that welfare-reliant mothers engaged in these cash-generating strategies only occasionally. In most months, mothers found they could live on their benefits if they spent frugally.

Rural Minnesota's wage-reliant mothers, however, faced a situation that more closely resembled that of their urban counterparts. Though rent was relatively cheap and the state provided its uninsured citizens with access to very low-cost health care (although the strong union presence ensured that most mothers got insurance from their employers), child care was nearly as expensive for these mothers as for mothers living in large cities. Public transportation was nonexistent, so working almost always required having a car. For these reasons, mothers who worked at or near the minimum wage nearly always had to supplement their wages with side-work, contributions from network members, or agency assistance. Thus, most mothers agreed that low-wage workers were worse off than they would have been on welfare.

Local welfare officials and the local JOBS agency recognized these realities. They believed it was short-sighted to place mothers in minimum-wage jobs, since most would only cycle back onto welfare. Instead, they required mothers to finish high school and then to find a job or enroll in a post–high school training program. Minnesota's system of technical and community colleges had a campus convenient to county residents, which provided high-quality two-year technical training. Nearly all of the college's programs trained mothers for occupations that paid a living wage (at least $8 an hour) upon completion. The state of Minnesota only funded technical-college programs that placed 60 percent of their students into jobs. Thus, the college's programs were quite closely aligned with the needs of employers in the region and state. The two-year programs took single mothers an average of three years to complete (presumably because of their childrearing responsibilities), but most mothers who completed their course eventually found employment earning $8 an hour or better (Zucker 1994). However, mothers often had to relocate. While in school, their children were cared for in a subsidized child care facility. After gaining employment and leaving welfare, mothers could keep these child care subsidies for two years.

In this high-benefit/low-cost-of-living site, welfare-reliant mothers generally came within $50 of balancing their budgets using their welfare checks and food stamps alone in 1991. As a result, they had time to attend school, mother their children, and plan for the future. Though this county's plan was expensive, it would probably have been just as expensive to create enough low-skill jobs in this rural county for all of the single mothers who would need them in the absence of welfare.

## CONCLUSION

In the early 1990s, single mothers chose the harsh world of welfare because that of low-wage work was even more grim. Both our data and national data provide overwhelming evidence for this claim. In the early 1990s, those who managed to survive the low-wage labor market did so because they were unusually fortunate. But, we cannot base policy on the hope that all mothers will be so lucky.

Either substantial wage supplements or high-quality training are essential if the current population of unskilled and semiskilled women is ever to attain self-sufficiency through work. In addition, each of these solutions must include affordable access to reliable child care and health care. While current welfare-to-work programs might move women into jobs in the short term, these mothers and their children will experience much material hardship if they remain trapped in jobs that pay $5, $6, or $7 an hour and offer few benefits.

If, on the other hand, states elect to pay welfare benefits that are even less generous than what the women in this book received, our data suggest that some mothers will elect to work merely because welfare is even less viable, though the effect will likely be small. Time limits might have a larger effect on family well-being, since mothers will not be able to withdraw from the low-wage labor market to get more schooling or attend to their children's needs. Both of these changes mean that single mothers' children will receive less supervision, spend more time home alone, and become even more vulnerable to the harmful influences of inner-city neighborhoods than is now the case. They will also suffer more material hardship.

It is not unreasonable, therefore, to predict that these children might suffer even higher delinquency, dropout, pregnancy, and incarceration rates than they currently do.[3] These problems, which may not become fully evident for a generation, will certainly prove far more costly in the long run than the "welfare problem" Americans have complained so bitterly about during the 1980s and early 1990s. For those states that choose to invest substantial sums in education and training, child care subsidies, and health care plans for single mothers who work, the future could be much brighter.

# —— Appendix A ——

# Interview Topics

ALL OF OUR interviews were as informal and unstructured as we could make possible. Thus, the questions below were never asked in the precise manner, or in the same order, as we have arranged them here. We did, however, collect data from each respondent in each of these areas. After coding the first interview, we made a list of questions that had not been covered. We asked these questions in subsequent interviews.

LEAD-IN

What is it like living in this neighborhood?

    What do you like best/least? Example?

    What are your neighbors like?

        Mostly on welfare?

        Mostly working?

    Are most of your friends and relatives nearby? Do they live in other neighborhoods?

        Mostly on welfare?

        Mostly working?

What is it like being a single mother?

    What are the advantages/disadvantages?

    How many children do you have?

        At home?

In school?

Which school does each of your children attend?

What do you have to spend for school supplies for your kids?

$ books?

$ paper, pencils, crayons, backpacks or book bags, other supplies?

$ special clothing (uniforms/gym clothes)?

$ field trips/activities/sports/PTA?

$ after-school activities/after-school care?

## FOOD

It's hard to feed a family these days. How do you manage?

School breakfast/lunch program?

Use now/ever?

Biggest problem?

Biggest advantage?

Last incident?

Food Stamps/WIC?

Use now/ever?

Biggest problem?

Biggest advantage?

Last incident?

Government surplus?

Use now/ever?

Biggest problem?

Biggest advantage?

Last incident?

Food pantries?

   Use now/ever?

   Biggest problem?

   Biggest advantage?

   Last incident?

Food sharing?

   Use now/ever?

   Biggest problem?

   Biggest advantage?

   Last incident?

Shopping strategies?

   Use now/ever?

   Biggest problem?

   Biggest advantage?

   Last incident?

   $ food for holidays and special occasions?

   $ treats for kids (eating out, etc.)

   $ cash spent for food that food stamps do not cover?

## NONFOOD GROCERY STORE ITEMS

What else do you buy at the grocery store other than food?

  Expenditures for bathroom products?

    $ toothpaste/mouthwash?

    $ shaving lotion/razors?

    $ soap/shampoo/conditioner?

    $ hairspray/cosmetics?

    $ deodorant/tub and bowl cleaner?

    $ toilet paper/Q-tips/band-aids?

Expenditures for kitchen products?

  $ dish soap/cleanser/disinfectant?

  $ floor cleaner/oven cleaner?

  $ other?

Baby care

  $ soap/bleach/machines?

  $ dry cleaning?

MEDICAL CARE

During the time you've been a single parent, have you had medical care? (Medicaid?)

  Biggest problem/advantage?

    $ debts and monthly payment toward debt?

    $ cash payments?

    $ over-the-counter (aspirin, cough medicine)?

  How did you pay for the birth(s) of each of your children?

  Describe the last time you or one of your children got sick enough to require care.

  What clinic or hospital did you use?

  What doctor did you use?

  When was the last time you or any of your children saw a dentist?

    Biggest problem/advantage?

    $ debts and monthly payments toward dental debt?

    $ cash payments for dentist?

  When was the last time you or any of your children saw an eye doctor?

    Biggest problem/disadvantage?

$ debts and monthly payments toward debt?

$ cash payments (eyeglasses, contact lenses, and over-the-counter products?)

Do you have any other source of medical care that I haven't mentioned (herbal healers, chiropractors, therapists, etc.)?

Biggest problem/advantage?

$ debts and monthly payments toward debt?

$ cash payments?

HOUSING

How long have you lived here?

What do you think about living here?

Biggest problem/advantage?

$ rent and utility costs?

Incidents?

When did you move here? What circumstances led you to move here?

FOR PUBLIC HOUSING

What do you think it would cost you to move to private housing?

Have you ever thought about moving to private housing?

What are the advantages/disadvantages of private housing?

Did you ever live in public housing when you were growing up? What was it like?

FOR PRIVATE HOUSING

What do you think it would cost you to move to public housing?

Have you thought about moving to public housing?

What are the advantages/disadvantages of public housing?

Did you ever live in public housing when you were growing up? What was it like?

CHILD CARE

If you have to go out, do you have someone who can watch the kids?

$ family/friends?

$ after-school care?

$ day care?

$ summer camp or recreation?

If you have to work and leave the house for several hours a day, could you arrange for child care?

$ how much do you think that would cost?

INCOME

When was your last job?

Type of job?

Advantages/problems?

$ how much did you make?

$ hourly/biweekly/yearly wage?

Number of hours worked per week?

Number of overtime hours worked per week?

$ hourly overtime pay?

Length of time on job?

$ starting pay?

$ last raise?

Did your employer provide some benefits? Specify.

$ did you pay for some benefits? specify.

$ how much would it have cost to have yourself or your family covered through your job?

IF NOT CURRENTLY WORKING

Could you get this job again?

Why did you leave this job?

Are you looking for a job now?

What kind of job are you looking for?

$ (Probe for what respondent expects to get in pay, hours, benefits, chances for promotion, types of work)

Do you know of a job that you could get but have decided not to take?

$ (Probe for reasons including pay, hours, benefits, chances for promotions, type of work)

If you did take a job, what kind of job would you take?

$ (Probe for expectations of pay, hours, benefits, chances for promotions, type of work)

IF CURRENTLY WORKING

Type of job?

Advantages/problems?

$ how much do you make? how much do you take home?

$ hourly/biweekly/yearly wage?

Number of hours worked per week?

Number of overtime hours worked per week?

$ hourly overtime pay?

Length of time on job?

$ starting pay?

$ last raise?

When do you expect next raise?

Does your employer provide some benefits? Specify.

$ do you pay for some benefits? specify.

$ how much would it cost to have yourself or your family covered through your job?

How do you feel about your current job?

Are you satisfied with this job, or would you like to switch jobs?

What kind of job would you ideally like to have?

How does your job compare with your friends' jobs?

Do you think your job matches your skills and experience?

What other kinds of jobs do you think you could get with your present education, skills, and experience?

Do you have a second job?

(REPEAT ABOVE QUESTIONS FOR EACH JOB.)

What other jobs have you had? (ASK FOR EACH.)

Type of job?

Advantages/problems?

$ how much did you make?

Could you get this job again?

Why did you leave this job?

Over the time you have been a single parent, have you ever received welfare?

| Yes | No |
| --- | --- |
| Advantages/problems? | Ever think about it? |
| Incident | Have any of these things |
| Have you been on steadily, | happened to you in the past |
| or on and off? | five years? How did you |
| | manage? |
| | |
| Why on each time? | You or your kids sick? |
| Why off each time? | Kids truant? |
| | New baby? |
| $ amount of grant? | transport problems? |
| $ amount of emergency | hassles at work? |
| assistance last year? | Cut in hours? |

Were you ever on welfare growing up?

IF WORKING NOW
Do you think you are better off working than on welfare (Probe in detail for perceptions of FINANCIAL and EMOTIONAL well-being.)

Do you think you are better off working than on welfare? (Probe in detail for perceptions of FINANCIAL and EMOTIONAL well-being.)

Do you receive welfare currently?

$ amount of grant?

For most people, it's hard to make ends meet. What do people in your neighborhood do? Have you ever tried to do something like that?

Informal jobs?

$ bartending for cash/cleaning/lawnmowing mechanic/babysitting

$ other cash work?

$ bottle collection/give blood/newspaper sales?

Child support?

   $ paid directly to you?

   $ pass-through/court ordered payment?

   Are you supposed to receive child support? (Has paternity been legally established?)

   Have you tried taking the father(s) to court to get child
   support? Has the state helped you to try to collect child
   support?

   Do you expect to receive child support in the near future?

Sales?

   $ door-to-door legal goods (Avon, Tupperware, Mary
   Kay)?

   $ illegal sales of legal goods (informal stores)?

   $ sale of sex, drugs, and/or stolen goods?

Contributions?

   $ Family and friends?

   $ Boyfriend/absent father?

   $ Did you get an earned income tax credit last year?

Other?

   Did you get money back from the IRS last year? (Probe
   for whether respondent filed a tax return.)

   Do you have any savings?

      In checking or savings account?

      IRAs, CDs, stocks, bonds, or other assets?

      Did you receive cash from a legal settlement last year?

   $ Do you ever get financial help from a church or com-
   munity organization?

   $ Do you receive any kind of energy assistance?

   $ Do you receive any child care subsidy?

OTHER EXPENSES

No list really covers all your expenses. Let me ask you about how much other items cost.

Transportation?

Own car?

$ car payment?

$ car insurance?

$ city sticker?

$ licensing?

$ taxes?

$ repairs?

$ gasoline?

$ tune up/oil change/other servicing?

$ tolls?

$ taxis (neighborhood or official)?

$ public transportation?

$ pay someone to use their car?

$ phone?

$ gifts?

$ life/health/burial/renter's insurance?

$ entertainment?

$ movies?

$ amusement parks/special outings?

$ trips?

$ videos?

$ cable?

$ bingo?

$ lottery?

$ dog races?

$ numbers?

$ tobacco products?

$ alcohol?

$ illegal substances?

$ layaway payments?

$ credit card payments?

$ jewelry?

$ other?

## MATERIAL HARDSHIP

Has there ever been a time when you needed food, but could not afford to buy it? When was the last time that happened to you?

Have you gone hungry because you could not afford to buy food? When was the last time that happened to you?

Has there been a time when you could not afford a place to stay or when you could not pay your rent? When was the last time that happened to you?

Have you been evicted from your home for not being able to pay your rent? When was the last time that happened to you?

Has your electricity or heat been turned off because you could not afford to pay the bill? When was the last time that happened to you?

Has your phone been disconnected, or have you gone without a phone, because you could not afford to pay the bill? When was the last time that happened to you?

I'm going to name some problems with housing that sometimes cause people difficulty. Do any of these things apply to your situation?

A leaky roof or ceiling?

A toilet, hot-water heater, or other plumbing that does not work right?

Rats, mice, roaches, or other insects?

Broken windows?

Heating system that does not work properly?

Exposed wires or other electrical problems?

A stove or refrigerator that does not work properly?

Inadequate garbage pickup?

Was there any time last year that you needed to see a doctor or dentist, but could not afford to go? When was the last time that happened to you?

Did you or your children ever go without proper winter clothing because you could not afford it? When was the last time that happened to you?


CLOTHING AND COSMETICS

How do you manage to buy all the clothes your kids need each year?

$ cost of clothes you buy at the store (winter coats and boots and shoes)?

$ thrift store, Salvation Army/free clothes? hand-me-downs?

Costs related to appearance?

$ haircuts/getting hair "done" at shop?


CONCLUSION

How would you sum up your experiences? Your situation?

How do you think things will look six months from now? A year? Five years? Ten years?

If you had to give advice to a young woman like yourself, one that was still in school and had no children yet, what would you tell her?

If the president were to ask you what the government could do to assist single mothers, what advice would you give him?

# — Appendix B —

# Regression Results

THE TABLES IN this appendix summarize the findings discussed in chapter 7. We employed a multistep model for each of the dependent variables, moving from those variables that are exogenous to those that are more endogenous. We only present those steps in which the coefficients changed significantly, however. If, for example, the coefficient on the dummy variable "African American" changed between step 1 and step 2, but there were no substantial changes in any of the coefficients between steps 2 and 4, we present step 1 followed by step 5 (but labeled "step 1" and "step 2"). If there were no appreciable changes in any of the coefficients in any of the steps, we present only the last step.

The variable labeled "background" refers to the respondent's family background. Respondents who grew up in welfare-reliant households received a score of 1, whereas those who did not scored 0. The same is true of the dummy variables "African American" and "Mexican American," the site dummies, "ever married," "rent subsidy," "current welfare," and "poor area."

"Age" refers to the mother's age at the time of the interview. "Family size" refers to the mother and her children, excluding other relatives or household members. We did separate runs (not shown) using dummies for families of different sizes. These equations did not yield significantly different results than those presented here. Because variation in expenditures, income, and hardship might matter more at the bottom of the scale, we did yet another set of runs (not shown) using the natural log of each of these variables. These did not result in a better fit.

Because relatively small sample sizes frequently yield false negatives, we note all those variables with a $p$ value of less than

.10, but distinguish between these variables and those variables with a *p* value of less than .05 or .01.

Tables 1–14 use roughly the same variables. Table 15 includes one additional variable: the amount of total network-based support available in the average month. We added this variable because our qualitative analysis, presented in chapter 6, suggested that networks might be important buffers against hardship. Another unique feature of table 15 is that we took into account the possibility that "poor areas" are endogenous, that they depend on income. Therefore, we controlled for income when estimating those effects. Table 15 shows, however, that this was not the case. Finally, in looking at material hardship we also assessed potential interaction effects between income and personal characteristics that might affect budgetary efficiency (that is, poor African Americans seem to budget more efficiently than poor whites do). Because these interactive effects seemed to have little effect on the results, we do not present this analysis.

### TABLE B-1. OLS Regression of Effects of Group Differences on Total Monthly Expenses

| Variable | Coefficient |
| --- | --- |
| Background | −7.27 |
| African American | −72.30** |
| Mexican American | −155.92*** |
| Charleston | −37.43 |
| Boston | 57.38 |
| San Antonio | −226.90*** |
| Age | 7.72*** |
| Ever married | 28.80 |
| Family size | 93.76*** |
| Any welfare | −324.23*** |
| Poor area | −76.12* |
| Rent subsidy | −67.46* |
| (Constant) | 833.36*** |
| | |
| N | 379 |
| $R^2$ | .49 |
| $R^2$ adjusted | .48 |

*Source:* Authors' calculations using Edin and Lein survival strategies data.
*Note:* Significance levels given by * $= p > .10$; ** $= p > .05$; *** $= p > .01$.

**TABLE B-2. OLS Regression of Effects of Group Differences on Total Expenditures Minus Housing Costs**

| Variable | Step 1 | Step 2 |
|---|---|---|
| Background | −55.94* | −19.62 |
| African American | −30.58 | −45.33* |
| Mexican American | −93.84* | −124.41** |
| Charleston | −13.60 | −29.60 |
| Boston | 28.72 | 5.37 |
| San Antonio | −127.48*** | −124.14*** |
| Age | 4.24** | 1.15 |
| Ever married | 23.94 | 18.17 |
| Family size | 59.20*** | 70.23*** |
| Any welfare | | −255.95*** |
| Poor area | | −32.86 |
| Rent subsidy | | 70.73** |
| (Constant) | 510.93*** | 704.27*** |
| N | 379 | 379 |
| $R^2$ | .16 | .35 |
| $R^2$ adjusted | .14 | .33 |

*Source:* Authors' calculations using Edin and Lein survival strategies data.
*Note:* Significance levels given by * = $p >$ .10; ** = $p >$ .05; *** = $p >$ .01.

TABLE B-3. **OLS Regression of Effects of Group Differences on Monthly Expenses for Nonhousing Necessities**

| Variable | Step 1 | Step 2 |
|---|---|---|
| Background | −61.78** | −26.45 |
| African American | −6.04 | −17.01 |
| Mexican American | −85.19* | −111.28** |
| Charleston | 26.45 | 12.52 |
| Boston | 28.01 | 13.44 |
| San Antonio | −90.63** | −85.07*** |
| Age | 2.71 | −.09 |
| Ever married | 23.90 | 18.87 |
| Family size | 8.98 | 20.58** |
| Any welfare | | −232.69*** |
| Poor area | | −30.22 |
| Rent subsidy | | 46.05* |
| (Constant) | 352.72*** | 527.40*** |
| N | 379 | 379 |
| $R^2$ | .11 | .32 |
| $R^2$ adjusted | .09 | .30 |

*Source:* Authors' calculations using Edin and Lein survival strategies data.
*Note:* Significance levels given by * = $p > .10$; ** = $p > .05$; *** = $p > .01$.

## TABLE B-4. OLS Regression of Effects of Group Differences on Monthly Expenses for Nonnecessary Items

| Variable | Step 1 | Step 2 | Step 3 |
|---|---|---|---|
| Background | 6.75 | 5.01 | 6.81 |
| African American | −3.25 | −6.86 | −8.96 |
| Mexican American | −31.35** | −25.56* | −30.36** |
| Charleston | −7.94 | −7.15 | −8.31 |
| Boston | 31.57*** | 30.71*** | 26.26*** |
| San Antonio | 2.32 | 3.53 | 2.25 |
| Age | −.15 | .22 | −.15 |
| Ever married | | −15.72** | −15.34** |
| Family size | | −4.89* | −4.73 |
| Any welfare | | | −25.75*** |
| Poor area | | | 10.68 |
| Rent subsidy | | | 4.81 |
| (Constant) | 74.51*** | 88.07*** | 111.14*** |
| N | 379 | 379 | 379 |
| R² | .07 | .09 | .13 |
| R² adjusted | .06 | .07 | .10 |

*Source:* Authors' calculations using Edin and Lein survival strategies data.
*Note:* Significance levels given by * = $p > .10$; ** = $p > .05$; *** = $p > .01$.

**TABLE B-5. OLS Regression of Effects of Group Differences on All Monthly Earnings from Supplemental Work**

| Variable | Step 1 | Step 2 |
|---|---|---|
| Background | 31.26 | 29.90 |
| African American | −10.99 | −20.42 |
| Mexican American | −86.54** | −96.43** |
| Charleston | −19.42 | −10.45 |
| Boston | −24.90 | −23.23 |
| San Antonio | −17.24 | −33.59 |
| Age | 1.57 | 1.91 |
| Ever married | 4.26 | 10.31 |
| Family size | −.96 | .29 |
| Any welfare | 45.93** | 33.38 |
| Poor area | −46.62 | −59.88** |
| Rent subsidy | 10.14 | 3.08 |
| Network | | −.21*** |
| Agency | | −.16* |
| (Constant) | 61.68 | 111.95** |
| | | |
| N | 379 | 379 |
| $R^2$ | .05 | .10 |
| $R^2$ adjusted | .02 | .07 |

*Source:* Authors' calculations using Edin and Lein survival strategies data.
*Note:* Significance levels given by * = $p > .10$; ** = $p > .05$; *** = $p > .01$.

## TABLE B-6. OLS Regression of Effects of Group Differences on All Monthly Earnings from Reported Supplemental Work

| Variable | Step 1 | Step 2 |
|---|---|---|
| Background | 2.66 | 3.06 |
| African American | −3.95 | −5.18 |
| Mexican American | −42.33** | −44.75** |
| Charleston | 11.22 | 11.10 |
| Boston | 32.05** | 30.47** |
| San Antonio | 29.63* | 26.09* |
| Age | .07 | .15 |
| Ever married | 12.35 | 13.25 |
| Family size | 1.62 | 1.88 |
| Any welfare | −6.36 | −5.25 |
| Poor area | −9.83 | −13.04 |
| Rent subsidy | −2.15 | −3.46 |
| Network | | −.04 |
| Agency | | −.02 |
| Informal job | | −.04 |
| Illegal job | | −.03 |
| (Constant) | 2.49 | 11.84 |
| N | 379 | 379 |
| $R^2$ | .031 | .038 |
| $R^2$ adjusted | −.001 | −.004 |

*Source:* Authors' calculations using Edin and Lein survival strategies data.
*Note:* Significance levels given by * = $p > .10$; ** = $p > .05$; *** = $p > .01$.

**TABLE B-7. OLS Regression of Effects of Group Differences on Monthly Earnings from Unreported Work**

| Variable | Step 1 | Step 2 |
|---|---|---|
| Background | −1.20 | −.55 |
| African American | −7.34 | −10.56 |
| Mexican American | −24.21 | −31.00 |
| Charleston | −26.90 | −23.14 |
| Boston | −43.36** | −40.65** |
| San Antonio | −1.66 | −7.30 |
| Age | 1.47 | 1.55 |
| Ever married | −6.66 | −2.96 |
| Family size | −2.55 | −1.72 |
| Any welfare | 72.59*** | 67.37*** |
| Poor area | −36.24* | −41.57** |
| Rent subsidy | 12.24 | 8.06 |
| Network | | −.09*** |
| Agency | | −.05 |
| Illegal job | | −.05 |
| Side-job | | −.07 |
| (Constant) | 11.26 | 33.32 |
| N | 379 | 379 |
| $R^2$ | .09 | .11 |
| $R^2$ adjusted | .06 | .07 |

*Source:* Authors' calculations using Edin and Lein survival strategies data.
*Note:* Significance levels given by * $= p > .10$; ** $= p > .05$; *** $= p > .01$.

TABLE B-8. **OLS Regression of Effects of Group Differences on Monthly Earnings from Underground Work**

| Variable | Step 1 | Step 2 |
|---|---|---|
| Background | 16.92* | 17.15* |
| African American | 16.23* | 15.04 |
| Mexican American | 5.03 | 2.40 |
| Charleston | −17.23 | −16.11 |
| Boston | −4.05 | −3.93 |
| San Antonio | −23.36* | −24.86** |
| Age | −.46 | −.46 |
| Ever married | 1.66 | 3.05 |
| Family size | 4.71 | 4.87 |
| Any welfare | 12.44 | 11.52 |
| Poor area | 5.25 | 3.49 |
| Rent subsidy | −11.55 | −13.24 |
| Network | | −.03 |
| Agency | | −.00 |
| Informal job | | −.02 |
| Side-job | | −.02 |
| (Constant) | 6.79 | 15.21 |
| N | 379 | 379 |
| R² | .062 | .068 |
| R² adjusted | .031 | .027 |

*Source:* Authors' calculations using Edin and Lein survival strategies data.
*Note:* Significance levels given by * − $p > .10$; ** − $p > .05$; *** − $p > .01$.

**TABLE B-9. OLS Regression of Effects of Group Differences on Monthly Cash Contributions from All Network-Based Sources**

| Variable | Step 1 | Step 2 |
|---|---|---|
| Background | 7.40 | 12.76 |
| African American | −33.48 | −37.83 |
| Mexican American | −45.17 | −66.08 |
| Charleston | 46.14 | 41.04 |
| Boston | 4.69 | −.74 |
| San Antonio | −73.25** | −78.09** |
| Age | −.90 | −.15 |
| Ever married | 43.72* | 42.54* |
| Family size | 5.64 | 5.46 |
| Any welfare | −69.28*** | −56.98** |
| Poor area | −31.14 | −47.05 |
| Rent subsidy | −66.03** | −58.82** |
| Side-job | | −.24*** |
| Agency | | −.11 |
| (Constant) | 286.31*** | 294.16*** |
| | | |
| N | 379 | 379 |
| R² | .16 | .20 |
| R² adjusted | .13 | .17 |

*Source:* Authors' calculations using Edin and Lein survival strategies data.
*Note:* Significance levels given by * = $p > .10$; ** = $p > .05$; *** = $p > .01$.

TABLE B-10. **Stepwise Regression of Effects of Group Differences on Monthly Cash Contributions from Family and Friends**

| Variable | Step 1 | Step 2 | Step 3 | Step 4 |
|---|---|---|---|---|
| Background | −6.59 | −2.00 | 3.32 | 7.00 |
| African American | −34.63*** | −23.36* | −18.64 | −21.42 |
| Mexican American | −50.75** | −52.50** | −45.15* | −52.60** |
| Charleston | 2.17 | −1.28 | −1.04 | 3.19 |
| Boston | −23.49 | −22.97 | −9.83 | −9.89 |
| San Antonio | −16.61 | −16.92 | −10.42 | −18.36 |
| Age | .67 | −.02 | .27 | .20 |
| Ever married | | 36.01*** | 34.12** | 36.51*** |
| Family size | | −4.40 | −.90 | −.26 |
| Any welfare | | | 11.39 | 5.30 |
| Poor area | | | −33.00* | −36.17** |
| Rent subsidy | | | −16.70 | −21.96 |
| Side-job | | | | −.08*** |
| Boyfriend | | | | −.10** |
| Child's father | | | | −.12*** |
| Agency | | | | .03 |
| (Constant) | 73.69** | 82.90*** | 64.31* | 95.44*** |
| N | 379 | 379 | 379 | 379 |
| $R^2$ | .05 | .07 | .09 | .13 |
| $R^2$ adjusted | .03 | .04 | .06 | .10 |

*Source:* Authors' calculations using Edin and Lein survival strategies data.
*Note:* Significance levels given by * = $p > .10$; ** = $p > .05$; *** = $p > .01$.

**TABLE B-11. OLS Regression of Effects of Group Differences on Monthly Cash Contributions from Boyfriends**

| Variable | Step 1 | Step 2 | Step 3 | Step 4 |
|---|---|---|---|---|
| Background | −13.84 | −17.93 | −16.20 | −12.52 |
| African American | 28.80** | 18.98 | 22.43 | 15.38 |
| Mexican American | 18.36 | 21.43 | 22.08 | 6.35 |
| Charleston | −10.15 | −7.23 | −5.55 | −4.03 |
| Boston | −27.61 | −28.27 | −19.29 | −20.21 |
| San Antonio | −58.01*** | −57.41*** | −55.06*** | −58.99*** |
| Age | −.82 | −.17 | −.23 | .10 |
| Ever married | | −32.64** | −30.96** | −24.57* |
| Family size | | 1.98 | 3.53 | 3.57 |
| Any welfare | | | −.59 | .27 |
| Poor area | | | 17.97 | 5.49 |
| Rent subsidy | | | −35.37** | −34.82** |
| Side-job | | | | −.10*** |
| Family/friends | | | | −.13** |
| Child's father | | | | −.07* |
| Agency | | | | −.06 |
| (Constant) | 96.21*** | 93.06*** | 96.41*** | 115.58*** |
| N | 379 | 379 | 379 | 379 |
| R² | .04 | .06 | .07 | .10 |
| R² adjusted | .02 | .03 | .04 | .06 |

*Source:* Authors' calculations using Edin and Lein survival strategies data.
*Note:* Significance levels given by * = $p > .10$; ** = $p > .05$; *** = $p > .01$.

TABLE B-12. **OLS Regression of Effects of Group Differences on Monthly Cash Contributions from Children's Father(s)**

| Variable | Step 1 | Step 2 |
| --- | --- | --- |
| Background | 20.29 | 21.39 |
| African American | −37.27** | −41.56** |
| Mexican American | −22.09 | −39.97 |
| Charleston | 52.73** | 49.29** |
| Boston | 33.813 | 27.09 |
| San Antonio | −7.71 | −18.38 |
| Age | −.93 | −.43 |
| Ever married | 40.56** | 43.57** |
| Family size | 3.01 | 3.11 |
| Any welfare | −80.08*** | −71.25*** |
| Poor area | −16.07 | −30.46 |
| Rent subsidy | −13.97 | −16.53 |
| Side-job | | −.12*** |
| Family/friends | | −.22*** |
| Boyfriend | | −.11* |
| Agency | | −.08 |
| (Constant) | 125.59*** | 151.84*** |
| N | 379 | 379 |
| $R^2$ | .14 | .18 |
| $R^2$ adjusted | .11 | .16 |

*Source:* Authors' calculations using Edin and Lein survival strategies data.
*Note.* Significance levels given by * = $p > .10$; ** = $p > .05$; *** = $p > .01$.

**TABLE B-13. OLS Regression of Effects of Group Differences on Covert Child Support Payments (Welfare-Reliant Mothers Only)**

| Variable | Step 1 | Step 2 |
|---|---|---|
| Background | 30.47** | 29.56** |
| African American | 7.84 | 4.50 |
| Mexican American | −7.09 | −22.35 |
| Charleston | 22.04 | 20.36 |
| Boston | −16.71 | −23.72 |
| San Antonio | −12.36 | −17.15 |
| Age | −.22 | .23 |
| Ever married | 12.36 | 12.58 |
| Family size | −5.56 | −7.11 |
| Poor area | .75 | −9.15 |
| Rent subsidy | −16.73 | −18.02 |
| Side-job | | −.10*** |
| Family/friends | | −.14*** |
| Boyfriend | | −.05 |
| Formal | | .41 |
| Agency | | −.06 |
| (Constant) | 48.78 | 72.90** |
| | | |
| N | 214 | 214 |
| $R^2$ | .08 | .16 |
| $R^2$ adjusted | .03 | .09 |

*Source:* Authors' calculations using Edin and Lein survival strategies data.
*Note:* Significance levels given by * = $p > .10$; ** = $p > .05$; *** = $p > .01$.

**TABLE B-14. OLS Regression of Effects of Group Differences on Monthly Cash Contributions from Agencies**

| Variable | Step 1 | Step 2 |
|---|---|---|
| Background | −18.47 | −16.22 |
| African American | −15.42 | −17.42 |
| Mexican American | −2.95 | −10.17 |
| Charleston | −4.30 | −3.70 |
| Boston | 4.40 | 3.02 |
| San Antonio | −6.56 | −10.52 |
| Age | 3.38*** | 3.44*** |
| Ever married | −19.58 | −17.59 |
| Family size | .41 | .57 |
| Any welfare | 12.19 | 12.35 |
| Poor area | −42.82** | −46.97** |
| Rent subsidy | 42.71*** | 40.75** |
| Side-job | | −.06* |
| Network | | −.04 |
| (Constant) | −60.65* | −45.51 |
| N | 379 | 379 |
| $R^2$ | .07 | .08 |
| $R^2$ adjusted | .04 | .05 |

*Source:* Authors' calculations using Edin and Lein survival strategies data.
*Note:* Significance levels given by * $= p > .10$; ** $= p > .05$; *** $= p > .01$.

**TABLE B-15. Stepwise Regression of Effects of Group Differences on Material Hardship (Weighted Core Hardship Scale)**

| Variable | Step 1 | Step 2 | Step 3 | Step 4 | Step 5 |
|---|---|---|---|---|---|
| Background | .16 | .15 | .19** | .19* | .20** |
| African American | -.23*** | -.26*** | -.27*** | -.33*** | -.33*** |
| Mexican American | -.04 | -.14 | -.16 | -.25 | -.23 |
| Charleston | .08 | .09 | .08 | .09 | .07 |
| San Antonio | .32** | .29** | .30** | .19 | .19 |
| Chicago | -.25** | -.26** | -.26** | -.27** | -.28** |
| Age | .02*** | .02*** | .01** | .02*** | .02*** |
| Ever married | | -.01 | -.01 | .02 | .01 |
| Family size | | .13*** | .14*** | .17*** | .18*** |
| Any welfare | | | -.22*** | -.41*** | -.41*** |
| Rent subsidy | | | | .04 | .12 |
| Network support[a] | | | | -.04*** | -.04*** |
| Total expenditures[b] | | | | -.06*** | -.06*** |
| Poor area | | | | | -.20* |
| (Constant) | .23 | -.09 | .07 | .50*** | .48* |
| | | | | | |
| | N = 379 | N = 379 | N = 379 | N = 379 | N = 379 |
| $R^2$ | .11 | .14 | .15 | .19 | .20 |
| $R^2$ adjusted | .09 | .12 | .13 | .16 | .17 |

*Source:* Authors' calculations using Edin and Lein survival strategies data.
*Note:* Significance levels given by $*$ = $p > .10$; $**$ = $p > .05$; $***$ = $p > .01$.
[a] Total monthly network-based support * 100.
[b] Total monthly expenditures * 100.

## TABLE B-16. Means and Standard Deviations for Selected Variables

| Variable | Mean | Standard Deviation | N |
|---|---|---|---|
| Total expenses | 1035.67 | 365.46 | 379 |
| Total minus housing | 767.06 | 272.25 | 379 |
| Non-housing necessities | 694.39 | 259.31 | 379 |
| Non-necessities | 72.68 | 65.38 | 379 |
| Work-based strategies | 110.49 | 192.62 | 379 |
| Reported work | 22.39 | 95.52 | 379 |
| Unreported work | 61.39 | 133.13 | 379 |
| Underground work | 11.75 | 78.21 | 379 |
| Network based strategies | 198.80 | 218.31 | 379 |
| Family | 63.50 | 115.32 | 379 |
| Boyfriends | 57.62 | 125.65 | 379 |
| Absent fathers | 77.68 | 160.20 | 379 |
| Covert support | 32.85 | 85.41 | 214 |
| Formal support | 6.62 | 16.51 | 214 |
| Agency-based strategies | 36.36 | 120.44 | 379 |
| Weighted core hardship scale | .75 | .82 | 379 |
| Background | .27 | .44 | 379 |
| White | .46 | .50 | 379 |
| African American | .45 | .50 | 379 |
| Mexican American | .09 | .29 | 379 |
| San Antonio | .27 | .45 | 379 |
| Charleston | .24 | .43 | 379 |
| Chicago | .28 | .45 | 379 |
| Boston | .21 | .41 | 379 |
| Mother's age | 31.01 | 7.88 | 379 |
| Ever married | .56 | .51 | 379 |
| Family size | 3.05 | 1.18 | 379 |
| Rent subsidy | .45 | .50 | 379 |
| Poor area | .23 | .42 | 379 |
| Any welfare | .56 | .50 | 379 |

*Source:* Authors' calculations using Edin and Lein survival strategies data.

**TABLE B-17. Correlation Coefficients for Selected Variables**

| | Total Expenses | Total $ Minus Housing | Necessities | Non-Necessities | Work-Based | Reported Work | Unreported Work | Underground Work | Network-Based | Family | Boyfriend |
|---|---|---|---|---|---|---|---|---|---|---|---|
| Total $ minus housing | .8569 | | | | | | | | | | |
| Necessities | .8430 | .9709 | | | | | | | | | |
| Non-necessities | .2247 | .3132 | .0767 | | | | | | | | |
| Work-based | .2361 | .1840 | .1499 | .1719 | | | | | | | |
| Reported work | .1554 | .0938 | .0778 | .0819 | .4313 | | | | | | |
| Unreported work | .0616 | .0406 | .0185 | .0955 | .5871 | -.0531 | | | | | |
| Underground work | .1202 | .1430 | .1277 | .0890 | .3798 | -.0353 | .0026 | | | | |
| Network-based | .5637 | .4589 | .4694 | .0490 | -.1823 | -.0345 | -.1550 | -.0855 | | | |
| Family | .2503 | .1497 | .1510 | .0245 | -.0676 | -.0301 | -.0601 | -.0442 | .4307 | | |
| Boyfriends | .2087 | .1581 | .1442 | .0864 | -.1057 | -.0233 | -.0617 | -.0546 | .4899 | -.0870 | |
| Absent fathers | .4243 | .3936 | .4179 | -.0186 | -.1168 | -.0071 | -.1196 | -.0418 | .6685 | -.0647 | -.0542 |
| Covert support | .0600 | .0079 | .0114 | -.0094 | -.1472 | -.0471 | -.1557 | -.0055 | .4295 | -.1070 | .0049 |
| Formal support | .0297 | .0945 | .1239 | -.0717 | -.0883 | -.0321 | -.0856 | -.0124 | .1056 | -.0340 | -.0010 |
| Agency-based | .2205 | .2064 | .2069 | .0388 | -.0655 | -.0126 | -.0154 | -.0219 | -.0401 | .0560 | -.0575 |
| Core hardship scale | -.0400 | -.0481 | -.0443 | -.0246 | -.0565 | .0068 | -.0454 | -.0719 | -.1434 | .0067 | -.1324 |
| Background | -.1436 | -.1091 | -.1333 | .0744 | .0564 | -.0335 | .0074 | .1618 | -.0811 | -.0736 | .0029 |
| White | .1846 | .1123 | .1030 | .0592 | .0610 | .0685 | .0262 | -.1038 | .1739 | .1730 | -.0739 |
| African American | -.0755 | -.0341 | -.0417 | .0232 | .0177 | -.0263 | -.0063 | .1284 | -.1008 | -.1131 | .1178 |
| Mexican American | -.1903 | -.1364 | -.1070 | -.1437 | -.1373 | -.0737 | -.0348 | -.0425 | -.1276 | -.1048 | -.0763 |
| San Antonio | -.3442 | -.2238 | -.2104 | -.0977 | -.0937 | .0120 | .0275 | -.0853 | -.2161 | -.0910 | -.1462 |
| Charleston | .1260 | .0689 | .0973 | -.0992 | .0111 | .0025 | -.0368 | -.0727 | .1996 | .0855 | .0574 |
| Chicago | .1111 | .0660 | .0744 | -.0203 | .0890 | -.0909 | -.0980 | .1188 | .0388 | .0526 | .1160 |
| Boston | .1232 | .1007 | .0467 | .2340 | -.0068 | .0844 | -.0996 | .0392 | -.0153 | -.0479 | -.0275 |
| Mother's age | .3378 | .1996 | .2178 | -.0327 | .0237 | .0248 | .0034 | -.0748 | .0726 | .0642 | -.0211 |
| Ever married | .1828 | .1274 | .1712 | -.1487 | -.0027 | .0635 | -.0144 | -.0775 | .1348 | .1702 | -.1414 |
| Family size | .1481 | .2104 | .2533 | -.1285 | -.0329 | -.0070 | -.0055 | .0663 | -.0706 | -.0602 | -.0098 |
| Rent Subsidy | -.1959 | .0334 | .0200 | .0596 | -.0230 | -.0201 | .0015 | .0072 | -.2479 | -.1691 | -.1078 |
| Poor area | -.2057 | -.0406 | -.0585 | .0627 | -.0792 | -.0461 | -.0539 | .0454 | -.2349 | -.2044 | -.0332 |
| Any welfare | -.4990 | -.4374 | -.4206 | -.1534 | .1016 | -.0445 | .2431 | .1089 | -.2166 | -.0129 | -.0177 |

## TABLE B-17. Correlation Coefficients for Selected Variables (*continued*)

| | Absent Father | Covert Support | Formal Support | Agency-Based | Core Hardships | Background | White | Black | Latina | San Antonio | Charleston |
|---|---|---|---|---|---|---|---|---|---|---|---|
| Total $ minus housing | | | | | | | | | | | |
| Necessities | | | | | | | | | | | |
| Non-necessities | | | | | | | | | | | |
| Work-based | | | | | | | | | | | |
| Reported work | | | | | | | | | | | |
| Unreported work | | | | | | | | | | | |
| Underground work | | | | | | | | | | | |
| Network-based | | | | | | | | | | | |
| Family | | | | | | | | | | | |
| Boyfriends | | | | | | | | | | | |
| Absent fathers | .9824 | | | | | | | | | | |
| Covert support | .2550 | | | | | | | | | | |
| Formal support | -.0499 | .0698 | | | | | | | | | |
| Agency-based | -.0963 | -.0852 | -.0223 | | | | | | | | |
| Core hardship scale | -.0599 | -.1352 | .0688 | .0386 | | | | | | | |
| Background | .1704 | .1452 | -.1357 | -.0974 | -.0263 | | | | | | |
| White | -.1485 | -.0257 | .0036 | .0571 | .0827 | -.2128 | | | | | |
| African American | .0777 | .0777 | -.0743 | -.0422 | -.1605 | .2030 | -.8353 | | | | |
| Mexican American | -.0386 | -.0914 | .1239 | -.0262 | .1354 | .0177 | -.2892 | -.2846 | | | |
| San Antonio | -.1142 | -.1191 | .1449 | -.0544 | .1901 | -.1065 | -.1750 | -.1179 | .5105 | | |
| Charleston | .1655 | .1628 | .0763 | -.0034 | .0376 | -.1500 | .1019 | -.0007 | -.1765 | -.3457 | |
| Chicago | -.0759 | .0547 | -.0848 | .0464 | -.2166 | .1428 | -.0024 | .1140 | -.1943 | -.3807 | -.3480 |
| Boston | .0352 | -.0848 | -.1434 | .0464 | -.0097 | .1280 | .0877 | .0046 | -.1611 | -.3156 | -.2885 |
| Mother's age | .0693 | -.0891 | .0245 | .1968 | .1309 | -.2311 | .0303 | -.0296 | -.0014 | -.1327 | .1072 |
| Ever married | .1721 | -.0302 | .2065 | .0320 | .1197 | -.2537 | .2484 | -.3409 | .1605 | .0499 | .1051 |
| Family size | -.0452 | -.0005 | .2211 | .0026 | .2058 | .0146 | -.1386 | .0245 | .1990 | .1551 | -.0766 |
| Rent Subsidy | -.1315 | -.1105 | .0383 | .0815 | .0698 | .1552 | -.1650 | .1262 | .0679 | .0484 | -.1373 |
| Poor area | -.1469 | -.1235 | | -.0428 | .0263 | .1972 | -.1856 | .0981 | .1528 | .1336 | -.1948 |
| Any welfare | -.2720 | -.0989 | -.0043 | .0020 | -.1219 | .1849 | -.0240 | .0262 | -.0037 | .0510 | -.0920 |

**TABLE B-17. Correlation Coefficients for Selected Variables (*continued*)**

| | Chicago | Boston | Mother's Age | Ever Married | Family Size | Rent Subsidy | Poor Area |
|---|---|---|---|---|---|---|---|
| Total $ minus housing | | | | | | | |
| Necessities | | | | | | | |
| Non-necessities | | | | | | | |
| Work-based | | | | | | | |
| Reported work | | | | | | | |
| Unreported work | | | | | | | |
| Underground work | | | | | | | |
| Network-based | | | | | | | |
| Family | | | | | | | |
| Boyfriends | | | | | | | |
| Absent fathers | | | | | | | |
| Covert support | | | | | | | |
| Formal support | | | | | | | |
| Agency-based | | | | | | | |
| Core hardship scale | | | | | | | |
| Background | | | | | | | |
| White | | | | | | | |
| African American | | | | | | | |
| Mexican American | | | | | | | |
| San Antonio | | | | | | | |
| Charleston | | | | | | | |
| Chicago | | | | | | | |
| Boston | −.3177 | | | | | | |
| Mother's age | .0168 | .0145 | | | | | |
| Ever married | −.0849 | −.0719 | .3543 | | | | |
| Family size | −.0214 | −.0662 | .0471 | .1122 | | | |
| Rent Subsidy | −.1348 | .2396 | −.0148 | −.0372 | .2143 | | |
| Poor area | −.0926 | .1601 | .0020 | −.0892 | .2574 | .6110 | |
| Any welfare | .0323 | .0052 | −.2355 | −.1034 | .1191 | .2187 | .1977 |

Source: Author's calculations using Edin and Lein survival strategies data

# ——— Chapter Notes ———

## Foreword

1. For data on both cash income and the value of noncash benefits, see U.S. Bureau of the Census (1994f) table 1.
2. The CES income questions are similar to those that the Census Bureau uses in other surveys, but the CES does not impute values to those who fail to answer one of the income questions. Instead, it excludes those who fail to report their major source of income and sets other missing amounts to zero. Excluding respondents with missing data does not, however, greatly reduce the ratio of expenditure to income among those with very low reported incomes. For 1992 data, see U.S. Bureau of Labor Statistics (1993) table 2.
3. The national median in 1990 was $364 (U.S. House of Representatives 1994, p. 377).
4. Mayer and Jencks (1989) pp. 88–114.
5. The 1992 CPS found 26.6 percent of children living with one parent (23.3 percent with their mother and 3.3 percent with their father), and 70.7 percent living with two parents (a category that includes children who live with one natural and one stepparent). All the CPS estimates exclude children in institutions and count adopted children as living with their parents. The overall percentage of all children not living with either of their natural parents is therefore more than 2.6 percent. I am indebted to David Knutson for the CPS tabulations.
6. TANF penalizes states that cut their contribution to the support of single mothers below 75 percent of its 1996 level (in nominal dollars). States can, however, count all sorts of activities besides cash transfers to the poor in meeting this "maintenance of effort" requirement. In any event, inflation will make the requirement steadily weaker as time goes on.
7. The National Research Council's panel on poverty measurement recently recommended the exclusion of work-related expenses from allowable income (Citro and Michael 1995).

271

8.   The minimum wage will rise to $5.15 an hour in September 1997.
     If the Consumer Price Index (CPI) is an accurate measure of infla-
     tion, this should put its real value close to what it was after the
     last rise in 1991, and somewhat above its level from 1988 to 1990.
     Most economists think the CPI overstates inflation, but that does
     not necessarily mean that it overstates the increase in single moth-
     ers' need for cash. The fact that the CPI ignores qualitative
     improvements in medical care, for example, means that it over-
     states the cost of buying medical services of constant quality. But
     if a mother takes her child to the emergency room in 1997, buy-
     ing 1990 services at 1990 prices will not be a real option. She will
     have to pay for 1997 services at 1997 prices. If higher prices lead
     to more effective treatment, she will be better off, but her need for
     cash will still have risen.

9.   For a good review of public opinion on welfare, see Blendon et al.
     (1995) pp. 1065–1069.

10.  Mayer (1997).

11.  For a good summary of this literature, see Moffitt (1992) pp. 1–61.
     Charles Murray, who has staked his reputation on the idea that
     generous welfare benefits encourage unwed motherhood, also
     finds that little evidence that state-to-state differences in benefit lev-
     els have much effect (Murray 1993, pp. S224–S262). For a recent
     study suggesting much larger effects but making somewhat uncer-
     tain assumptions, see Rosenzweig (1995).

12.  In principle, one could also ask how the risk of poverty affects
     the fraction of children born out of wedlock. In practice, this is
     difficult for two reasons. First, while household surveys usually ask
     who lives in the household, they do not ask whether the children
     were born out of wedlock. This makes it harder to ascertain the
     economic effect of having had a baby out of wedlock in the past
     than to determine the effect of current living arrangements. Sec-
     ond, while the rate of out-of-wedlock childbearing is higher in
     Scandinavia than in other rich countries, its effect on living
     arrangements is also different. In the United States, unmarried cou-
     ples seldom live together for a protracted period after the birth of
     their child without marrying. In America, therefore, a woman who
     has a baby out of wedlock is quite likely to be the only adult with
     clear responsibility for its support. In Scandinavia, couples who
     have children out of wedlock often live together for many years,
     so the connection between marital status and living arrangements
     is weaker. For economic purposes, living arrangements are what
     matter.

13. Lee Rainwater and Timothy Smeeding describe their analytic framework and present their preliminary results in Rainwater and Smeeding (1995). In December 1996, Rainwater sent me corrected estimates, which I use here.

14. If one regresses the percentage of children living with a single mother ($P$) on the difference between the poverty rates for children living with single and married mothers ($D$), the equation is $D = 8.13 + .17D$ ($R^2 = .26$; $t = 2.05$). (Using logged odds ratios, $R^2$ rises to .44 and the $t = 2.85$.) This positive relationship can hardly be causal. An alternative hypothesis is that in countries where voters oppose single motherhood, they respond to its increase by limiting benefits for single mothers.

15. Because the LIS data come from national surveys that ask different questions, the data describing children's living arrangements may not be precisely comparable across countries, though they appear to be better than estimates from any other source. One worrisome finding is that the LIS data show 9 percent of U.S. children living in a household headed by a single woman that also includes other adults over the age of eighteen. This figure is below 3 percent in other countries. Since the percentage of children living in one-adult households headed by unmarried women is about the same in the United States, Britain, and Scandinavia, it is not clear why two-adult households headed by unmarried women should vary so much. I can see no obvious reason why children over eighteen would be less likely to live with their mother in Britain and Scandinavia than, for example, in the United States. A more rigorous analysis of the LIS data would need to use continuous rather than dichotomous measures of economic status and would control for demographic differences between single and unmarried mothers, the magnitude of which presumably varies from country to country.

## Chapter One

1. Roughly two-thirds of children across race groups lived with two parents, while 22 percent lived with a single mother. The remainder lived with a single father, with other relatives, in foster care, and in group homes and other institutional settings.

2. African American mothers like Mary Ann Moore have always worked in large numbers. For white mothers, work outside the home was rare in the 1950s and 1960s, but has increasingly become the norm. Thus, there is now more public pressure for all mothers to work, even for those who are raising young children alone.

3. The term "welfare reliant" is not our invention. Heidi Hartmann and Roberta Spalter-Roth developed the term for many of the same reasons we have decided to adopt it.

4. Cleaning crews in northern cities tended to charge quite a lot for cleaning houses, but in the South cleaning jobs paid much more poorly. Mothers in both cities cleaned their neighbors' houses for cash, but these neighbors hired them precisely because they could not afford a commercial cleaning company's services. Welfare-reliant mothers went along with this arrangement both because they knew what their neighbors could afford and because the commercial crews would have offered the mothers less flexible schedules and long commutes.

5. The survey was conducted by Fay Cook and Christopher Jencks, of the Center for Urban Affairs and Policy Research at Northwestern University.

6. Central-city unemployment rates were substantially higher in all of these cities. However, since most of the central-city low-wage working women we interviewed worked outside the central city, we take the view that labor-market strength should be measured by citywide, rather than central-city, rates.

7. Respondents commonly reported inaccurate information. For a more thorough description of respondents' motivations, see Bernard (1995, 233–35).

8. The term "boosting" is used in many African American neighborhoods, but usually as a synonym for general shoplifting and not in the specific "for hire" sense used in San Antonio. See Donaldson (1993) for examples of the term's use in this more general sense among the young men of the Brownsville section of Brooklyn, New York.

9. Though income data are collected by the Consumer Expenditure Survey, we had reasons to doubt its veracity. No survey satisfactorily gets at the range of income-generating strategies single mothers must employ to pay their bills, probably because so many of the strategies are illegal (see chapters 6 and 7).

## Chapter Two

1. In 1994, 49 percent of Americans thought that welfare programs discouraged people from working, and two-thirds believed that welfare encouraged women to have more children than they would have had if welfare were not available (Blendon and others 1995).

2. These responses were gathered during the center's General Social Survey.
3. Due to rounding, these estimates do not total $876.
4. We did not include any teenage mothers living at home. Mothers under age eighteen constitute only a tiny portion of all mothers on the welfare rolls (U.S. House of Representatives 1995, table 10-27). We did interview seventeen teenage mothers and found that they paid almost none of their own bills because most of them lived rent-free with their mothers while they tried to finish school. Therefore, these teenage mothers could not construct a household budget.
5. Nor could families with housing subsidies, disability income, or reported outside income buy all of their food with food stamps.
6. There is a reduction in food stamp benefits as cash benefits rise.
7. (69/3.17)*12
8. In terms of nonnecessary spending, more than a third of families spent nothing whatsoever on entertainment during the previous year, two-thirds never ate out; nearly half had spent nothing on cigarettes or alcohol during the year; and four-fifths had gone without cable television.
9. Only about half the states have ever funded the General Assistance Program, and of these, nineteen cut or reduced benefits by 1991 (Center on Social Welfare Policy and Law 1992).
10. Prior to 1997, a small proportion of families were eligible for AFDC UP (AFDC-Unemployed Parent program).
11. Benefits in the states we studied did not change significantly over the period we observed, with the exception of South Carolina, which had offered the typical family $5 a month more in 1991 than in 1993.
12. While administered by states, the food stamp program is entirely funded by the federal government and offers benefits on a sliding scale to poor families. AFDC recipients who lived rent-free with their parents could receive food stamps only if the entire household was poor. Mothers who established technical "independence" by paying a portion of the rent could get food stamps based on their own incomes. AFDC mothers who received disability or death benefits for themselves or one of their children usually took in too much cash income to qualify. Mothers living with their mothers rent-free and mothers receiving disability or social security made up the vast majority of AFDC recipients who did not participate in the program.
13. One in ten AFDC families did not participate because they were subfamilies living in households with higher incomes or because

they received other benefits (SSI or social security) that brought their total incomes above the food stamp eligibility threshold.

14. In Minnesota, Wisconsin, Vermont, New Hampshire, Massachusetts, and other relatively generous states, it is possible to imagine areas in which AFDC families received enough cash in the early 1990s to rent a private apartment. However, rural areas do not generally have public transportation. Therefore, in order to take advantage of the savings, a family would have had to own and maintain a car. In addition, all of these states but California are in the North, where fuel costs are usually high in winter months.

15. In the Boston area, we conducted most of our interviews north of the Charles River, where low-income mothers had to compete with students for apartments in even the worst neighborhoods and where rents were even higher than for the area as a whole.

16. Many of these dwellings had no heat or electricity. Mothers either used kerosene stoves, heaters, and lanterns or "ran a cord" to the home of a cooperative neighbor who had electricity. Some of the homes we saw also had portions of the floor and ceiling missing.

17. Initially, the Federal Emergency Management Agency (FEMA) and community groups joined forces to provide temporary housing for the poor. By the fall of 1991, when our interviews in Charleston began, relatives were tired of living in overcrowded conditions, and the FEMA money and other charitable funding had largely run out.

18. This category is mostly comprised of disability payments, which the government calls supplementary security income (SSI). However, we have also included the income that families received for the care of foster children and the social security survivor's benefits paid to a child whose father is deceased. We included this amount in welfare benefits because SSI, foster care, and survivor's benefits affect both a family's AFDC payment and their food stamps. According to the AFDC rules of the early 1990s, these benefits were not "taxed," but the family member who was the beneficiary was excluded from the assistance unit, and the cash awarded to that unit was adjusted downward. The food stamp rules worked a bit differently. The food stamp program included the beneficiary in the assistance unit and taxed all forms of assistance awarded to families.

19. Four percent of all welfare-reliant families received either SSI or survivor's benefits (U.S. House of Representatives 1993, 719).

20. For those mothers who sold illegal drugs, a small personal supply was sometimes an in-kind benefit of the job.

21.  These small differences are due to the fact that we did not interview any teenage recipients, who often lived with better-off family members and were thus not eligible for food stamps.

22.  Fourteen percent had received payments through the Child Support Enforcement system in the last year, which was slightly above the national average of 12 percent for welfare recipients (U.S. Department of Health and Human Services 1990, 43).

23.  This poorest income group included individuals and families reporting household incomes of less than $5,000 a year. Of course, this group spent far more than their reported incomes, and the CES could not account for the discrepancy.

24.  The Survey of Income and Program Participation now collects hardship data.

25.  Those Chicagoans who failed to answer one or more questions were fairly evenly distributed according to race, age, and material hardship, so the incomplete reporters were dropped from the analysis.

26.  In our sample and the Cook and Jencks data, most hardships were positively related to family size.

27.  We excluded the elderly Cook and Jencks respondents in our analysis of the Cook and Jencks data for these comparisons.

28.  Despite being in the South, Charleston and San Antonio do have periods when children need a coat to keep warm.

29.  Again, family size was positively related to a lack of phone service, and this hardship affected 44 percent of the children.

30.  Because we did not distinguish between those mothers who went without medical care for themselves and for their children in our coding of the data, we cannot estimate the percentage of children affected by medical hardship.

31.  The families of those mothers reporting eviction during the prior twelve months were somewhat larger than the average family. Thus, 11 percent of the 464 children of our 214 welfare-reliant mothers had experienced eviction. The family sizes of those who had gone homeless were about the same (3.18 as compared with 3.17), so 16 percent of the children went homeless for some period.

32.  In Charleston, homelessness resulted from the combination of low benefits and high rents, and from Hurricane Hugo, which damaged or destroyed much of the low-rent housing stock in some portions of the city.

33.  Nationally, about one-fifth of welfare families reported sharing housing with another individual or family in 1989 (U.S. Bureau of the Census 1992). The discrepancy with our figures results from

the fact that we did not interview any teenagers, who are the most likely to double up.

34. They worked with Cook and Jencks's data.

35. There was no variance in the insurance variable for welfare-reliant mothers because Medicaid was available to all of them.

36. Edin's calculations show that both are significantly correlated with respondents' satisfaction with their standard of living in the 1985 Cook and Jencks data. See appendix B for these correlations.

37. Readers should note that we did not include homelessness or eviction in any of our hardship scales because too few Cook and Jencks respondents had experienced them to reliably estimate their importance relative to the other hardships. Nor did we include the telephone or clothing hardships, because Cook and Jencks did not ask about them. We have, however, reported how frequently our mothers experienced these four hardships in table 2-8; they were more common in the South than in the North.

38. This estimate is based on ordinary least squares regression, in which we controlled for our sample selection criteria (site, race and ethnicity, and housing subsidy status), and on a mother's family size. When we added controls for a mother's age and the age of her youngest child, our results did not change substantially.

39. Whereas Charles Murray portrayed an overly generous welfare system that kept the poor in poverty because it rewarded their indolence, mothers saw welfare as a stingy and punishing system that placed them and their childen in a desperate economic predicament.

## Chapter Three

1. Evaluations from the Manpower Demonstration Research Corporation have shown that when asked, welfare-reliant mothers often say they favor work requirements (Gueron and Pauly 1991). One must interpret these statements with care. Gerald Suttles (1968) has suggested that stigmatized groups take on society's negative evaluations of their own group and express stereotypical views of others who share their status in an effort to distance themselves from the stigma. In our experience, this is particularly likely to occur when outsiders, such as survey researchers, ask these kinds of questions, since they have not established rapport with their respondents.

2. Dead-end jobs affected informal support systems as well, since mothers who worked on the books had to rely more heavily on their personal networks than mothers who relied on welfare (as we show later). While relatives might be willing to help in the short

term, if an end is in sight, they could not and would not help indefinitely. Thus, the job would eventually have to pay enough to buy a mother's independence from her network's financial support (at which point she might be expected to begin to contribute toward the needs of other poor members of the network).

These mothers' experiences were consistent with the findings of social scientists, who have long documented that jobs in the low-wage labor market provide little or no return to age or experience for women workers, a point to which we return in chapter 5 (Burtless 1994; Danziger and Gottschalk 1993; Levitan and Shapiro 1987, 30).

3. About one-third of these years of work experience occurred before the respondent became a mother.

4. Of these mothers who worked in the informal economy, all but three occasionally participated in the underground economy as well. One respondent worked exclusively in the underground economy and did no informal work.

5. If we add these twenty-seven mothers to the twenty permanently disabled ones receiving SSI, then a total of thirty-seven mothers, or 17 percent of the sample, reported that a disability prohibited them from working. In his analysis of the PSID, David Ellwood found that 18 percent of respondents said they had a disability that limited work (U.S. House of Representatives 1993, 718).

6. Statistics from the JOBS program show that 26 percent of JOBS participants are engaged in educational activities (U.S. House of Representatives 1993).

7. It was striking to us how many women had already been through low-level training programs such as those for work as a nurse's aide, for housekeeping, or for basic typing or word processing and had found they could not make ends meet on the jobs that resulted. These women knew, even if policymakers and workfare caseworkers turned a blind eye, that low-level training does virtually nothing for their long-term earning power. Social scientists, for their part, have long recognized this fact. See, for example, Gueron and Pauly (1991).

8. The reason these estimates are lower than those generated by CES data is probably twofold: first, the CES subsample of working mothers was not restricted to low earners; second, we intentionally oversampled working mothers with housing subsidies so they would compare as closely as possible with our welfare sample.

9. Because we oversampled working mothers with housing subsidies, this figure is probably an underestimate.

10. This figure is in 1991 dollars. The authors made the cost of living adjustments.
11. Unpublished tabulations from Kathleen Mullan Harris of the Department of Sociology, University of North Carolina at Chapel Hill and of the Carolina Population Council (1997).
12. For these mothers, their EITC (in 1991) would amount to slightly less than what they paid in FICA contributions. They would pay no federal taxes and only a small amount in state taxes.

## Chapter Four

1. Others might wonder why none of them was living with her. Still others might wonder why she had had three children. These questions, while important, were not the focus of our study.
2. Because of the limitations imposed by the twenty-year window, Harris's estimates are somewhat right-censored. In some cases, spells of work and welfare overlapped. The 5.5 years the typical respondent reported neither working nor earning income were generally spent married and/or in school (Harris 1997).
3. Formal-sector work and welfare are not always mutually exclusive. Very low earners and part-time workers can retain some of their welfare benefits.
4. This average includes the cash payments of mothers who had child care subsidies.
5. SIPP respondents with preschool-aged children paid more than mothers with older children: $312 versus $173 a week (U.S. Bureau of the Census 1994e).
6. Unionized workers are more likely to have health insurance than nonunionized workers.
7. In terms of nonnecessary spending, more than a third of families spent nothing whatsoever on entertainment during the previous year; two-thirds never ate out; nearly half spent nothing on cigarettes or alcohol during the year; and four-fifths went without cable television.
8. We follow the Census Bureau's determinations regarding the skill levels of certain occupations.
9. Other jobs in this category include retail salespersons, janitors, waitresses, fast food or other food workers, seamstresses, and factory workers.
10. This standard deduction applies to all AFDC recipients who have worked for twelve or more months; it is only slightly more generous for mothers who have worked for less than twelve months.

We then subtracted $10 from the total because mothers who are eligible for less than $10 of AFDC assistance get no benefits.

11. As of 1989, states were required to disregard the EITC in calculations of eligibility and benefit levels (U.S. House of Representatives 1993, 568).

12. In 1991, when we conducted most of the interviews, the maximum for a family of three was slightly lower—$277 a month (U.S. House of Representatives 1991, 1396).

13. The agency figure includes the portion of student grants and loans left over after paying for tuition and books.

14. Not all of the insured mothers could insure their children. Some children were covered by their father's health plan or by Medicaid.

15. For example, working mothers were less likely to run out of food or go hungry and less likely to live in the projects, but they were far more likely to say they had untreated medical problems.

## *Chapter Five*

1. Recently, Judith Smith and Jeanne Brooks-Gunn (1995) have found that the cognitive abilities of children of welfare recipients who go to work and remain in poverty decrease significantly.

2. A detailed discussion of the economic factors that have led to these very slow gains is beyond the scope of this book. However, Blank (1994) and others argue that the changes are partly due to the fact that the demand for less-skilled workers has declined faster than the supply of such labor. Returns to experience also may have declined as job ladders have become more attenuated. Though the expansion of the earned income tax credit somewhat eased the impact of these harsh realities by the early- to mid-1990s, it did not go far enough. Full-time, year-round working mothers who received the EITC in 1996 (when it was fully phased in) could raise their families above the official poverty line, but not to a level of self-sufficiency.

3. The Census Bureau defines "very low earners" as all full-time, year-round workers who are unable to earn enough to bring a family of four out of poverty ($14,228 in 1992). In 1992, 55 percent of women workers with no high school diploma were classified as very low earners—up 15 percent from 1979. For women with a high school diploma, 30 percent were very low earners, compared with 21 percent in 1979.

4. Hence, as this chapter discussed, most mothers planned to continue their education in the near or medium term. The costs of

schooling and the time needed to complete classes sometimes delayed a mother's ability to take this step, however.

## Chapter Six

1. Furthermore, our data show that mothers' constraints, and thus their range of alternatives, varied by mothers' characteristics and situations at a given point in time and by changes in these characteristics and situations over time.

2. Some mothers could not get (or did not want) their children's father or a boyfriend to help pay the bills. In other cases, the mother's current or past partner was incarcerated and could not contribute.

3. Our data show a lot of variety in which strategies a given mother thought were most acceptable. Though we do not want to diminish the importance of this variation, our data do suggest some widely shared agreement about the overall acceptability of a given strategy.

4. Most did use two or more strategies during the twelve-month period covered by our tables.

5. A mother's individual characteristics and her family background also influenced her likelihood of getting network-based help. In general, the younger the mother and the better off her network, the more she could expect from her relatives.

6. In this regard, the patterns we observed were virtually identical to those Elliot Leibow described in *Tally's Corner* (1967), his classic study of black street-corner men in Washington, D.C.

7. The likelihood of receiving covert support did not vary significantly by site.

8. Sixty-two percent of those who did not pursue formal support did not get informal support either. These women voluntarily gave up their rights to support for four reasons. First, some traded material support for the emotional support their children gained because of a strong father-child tie, which may have been severed if support were sought. Second, some valued exclusive rights of control over their children—rights they felt would be compromised if they received support from the absent father. Third, some chose to forgo their claims of support because they feared physical abuse or other forms of reprisal. Fourth, several did not pursue support because they had no long-term or substantial relationship with the child's father. These women did not feel they deserved support from men they barely knew. These four types of responses may

help to explain why a U.S. Census Bureau (1991, 10) survey showed that 42 percent of the single mothers without an award said they did not want one.

9. Unfortunately, once mothers turned in fathers, their chances of getting covert support were further diminished.

10. As we saw with boyfriends, the rules governing welfare may reduce men's willingness to pay, since their children received hardly any of the money paid through official channels.

11. We have not divided absent fathers' contributions to wage-reliant mothers into the subcategories we used for welfare-reliant mothers. Our interviewers found it difficult to determine whether mothers were receiving support as a result of a court order or an informal agreement. Our best guess is that at least half of the wage-reliant mothers received the support informally.

12. James Wetzel (1995) has estimated that the average annual incidence of employment is typically 10 to 15 percent greater than the average monthly incidence. If this holds true for single mothers at the low end of the income distribution, which it may not, we could expect that the percent of welfare-reliant mothers who worked at reported jobs at some point during 1991 did not exceed 8 percent.

13. At the time of our early Chicago interviews, caseworkers had to make these comparisons manually. Later, computers handled more and more of these checks.

14. Employers were supposed to report even former employees who had quit, but our data suggest that many did not follow this rule.

15. See Edin (1993) for a more detailed account of caseworkers' motivations in reporting violations.

16. If we take taxes and the EITC into account, the picture does not change much. Mothers who reported their work would receive benefits from the EITC if they knew how to claim them, but these benefits were offset somewhat by the state and social security taxes they would be forced to pay. The net gain (EITC minus taxes) would equal far less than a mother would lose in AFDC and food stamp benefits. Mothers who engaged in unreported work in the formal sector (usually using false social security numbers) had some taxes deducted from their checks, but they were usually not brave enough to "tempt fate" by submitting a tax return. Therefore, they were unlikely to claim anything from the EITC program. Mothers who work at unreported jobs in the informal sector neither paid taxes nor were eligible for the EITC.

17. Unreported jobs in the formal sector included work as cashiers, waitresses, secretaries, teacher's aides, telephone salespersons, and child care providers.

18. False IDs could be purchased on the street for about $20, assuming a mother "knew someone who knew someone." Typically, vendors of false IDs worked out of small local groceries and other community-based businesses.

19. These employers also could not claim the wages as a business expense, however, so either they showed up as taxable profits or else the employer had to conceal the income used to pay the wages too.

20. This is because caseworkers relied on the Department of Labor Statistics, which were generated every quarter.

21. For this reason, we chose not to assign cash values to any in-kind assistance.

22. Mothers who can find them also use agencies for dental care, which Medicaid sometimes provides to children but seldom to mothers.

23. For Boston and Chicago we use the Partial Metropolitan Statistical Area, whereas for Charleston and San Antonio we use the Metropolitan Statistical Area.

24. Such raids by AFDC caseworkers (which rendered a mother ineligible for AFDC if they found evidence of a man in the house) were ruled unconstitutional in 1967. We know of no legal challenge to similar practices among housing authority officials, however.

25. Overall, the Charleston welfare-reliant mothers worked at side-jobs as often as any group except the Chicago mothers. However, Charleston's African American recipients performed almost all of this work.

26. In all sites except San Antonio, mothers were more likely to receive covert support than formal support. In San Antonio, a greater proportion of welfare-reliant respondents had been married (solely because of the marriage rates of Latinas). Consequently, these mothers found it harder to deny that they knew who the father was, name the wrong man, or claim not to know his social security number.

## Chapter Seven

1. It would be useful to look at whether these group differences could predict welfare use, after controlling for demographic differences and structural constraints (see chapters 3 and 5). The latter include a mother's education, her wage rate (either current or prospective), her child care costs (current or prospective), and so on. We cannot observe, however, what welfare mothers would *actually* earn if they left welfare for a job. The same is true of child care costs.

In addition, since most of the women we interviewed had little education, we could not get an accurate measure of how educational levels might affect the welfare/work choice. Finally, since we stratified our sample by race (in San Antonio, by ethnicity) for both welfare-reliant mothers and workers, we could not assess whether mothers' racial or ethnic backgrounds predicted the choice between welfare or work.

2. More specifically, 56 percent of respondents agreed that welfare did more harm than good because it encouraged family breakup and discouraged work.

3. Yet Moyers did not discuss the dramatic decline in wages among young urban African American males over the last two decades (despite increases in educational attainment), nor did he mention the dramatic growth in unemployment rates for young minority men in Newark and other American cities during the 1980s. John Kasarda's analysis of Current Population Survey data shows that between 1968 and 1970 approximately eight of every ten African American men living in central cities like Newark who were without a high school diploma worked; by the early 1990s, that figure had dropped to less than one in two. For those central-city African American males who had completed high school but had no college or technical training, jobless rates grew from 11 to 31 percent in the Northeast and more elsewhere (Kasarda 1995, 257–58).

4 Mexican American households were marked by distinctions ranging from food preferences to the propensity to seek some kinds of medical care in Mexico.

5. For the sake of analysis, family background here means the welfare history of the low-income mother as a child.

6. Regression results are shown in appendix B.

7. Welfare status could not affect covert support, since this category applies only to welfare-reliant mothers.

8. Mothers were less open with each other in casual settings with regard to income-generating strategies. This was because they were afraid that neighbors or more casual acquaintances might get them in trouble.

9. If we had more precise measures of the socioeconomic status of mothers' families of origin, this difference might prove spurious.

10. Wage-reliant ghetto residents also spent less overall than nonghetto, wage-reliant mothers, but this difference is almost entirely due to the fact that more of the ghetto residents have housing subsidies.

11. Our hardship scale was based on responses to questions asking whether respondents had experienced a particular hardship during the last twelve months. It did not distinguish among frequencies

during the twelve-month period. Furthermore, it did not distinguish among the seriousness of problems within each hardship category.

12. Though it initially appeared that African American mothers were more likely to engage in underground work, the difference was not significant once we controlled for earnings from other income-generating strategies.

13. Ann Swidler (1986), who introduced the idea of a cultural tool kit, wanted to move away from the idea that culture consisted mainly of values. She suggested that members of different cultures or sub-cultures may share practical strategies, or tools, for resolving common problems.

14. A few notable exceptions include the work of Nadine Marks and Sara McLanahan (1993), Dennis Hogan, Ling Hao, and William Parrish (1990), and Roberto Fernandez and David Harris (1991), which deal generally with the subject of social support among poor populations.

## Chapter Eight

1. The poverty line is based on the percentage of total income Americans spent for food in the early 1960s (33 percent). At that time, the Department of Agriculture drew up estimates of bare-bones or "minimally nutritious" food budgets for families of various sizes and multiplied it by three. Although this amount is adjusted annually for inflation, the spending patterns of Americans have changed dramatically, and the official measure has not been adjusted to reflect these changes.

   Between the mid-1960s and 1980 the proportion of Americans' budgets spent on food decreased to one-fifth. This was because the prices of nonfood items went up, while food costs stayed roughly constant. If we adjusted the poverty line to reflect these changes, the official threshold would need to be raised to 140 percent of the official poverty threshold for a family of four (Ruggles 1990).

2. In sum, a strong enforcement system seemed to be good for mothers' budgets. We are not so sure, however, about the effects of strong enforcement for the well-being of men. In some states with strong enforcement, fathers who fail to pay are jailed. Less dramatically, their driver's licenses can be revoked, their tax returns seized, and so on. These things can occur even when the father loses his job and cannot meet his monthly obligation. Fathers who want to change the award amount they pay must hire a lawyer and go to court, which many cannot afford to do. We suspect that a

system of this kind may actually force the least able and willing of fathers to deny paternity or, if paternity is proven, to "go underground"—to take jobs in the informal or underground economy. More research is needed in this area, but policymakers who advocate strong enforcement systems should attempt to learn more about how it affects men's behavior.

3. See McLanahan and Sandefur (1994) for a review of current rates of these social problems among children raised by a single parent.

# References

Auletta, Ken. 1982. *The Underclass.* New York: Random House.

Bane, Mary Jo, and David T. Ellwood. 1983. "The Dynamics of Dependence: The Routes to Self-Sufficiency." Report supported by U.S. Department of Health and Human Services under Grant no. HHS-100-82-0038. Cambridge, Mass.: John F. Kennedy School of Government, Harvard University. Mimeo.

———. 1994. *Welfare Realities: From Rhetoric to Reform.* Cambridge, Mass.:Harvard University Press.

Bernard, H. Russell. 1994. *Research Methods in Anthropology.* Thousand Oaks, Calif.: Sage Publications.

Bianchi, Suzanne. 1995. "Changing Economic Roles of Women and Men." In *State of the Union*, edited by Reynolds Farley. New York: Russell Sage Foundation.

Blank, Rebecca M. 1994. "The Employment Strategy: Public Policies to Increase Work and Earnings." In *Confronting Poverty*, edited by Sheldon H. Danziger, Gary D. Sandefur, and Daniel H. Weinberg. Cambridge, Mass.: Harvard University Press; New York: Russell Sage Foundation.

———. 1995. "Outlook for the U.S. Labor Market and Prospects for Low-Wage Entry Jobs." In *The Work Alternative*, edited by Demetra Smith Nightingale and Robert H. Haveman. Washington, D.C.: The Urban Institute Press; Cambridge, Mass.: Harvard University Press.

Blendon, Robert J., Drew E. Altman, John Benson, Mollyann Brodie, Matt James,and Gerry Chervinsky. 1995. "The Public and the Welfare Reform Debate." *Archives of Pediatric and Adolescent Medicine* 149: 1065-1069.

Bobo, Lawrence, and Ryan A. Smith. 1994. "Antipoverty Policy, Affirmative Action, and Racial Attitudes." In *Confronting Poverty*, edited by Sheldon H. Danziger, Gary D. Sandefur, and Daniel H. Weinberg. Cambridge, Mass.: Harvard University Press; New York: Russell Sage Foundation.

Brooks-Gunn, Jeanne, and Greg J. Duncan, eds. Forthcoming. *Consequences of Growing Up Poor.* New York: Russell Sage Foundation.

Burtless, Gary. 1994. "Public Spending on the Poor: Historical Trends and Economic Limits." In *Confronting Poverty*, edited by Sheldon H. Danziger, Gary D. Sandefur, and Daniel H. Weinberg. Cambridge, Mass.: Harvard University Press; New York: Russell Sage Foundation.

———. 1995. "Employment Prospects of Welfare Recipients". In *The Work Alternative*, edited by Demetra Smith Nightingale and Robert H. Haveman. Washington, D.C.: The Urban Institute Press.

Center on Social Welfare Policy and Law. 1992. *1991: The Poor Got Poorer as Welfare Programs Were Slashed.* Publication 165. New York: Center on Social Welfare Policy and Law.

Citro, Constance, and Robert Michael, eds. 1995. *Measuring Poverty: A New Approach.* Washington, DC: National Academy Press.

Danziger, Sheldon, and Peter Gottschalk, eds. 1993. *Uneven Tides:Rising Inequality in America.* New York: Russell Sage Foundation.

Donaldson, Greg. 1993. *The Ville: Cops and Kids in Urban America.* New York: Anchor Books.

Duncan, Greg J., Martha S. Hill, and Saul D. Hoffman, 1988. "Welfare Dependence Within and Across Generations." *Science* 239: 467-471.

Edin, Kathryn. 1991. "Surviving the Welfare System: How AFDC Recipients Make Ends Meet in Chicago." *Social Problems* 38: 462-474.

———. 1993. *There's a Lot of Month Left at the End of the Money: How AFDC Recipients Make Ends Meet in Chicago.* New York: Garland Press.

———. 1994. "The Myths of Dependency and Self-Sufficiency." Working Paper. New Brunswick, N.J.: Center for Urban Policy Research, Rutgers University.

———. 1995. "Single Mothers and Child Support: The Possibilities and Limits of Child Support Policy." *Children and Youth Services Review* 17: 203-230.

Edin, Kathryn, and Kathleen Mullan Harris. Forthcoming. "Getting Off and Staying Off: Race Differences in the Process of Working Off Welfare." In *Race, Gender, and Economic Inequality*, edited by Irene Brown. New York: Russell Sage Foundation.

Edin, Kathryn, and Christopher Jencks. 1992. "Welfare." In *Rethinking Social Policy*, edited by Christopher Jencks. Cambridge, Mass.: Harvard University Press.

Edin, Kathryn, and Laura Lein. Forthcoming. "Work, Welfare, and Single Mothers' Economic Survival Strategies." *American Sociological Review.*

Fernandez, Roberto M., and David Harris. 1991. "Social Isolation and the Underclass." Paper presented at the Urban Poverty and Family Life Conference. Chicago (October 10-12, 1991).

Friedlander, Daniel, and Judith M. Gueron. 1992. "Are High-Cost Services More Effective Than Low-Cost Services?" In *Evaluating Welfare and Training Programs,*edited by Charles F. Manski and Irwin Garfinkel. Cambridge, Mass.: Harvard University Press.

Frisbie, Parker, and Rudolfo Cruz. 1992. "Violent Deaths: Ethnic and Life-Cycle Differentials Among Mexican Americans, Mexican Immigrants, and Anglos, 1970-1980." *Population Research Center Papers* 13.01. Austin: University of Texas.

Frisbie, Parker, et al. 1992. "The Mexican Origin Mortality Transition:Differentials by Age and Sex." *Population Research Center Papers* 13.06. Austin: University of Texas.

Furstenberg, Frank F., Jeanne Brooks-Gunn, and S. Philip Morgan. 1987. *Adolescent Mothers in Later Life.* Cambridge, Mass: Cambridge University Press.

Garfinkel, Irwin, and Sara McLanahan. 1986. *Single Mothers and Their Children.* Washington, D.C.: Urban Institute Press.

Gilbert, Dennis, and Joseph A. Kahl. 1993. *The American Class Structure: A New Synthesis.* 4th ed. Belmont, Calif.: Wadsworth Press.

Goodwin, Leonard. 1972. *Do the Poor Want to Work? A Social-Psychological Study of Work Orientation.* Washington, D.C.: The Brookings Institution.

Gottschalk, Peter, and Sheldon Danziger. 1986. "Unemployment Insurance and the Safety Net for the Unemployed." Working Paper.

Gueron, Judith M., and Edward Pauly. 1991. *From Welfare to Work.* New York: Russell Sage Foundation.

Handler, Joel F. 1995. *The Poverty of Welfare Reform.* New Haven: Yale University Press.

Harris, Kathleen Mullan. 1991. "Teenage Mothers and Welfare Dependency: Working Off Welfare." *Journal of Family Issues* 12: 492-518.

———. 1993. "Work and Welfare Among Single Mothers in Poverty."*American Journal of Sociology* 99: 317-352.

———. 1996. "Life After Welfare: Women, Work and Repeat Dependency."*American Sociological Review* 61: 207-246.

———. 1997. Unpublished Calculations. Chapel Hill, NC: Carolina Population Center, University of North Carolina at Chapel Hill.

Harris, Kathleen Mullan, and Kathryn Edin. 1996. "From Welfare to Work and Back Again." Paper presented at the New School for Social Research, Conference titled "After AFDC: Reshaping the Anti-Poverty Agenda." New York (November 16, 1996).

Heclo, Hugh. 1994. "Poverty Politics." In *Confronting Poverty,* edited by Sheldon H. Danziger, Gary D. Sandefur, and Daniel H. Weinberg. Cambridge, Mass.: Harvard University Press; New York: Russell Sage Foundation.

Hill, Martha S., and Michael Ponza. 1984. "Does Welfare Dependency Beget Dependency?" Ann Arbor, Mich.: Institute for Social Research.

Hofferth, Sandra L. 1995. "The Impact of Welfare Reform and Work Requirements on the Demand for Child Care." Testimony before the Senate Committee on Labor and Human Resources, 104th Cong., 1st sess., 1 March 1995.

Hogan, Dennis P., Ling Xian Hao, and William L. Parish. 1990. "Race, Kin Networks, and Assistance to Mother-Headed Families." *Social Forces* 68: 797-812.

Jencks, Christopher, and Kathryn Edin. 1990. "The Real Welfare Problem." *American Prospect* (1, Spring):31-50.

———. 1995. "Do Poor Women Have the Right to Bear Children?" *American Prospect* (20, Winter): 43-52.

Jencks, Christopher, and Susan E. Mayer. 1990. "The Social Consequences of Growing Up in a Poor Neighborhood." In *Inner-City Poverty in the United States*, edited by Laurence E. Lynn and Michael G. H. McGeary. Washington, D.C.: National Academy Press.

Kasarda, John D. 1995. "Industrial Restructuring and the Changing Location of Jobs." In *State of the Union*, edited by Reynolds Farley. New York: Russell Sage Foundation.

Katz, Michael B. 1986. *In the Shadow of the Poor House*. New York: Basic Books.

Leibow, Elliot. 1967. *Tally's Corner: A Study of Negro Streetcorner Men*. Boston: Little, Brown & Co.

Lein, Laura. 1994. "Welfare Mothers Use of Service Agencies." Proceedings of the National Association of Welfare Research and Statistics Annual Meeting (July).

Levitan, Sar A., and Isaac Shapiro. 1987. *Working but Poor: America's Contradiction*. Baltimore: Johns Hopkins University Press.

Levy, Frank. 1995. "Incomes and Income Inequality." In *State of the Union*, edited by Reynolds Farley. New York: Russell Sage Foundation.

Lewis, Oscar. 1959. *Five Families: Mexican Case Studies in the Culture of Poverty*. New York: Basic Books.

———. 1965. *La Vida: A Puerto Rican Family in the Culture of Poverty*. New York: Random House.

———. 1968. "The Culture of Poverty." In *On Understanding Poverty: Perspectives from the Social Sciences*, edited by Daniel Patrick Moynihan. New York: Basic Books.

Lichter, Daniel T., Diane K. McLaughlin, George Kephart, and David J. Landry. 1992. "Race and the Retreat from Marriage: A Shortage of Marriageable Men?" *American Sociological Review* 56: 781-799.

Lipsky, Michael. 1980. *Street-Level Bureaucracy*. New York: Russell Sage Foundation.

Marks, Nadine F., and Sara S. McLanahan. 1993. "Gender, Family Structure, and Social Support Among Parents." *Journal of Marriage and the Family* 55: 481-493.

Martin, Theresa Castro, and Larry L. Bumpass. 1989. "Report on Trends in Marital Disruption." *Demography* 26: 37-51.

Massey, Douglas, and Nancy A. Denton. 1993. *American Apartheid*. Chicago: University of Chicago Press.

Mayer, Susan E. 1997. *More Than Money*. Cambridge, Mass.: Harvard University Press.

Mayer, Susan E., and Christopher Jencks. 1989. "Poverty and the Distribution of Material Hardship." *Journal of Human Resources* 24: 88-113.

McLanahan, Sara, and Gary Sandefur. 1994. *Growing Up with a Single Parent: What Hurts, What Helps*. Cambridge, Mass.: Harvard University Press.

Mead, Lawrence M. 1992. *The New Politics of Poverty: The Nonworking Poor in America*. New York: Basic Books.

Merton, Robert King. 1957. *Social Theory and Social Structure*. Glencoe, Ill.:The Free Press.

Metropolitan Planning Council. 1985. "Chicago Housing Authority Rehabilitation and Reinvestment Study." Background Paper. Chicago: Metropolitan Planning Council, CHA Task Force. Mimeo.

Michalopoulos, Charles, and Irwin Garfinkel. 1989. "Reducing Welfare Dependence and Poverty of Single Mothers by Means of Earnings and Child Support: Wishful Thinking and Realistic Possibilities." Discussion Paper 882-89. Madison: Institute for Research on Poverty, University of Wisconsin.

Moffitt, Robert. 1992. "Incentive Effects of the U.S. Welfare System: A Review." *Journal of Economic Literature* 30 (March): 1-61.

Murray, Charles A. 1984. *Losing Ground: American Social Policy*. New York: Basic Books.

———. 1993. "Welfare and the Family: The U.S. Experience." *Journal of Labor Economics* 11: S224-S262.

Page, Benjamin I., and Robert Y. Shapiro. 1992. *The Rational Public: Fifty Years of Trends in American's Policy Preferences*. Chicago: University of Chicago Press.

Pavetti, LaDonna. 1992. "The Dynamics of Welfare and Work: Exploring the Process by Which Young Women Work Their Way Off Welfare." Paper presented at the Applied Public Policy and Management Association Annual Meeting. Boulder, Col. (1992).

Pearce, Diana. 1991. "Chutes and Ladders." Paper presented at the American Sociological Association Annual Meeting. Cincinnati, Ohio (August).

Pendry, DeAnn. 1995. "Gender and Family Roles in Treatment Strategies of Mexican-American Diabetes Patients." Paper presented at the Society for Applied Anthropology Annual Meeting. (March).

Penzerro, Rose Marie, and Laura Lein. 1995. "Burning Their Bridges: Disordered Attachment and Foster Care Discharge." *Child Welfare* 74(2): 351–367.

Piven, Francis Fox, and Richard A. Cloward. 1993. *Regulating the Poor: The Functions of Public Welfare.* New York: Random House.

Rainwater, Lee, and Timothy Smeeding. 1995."Doing Poorly: The Real Income of American Children in Comparative Perspective." Working Paper. Syracuse, N.Y.: Maxwell School of Citizenship and Public Affairs, Syracuse University.

Rank, Mark R. 1988. "Racial Differences in Length of Welfare Use." *Social Forces* 66: 1080-1101.

Reskin, Barbara. 1993. "Sex Segregation in the Workplace." *Annual Review of Sociology* 19: 241-270.

Rosenzweig, Mark. 1995. "Welfare, Marital Prospects, and Nonmarital Childbearing." Working Paper. Philadelphia: Department of Economics, University of Pennsylvania.

Rossi, Peter H. 1989. *Down and Out in America: The Origins of Homelessness.* Chicago: University of Chicago Press.

Ruggles, Patricia. 1990. *Drawing the Line: Alternative Poverty Measures and Their Implications.* Washington, D.C.: Urban Institute Press.

Schwarz, John E., and Thomas J. Volgy. 1992. "Social Support for Self-Reliance: The Politics of Making Work Pay." *American Prospect* (9, Spring): 67-73.

Skocpol, Theda. 1992. *Protecting Soldiers and Mothers: The Political Origins of Social Policy in the United States.* Cambridge, Mass.: Harvard University Press.

Smith, Judith R., and Jeanne Brooks-Gunn. 1995. "Transitions Between Welfare and Work: Effects on Young Children and Mothers." Paper presented at Workshop on Welfare and Child Development. Sponsored by Board on Children, Youth, and Families and the National Institute for Child Health and Human Development. Washington, D.C. (December 5, 1995).

Sorensen, Elaine, and Mark Turner. 1996. "Barriers in Child Support Policy: A Literature Review." Paper LB-SB-96-04. Philadelphia: National Center on Fathers and Families, University of Pennsylvania.

Spalter-Roth, Roberta, Beverly Burr, Heidi Hartmann, and Louise Shaw. 1995."Welfare That Works: The Working Lives of AFDC Recipients."

Report to the Ford Foundation. Washington, D.C.: Institute for Women's Policy Research.

Spalter-Roth, Roberta, Heidi Hartmann, and Beverly Burr. 1994. *Income Insecurity: The Failure of Unemployment Insurance to Reach Working AFDC Mothers.* Washington, D.C.: Institute for Women's Policy Research.

Stack, Carol B. 1974. *All Our Kin: Strategies for Survival in a Black Community.* New York: Harper & Row.

Suttles, Gerald D. 1968. *The Social Order of the Slum.* Chicago: University of Chicago Press.

Sweet, James A., and Larry L. Bumpass. 1987. *American Families and Households.* New York: Russell Sage Foundation.

Swidler, Ann. 1986. "Culture in Action: Symbols and Strategies." *American Sociological Review* 51: 273-286.

Testa, Mark, Nan Marie Astone, Marylin Krogh, and Kathryn M. Neckerman. 1989. "Employment and Marriage Among Inner-City Fathers." *Annals of the American Academy of Political and Social Sciences* 501: 79-91.

Tienda, Marta, and Haya Stier. 1991. "Joblessness and Shiftlessness: Labor Force Activity in Chicago's Inner City." In *The Urban Underclass,* edited by Christopher Jencks and Paul E. Peterson. Washington, D.C.: Brookings Institution.

U.S. Bureau of the Census. 1991. *Who's Supporting the Kids?* SB/91-18.U.S. Department of Commerce, Economics and Statistics Administration. Washington: U.S. Government Printing Office.

———. 1992. *Housing of Single Parent Families.* SB/91-15. U.S. Department of Commerce, Economics and Statistics Administration. Washington: U.S. Government Printing Office.

———. 1994a. *1990. Census of the Population.Detailed Population Characteristics: U.S. Summary.* Washington: U.S. Government Printing Office.

———. 1994b. *Financial Characteristics of Housing Units: 1990.* Washington: U.S. Government Printing Office.

———. 1994c. *Health Insurance Coverage—1993.* SB/94-28. U.S. Department of Commerce, Economics and Statistics Administration. Washington: U.S. Government Printing Office.

———. 1994d. *The Earnings Ladder.* SB/94-3. U.S. Department of Commerce, Economics and Statistics Administration. Washington: U.S. Government Printing Office.

———. 1994e. *Who's Minding the Kids.* SB/94-5. U.S. Department of Commerce, Economics and Statistics Administration. Washington: U.S. Government Printing Office.

————. 1994f. *Measuring the Effects of Benefits and Taxes on Income and Poverty: 1992* Series P-60-186RD. Current Population Reports. Washington: U.S. Government Printing Office.

U.S. Bureau of Labor Statistics. 1993. *Consumer Expenditure Survey 1990.* Washington: U.S. Government Printing Office.

U.S. Department of Health and Human Services. 1990. *Child Support Enforcement.* Annual Report to Congress 92-3301. Washington: U.S. Government Printing Office.

U.S. House of Representatives, Committee on Ways and Means. 1987. Overview of Entitlement Programs (Green Book). Washington: U.S. Government Printing Office.

————. 1991. Overview of Entitlement Programs (Green Book). Washington: U.S. Government Printing Office.

————. 1993. Overview of Entitlement Programs (Green Book). Washington: U.S. Government Printing Office.

————. 1994. Overview of Entitlement Programs (Green Book). Washington: U.S. Government Printing Office.

————. 1995. Overview of Entitlement Programs (Green Book). Washington: U.S. Government Printing Office.

U.S. Office of the Federal Register. 1994. *Federal Register* 59 (120). Washington: Superintendent of Documents, U.S. Government Printing Office.

Wetzel, James R. 1995. "Labor Force, Unemployment, and Earnings." In *State of the Union*, edited by Reynolds Farley. New York: Russell Sage Foundation.

Wilson, William Julius. 1987. *The Truly Disadvantaged.* Chicago: University of Chicago Press.

————. 1996. *When Work Disappears: The World of the New Urban Poor.* New York: Alfred A. Knopf.

Wolfe, Barbara. 1994. "Reform of Health Care for the Nonelderly Poor." In *Confronting Poverty*, edited by Sheldon H. Danziger, Gary D. Sandefur, and Daniel H. Weinberg. Cambridge, Mass.: Harvard University Press; New York: Russell Sage Foundation.

Zucker, Brian. 1994. Unpublished Calculations. Minneapolis, Minn.: Human Capital Research

# Index

Boldface numbers refer to tables.